Extended Power Cruising

A GUIDE TO

Extended Power Cruising

Marlin (Ben) Schuetz
and
Joan Schuetz

Seaworthy
PUBLICATIONS

SEAWORTHY PUBLICATIONS, INC. • PORT WASHINGTON, WISCONSIN

Extended Power Cruising
by Marlin (Ben) Schuetz and Joan Schuetz

Copyright © 2008 by Marlin (Ben) Schuetz and Joan Schuetz

ISBN 978-1-892399-26-7

Published in the USA by: Seaworthy Publications, Inc.
   626 W. Pierre Lane
   Port Washington, WI 53074
   PHONE: 262-268-9250
   FAX: 262-268-9208
   E-MAIL: orders@seaworthy.com
   WEB: www.seaworthy.com

All rights reserved. No part of this book may be reproduced, stored in a retrieval system, or transmitted in any form or by any means, electronic, mechanical, photocopying, recording, or by any storage and retrieval system without permission in writing from the Publisher.

PHOTO CREDITS: All of the photographs were taken by Marlin (Ben) Schuetz

COVER DESIGN: Ken Quant, Broad Reach Marketing & Design, Mequon, WI

Library of Congress Cataloging-in-Publication Data

Schuetz, Marlin, 1939-
   Extended power cruising / Marlin Schuetz and Joan Schuetz.
     p. cm.
   Includes bibliographical references and index.
   ISBN-13: 978-1-892399-26-7 (pbk. : alk. paper)
     ISBN-10: 1-892399-26-1 (pbk. : alk. paper) 1. Motorboats--Handbooks, manuals, etc. 2. Boats and boating--Handbooks, manuals, etc. I. Schuetz, Joan, 1939- II. Title.

GV835.S36 2008
797.12'5--dc22
                      2007044959

FOREWORD

Everywhere we look, books and seemingly endless magazine articles replay ad nauseum the glorifications of small, underpowered or non-powered, boats making ocean crossings and circumnavigations. Numerous others describe complicated anchoring techniques using two or more anchors or tactics for challenging icebergs or defeating hurricanes and so on. Living with hardships at the boundaries of reason makes fascinating reading and may stir the blood of armchair sailors, but it does not reflect reality in most of the cruising community. We find that little is said about the great majority of cruisers who, like us, select, equip and use our boats to cruise safely over long distances in all manner of situations and who do so with a first-world, live-aboard lifestyle. The written advice currently available to those who plan to join us as full-time cruisers often presents a daunting and truly distorted picture.

Extended Power Cruising is meant to change this picture. For those contemplating the cruising life, power or sail, who want to seek adventure, cultural contact and camaraderie beyond the range of the cruise ships and charter fleets, this is the handbook on how it's done. There are relatively few general, proven solutions to major cruising problems—fundamentally, power, safety, quality of life and comfort afloat—that face all of us who live and travel on cruising boats. *Extended Power Cruising* focuses on those, leaving the highly specialized, unique and bizarre approaches to others.

Extended Power Cruising will be especially useful to those relatively new to cruising, yet there may be some valuable surprises for experienced cruisers as well. The book is well organized, concise, readable and consistent with the realities of American, Canadian and Caribbean Cruising. For those about to start an extended cruising adventure it's a "must read" and it will make an excellent addition to personal cruising libraries ashore and afloat.

Bob and Barbara Gilmour
S/V ENKIDU

ACKNOWLEDGEMENTS

We wish to express our appreciation to all of the boaters with whom we have cruised during the last nine years. Those relationships and experiences were the wellspring for this book.

Our special thanks to Bob and Barbara Gilmour on s/v *Enkidu* and equally to Bill and Melinda Scott, s/v *Sovereign* with whom we have had many hours of discussions and abundant correspondence regarding the needs of cruisers. Their contributions and encouragement were extremely helpful in this endeavor.

Thanks also to Kathy Parsons, author of "Spanish for Cruisers" and "French for Cruisers," for her help and advice.

Contents

Foreword v

Acknowledgements vi

PART ONE: PREPARATIONS 01

   1. Introduction 03

   2. Selecting a Boat 06

   3. Dinghies and Dinghy Retrieval 15

   4. Vessel Tax and Insurance Issues 24

   5. Gaining Confidence 27

   6. Building Range 32

   7. Outfitting 35

   8. Communications 50

   9. Provisioning 57

   10. Spare Parts 74

   11. Preparing for Foreign Destinations 78

PART TWO: CRUISING 85

12. Cruise Planning and Operating Costs 87
13. Fuel Management and Availability 95
14. Maintenance 106
15. Maintenance Checklist 122
16. Weather 129
17. Overnighters 139
18. Anchorages and Anchoring 142
19. Medical Concerns, Issues and Opportunities 154
20. Security at Sea, Anchor and Ashore 163
21. Safety at Sea 172
22. Assisting Other Vessels 177
23. Money 181
24. Pets Aboard 183
25. Pest Infestations 185
26. Fishing, Catching Lobsters and Preparing the Catch 187
27. Home Schooling 195
28. Your Cruising Newsletter and Website 199
29. Cruising the ICW (Intracoastal Waterway) 200
30. Useful References 206

Index 207

PART ONE
PREPARATIONS

Chapter 1
Introduction

In 1997, Joan and I (Ben) retired from careers in business and engineering and decided to try full time cruising. We bought a 1979 44' Marine Trader classic trawler, which was renamed *Francesca*. It was clear to us that it would take time and miles before the realities of our boat's capabilities as well as our personal interests and abilities were understood. We had read many articles about trawler cruising, but most of them only dealt with cruising inland and intra-coastal waterways. So, it isn't too surprising that our cruising expectations were limited to the waters of the United States and perhaps the Bahamas. The idea that with appropriate preparation, we could cruise thousands of miles to foreign shores never even occurred to us. And, at that time, it would have seemed absurd to suggest such a thing. After all, trawlers and other modest powerboats aren't meant for such activities.

It then took several months to sort through layers of problems and to learn the various boat systems. Outfitting was accomplished, given a very limited understanding of the needs, and planning was superficial and mostly intuitive. Thereafter, the eight-month, first cruise from South Carolina to the Florida Keys and Bahamas turned out well, but were it not for luck, on two occasions, it could have gone badly. Among the deficiencies, our ability to obtain and interpret weather information was lacking and *Francesca's* ground tackle was too light. We resolved that more preparation was needed and that, in the future, luck would not be such an important player.

We came to understand that the *boat and crew* make up a cruising system. And, while it is obvious that safety and reliability are a first priority, minimizing inconvenience and discomfort follow closely in importance for the long-term happiness of the crew. During the next

8 years and 38,000 additional miles, our *cruising system* has evolved to include most of the comforts we had come to expect in a more conventional lifestyle and our vessel has provided all the range capability we could reasonably expect. Gradually increasing experience combined with a technical background helped make that possible. What we have learned we wish to share with you. This book is not a repetition of other cruising guides, books on seamanship or boat handling. Had this information been available to us, even before buying a boat, it could have saved us greatly in time, money and some unpleasant experiences.

Throughout the Caribbean, we found trawlers to be very underrepresented. During any of our Western Caribbean cruises, only three or four trawlers were seen to be actively cruising. Trawlers were similarly absent in the Eastern Caribbean. We find this odd since, in many ways, powerboats are better suited to cruising those areas than are sailing vessels. Trawlers and other powerboats can take advantage of no wind and calm sea conditions, can more easily cope with adverse currents and provide a comfortable home.

Parts of this book are weighted toward trawlers, but *power cruising* is not just about powerboats. For power or sail, a satisfactory lifestyle includes the convenience of appliances and equipment that we are accustomed to having. Power is needed for refrigeration, communications, water-maker, pressurized water system, television, computers, lights, radar, autopilot, fans, air conditioning, sanitary equipment, power tools and a host of other energy consumers. Trawlers most often rely upon generator sets and high output alternators to charge the house batteries. Sailboats, which don't usually have the room required for a generator, often do nicely using solar panels, wind generators, high output engine alternators and an adequate bank of house batteries. An ample supply of power makes the difference between living comfortably and camping out on your boat.

For someone new to cruising, it may be difficult to understand the realities and problems of energy production, storage, consumption, redundancy, and critical equipment failures. Therefore, a significant portion of this book is dedicated to providing guidance in that area.

But *Extended Power Cruising* is more than about power. It includes information that will help to prepare a boat, crew and pets for long duration voyages to foreign lands. When a vessel and crew are seaworthy, *extended cruising* will take them beyond the horizons to adventures and personal freedom that cannot be comprehended by non-cruisers.

The complete meaning of *Extended Power Cruising* can therefore be characterized as: long term cruising beyond the boundaries of North America, often anchoring at islands, in bays or behind reefs, while maintaining needed comforts and social fulfillment. For most of us in North America, the areas to explore include the whole of the Caribbean, both coasts of Mexico, Central America, the Baja Peninsula, and South America.

It is fascinating to realize that of the two hundred million or so people living near the coasts of the U.S. and Canada only a couple of thousand vessels, power and sail, are active in this type of cruising. Surprisingly, in the Western Caribbean, there are only a few hundred active boats for nearly 2000 miles of coastline. Even more stunning is the small number of trawlers; in all of the Caribbean, only a few dozen are actively cruising.

Once a cruiser breaks away from the inland waterways, towboat services, yacht clubs, and various other commercial security blankets, the emphasis shifts to self-reliance and the support of a small community of cruisers. In the lower latitudes, the cruising community is openly friendly and supportive of all cruisers, power or sail, who have chosen to join them. With few exceptions, those who participate have no desire to return to land-based living for as long as they are physically capable.

After five trips to Central and South America, each lasting one to two years, our expectations of adventure continue to be fulfilled. The friendly people, lands, history and foods of Latin America are bountiful. Fishing, diving and snorkeling can be excellent and occasionally we have caught and enjoyed lobster in abundance. Opportunities for inland excursions to such wonders as the ruins of ancient civilizations, active volcanoes, lakes, jungles, waterfalls and indigenous peoples are numerous and usually inexpensive. Recently we cruised up the Orinoco River of Venezuela and later made an inland trip to the land of Tepuis (high mesas) and stood at the base of the magnificent Angel Falls.

Yet, at times, there have been problems. In that regard, parts of this book relate to negative experiences of the authors or the authors' friends. These should not be taken as experiences to be expected, but as situations that can be avoided. Remember that throughout our working lives, we have been immersed in a sea of regulations, restrictions, policies, barriers and overbearing protectivism. We have been pummeled with propaganda, taxes, sleazy advertising, competition, pollution, traffic, scams, tinsel and all manner of plastic pretense. Looking back on all of that, our few difficulties at sea seem rather insignificant.

The cruising life is a great departure from convention, but making the break is difficult and maybe even a little frightening. This book is about helping people make this transition, avoid costly mistakes, enjoy a richly rewarding lifestyle and safely experience a sense of freedom they did not know existed.

Angel Falls

Chapter 2
Selecting a Boat

BY THE TIME MOST PEOPLE ARE READY TO BUY A BOAT, they already have some idea of what they want. But without cruising experience, a mindset can be a bad thing. The criteria of boat selection should include consideration for the greatest range of uses the buyer reasonably anticipates. If the buyer limits his or her cruising expectations to inland waters or local cruising, the boat selected may not be capable of anything greater. Everyone knows that buying a boat can be quick and easy, but selling one can take many months. Thus, a wrong buying decision can have long-term consequences and the time and expense of changing boats can ruin a life plan.

2.1 SAILBOATS

The authors are not qualified to offer much advice regarding sailboat selection, however, one thing is clear, cruising sailboats (in the context of this book) sail far less than is often supposed. Mostly, they either motor or motorsail. Cruisers with sailboats, only rarely disagree with those statements. Thus, as opposed to overemphasizing sailing characteristics, primary consideration should be given to reliability, maintenance requirements, comfort, storage space, energy production, and performance while under power.

The motorsailer is a design compromise between the sailboat and motorboat. Typically, vessels in this class are equipped with a substantial single diesel engine, they often have a generator, have good fuel range and fair to good motoring characteristics. However, motorsailers do not usually perform well on sails alone and sail assisted motoring is favored when possible. In the event of an engine failure, motorsailers maneuver reasonably well under sail power alone. The main benefits of a motorsailer are that they are roomier and more airy than sailboats, have good fuel efficiency and the sails add stability in rough water. On the downside, motorsailers have all the complexities of a sailboat, require more effort while cruising and consume more fuel than a sailboat. They also retain some of the basement-like living characteristics of a sailboat.

The rest of this chapter is weighted more for powerboats, but there are many aspects common to both power and sail.

2.2 TRAWLERS AND OTHER POWERBOATS

Trawler configurations are as broadly varied as sailboats. There are trawlers with semi-planing, full displacement and modified displacement hulls. A few trawlers have active stabilization and a few are equipped with paravanes (birds or flopper stoppers) for stabilization. Some make good sea boats and others are uncomfortable in any sea state. Some burn gasoline (oh, no!) while most use diesel fuel. Many are fuel-efficient while others are not.

There are yet further variations on the theme. There are round sterns, square sterns, dry stack (exhaust), wet exhaust, keel cooled, seawater cooled, fly-bridges, pilot houses, sun decks, classic designs, masts and booms, radar arches, and on and on. So where does the buyer start? For the purposes of this book, the start begins when the buyer makes a commitment to experience *extended* cruising. From that point, the boat selection filtering process can be done thoughtfully.

The rest of this chapter covers a few of the main topics and makes suggestions that may be helpful to avoid bad decisions.

2.2.1 Hull Configurations

Planing and semi-planing hull designs are typical of vessels with short range and higher speeds in mind. However, if the boat has adequate fuel capacity, they can be cruised at low speeds reasonably efficiently. Boats with this type of hull will not be built as heavily as displacement hulls and are often less comfortable in higher sea conditions. Semi-planing hulls usually have no keel, thus leaving the propeller(s) and rudder(s) exposed to potential damage from an accidental grounding. There are many "trawlers" on the market with this hull configuration.

Full displacement hulls are generally round bottomed. This type of hull tends to roll to extremes and for that reason, active stabilization is desirable. When properly stabilized they handle diverse sea conditions very well. Deep keels are usual for this design and these offer good protection to the propeller(s) and rudder(s). This configuration generally offers good fuel efficiency in the speed range of 7 to 9 knots.

Modified displacement hulls have less of a round bottom, often having hard chines. This type hull usually has less of a roll problem than round bottom hulls and most often, they have a full keel for propeller(s) and rudder(s) protection. Active stabilization is also an option with these hulls. The speed range is usually 7 to 9 knots with good fuel efficiency.

So, what is the best choice? There's no single answer unless one also specifies all the needs, budget and intended use. However, the modified displacement hull

In larger sea conditions a well-flared bow reduces the likelihood of burying the bow.

without stabilization is a good all around compromise.

Power Catamarans are fairly recent entries to cruising. They have the advantages of speed, excellent fuel economy and roominess. But, at present, they are relatively expensive and because of the wide separation between the propellers, their single engine performance may be problematic. Multi-hulls also have a very different ride than single hulled vessels and it can take some getting used to. In time, it is likely that power cats will grow in popularity.

2.2.2 Engines

The various engine configurations available for trawlers cover a wide range. For the most part, trawlers with displacement hulls operated in the high efficiency speed range of 6 to 8 knots and require very little power to do so. As an example, a 44 foot displacement hull trawler requires a total of only about 60 horsepower to cruise at 7 knots or a bit more. Trawlers are generally equipped with more than 200 horsepower total capability and the engine(s) can thus be operated in a speed range that yields high reliability, good fuel efficiency and extended lifetime.

Because of rising fuel costs and trawler's low horsepower requirements, trawler manufacturers may eventually offer boats with smaller, more efficient engine packages. Smaller engines will mean less weight, more engine room space and less original and operating costs.

Turbo charged engines are sometimes fitted in trawlers, but for extended cruising where fuel efficiency is more important than speed, they are not

This boat, has an extremely weak bow pulpit. If it were cruised, the bow pulpit would likely suffer early damage due to the rigors of anchor recovery during adverse conditions or during a dragging incident. Untimely damage to this critical component can quickly lead to more serious problems. A weak bow pulpit can usually be reinforced with stainless steel tubular members. Two anchors and a husky windlass are also favored.

particularly desirable. However, most turbo-equipped diesel engines can be operated reasonably efficiently at low rpms (turbo inactive) without concern for either engine or turbocharger damage. Periodic short-term operation at higher power settings will keep the turbochargers from loading up.

Deciding on *single engine or twins* is not as straightforward as one might think. For instance, with a single engine, there can be better fuel efficiency because there is less engine/transmission/shaft bearing overhead (frictional losses). Also, on the positive side, a single engine leaves more space in the engine room, is easier and less costly to maintain and fewer spare parts are needed. But, on the negative side, single engine vessels, especially those without bow thrusters, are more difficult to maneuver. They may also be a little slower than their twin-engine counterpart and, of course, there is the lack of a redundant means of propulsion.

A properly installed and maintained diesel propulsion system is a marvel of reliability. A few of the high-end ocean crossing capable trawlers have only single engines. In the unlikely event of the loss of the main propulsion system, single engine trawlers may have get-home propulsion alternatives. For example, if a transmission clutch or hydraulic system packs it in, it may be possible to lock the transmission in forward gear. Or, there may be a means of using the generator engine or a small auxiliary engine for propulsion.

Another consideration is that it is not possible to cruise the Caribbean without making overnighters. During the past 8 years, *Francesca* has hit logs twice at night. Thankfully, propeller damage was experienced only once, but it was significant and happened 100 miles off the coast of Panama in an area where the ocean current was quite strong. Had *Francesca* been equipped with only one engine, assistance from another vessel would probably have been needed. As it was, we were able to continue on course, albeit more slowly, and make repairs without much inconvenience or expense.

Another important argument to be made for twin engines is that once in a while dirty fuel can overwhelm the filters. With a properly designed filtering system and plenty of spare filters, that should not be too much of a problem. This is true even for a vessel with a single engine. However, until the problem has been experienced and sorted through it should not be assumed that all would be well. Changing fuel filters at sea can be a miserable experience. If the fuel system is not well designed, additional problems can crop up. As a minimum, there will be a bit of spilled diesel fuel, large doses of sweat and a few choice words. In more extreme cases, there can be an extended period of power loss due to air in the fuel lines. How well that sort of situation turns out depends upon yet other factors such as experience, sea conditions, fuel system accessibility, etc. However, with two engines and separate fuel filtration systems, it is very unlikely that both engines would falter at the same time with bad fuel.

In your decision making process, mull these thoughts over, do more research, talk to knowledgeable cruisers and work through all the pros and cons. A good single engine package may yet be the right answer.

With only a few exceptions and for obvious reasons, little discussion is offered regarding the types of engines, transmissions or propellers. One of those exceptions is a very old version of the Borg-Warner Velvet Drive™ transmission known as the CR or drop center unit. This transmission was installed in a few 1970s and early 80s trawlers. There aren't many left out there, but if you buy a trawler so equipped, it or they will need to be replaced before any serious cruising is done. The design was weak and repair parts are almost impossible to find.

The second recommendation is that, given a choice, transmissions such as the Twin Disk or equivalent have one big advantage. Rotational differences are accommodated with linkage changes only. Thus, the right hand rotating transmission is identical with the left hand rotating transmission. This makes repairs and parts less demanding.

Probably most important of all, however, is to understand just how bad a bad buying decision can be regarding the engine package. Some engines have sleeved cylinders and can be overhauled or repaired relatively inexpensively without removal from the boat. Other engine packages, however, require complete removal from the boat to be repaired or rebuilt. A worst case scenario might be that the cost of repair would exceed the value of a functional boat. Also, the parts for some European/Scandinavian engines can be hard to find and extremely pricey. That's bad anywhere, but a lot worse in the Caribbean. Your fellow boaters, the Internet and knowledgeable mechanics can save a big time headache.

2.3 OTHER VESSEL SELECTION CONSIDERATIONS

Personal preferences will likely override arguments that might be made here regarding which type of trawler to purchase. But, here are a few general thoughts and associated pitfalls to keep in mind when looking for a boat.

2.3.1 Vessel size

For most people the minimum length trawler for long duration cruising is about 40 feet. In addition to seaworthiness, that minimum length supports the needs of storage, equipment, fuel range, living space and comfort. Does bigger therefore mean better? In situations where budget is only secondarily important, bigger may be better. But given the budget restrictions of most cruisers, the increased costs of fuel, maintenance, additional crew and marina fees often put a limit on size. Thus, most long-range cruising powerboats are 40 to 55 feet in length.

2.3.2 Cabin layout and integrity

Traveling in the southern latitudes and spending lots of time at anchor requires good, screened ventilation throughout the boat. At anchor there is generally a nice breeze and the sleeping quarters can be quite comfortable. But, there are trawler layouts for which the sleeping quarters become stifling pits of hell without air conditioning. That problem can be mitigated with modest fans, but it's one more thing to have to deal with.

Most boats experience leaks around window frames or hatches at sometime or other. Frequently these leaks cause significant inside wood damage. Be aware that in a few areas of the tropics, there can 200 inches or more of rainfall annually. Think about the issues involved in repairing and preparing a vessel for that environment.

2.3.3 Teak decks

Teak decks are lovely, but they can be the worst attribute on a boat. Deck leaks are nearly impossible to localize/repair and complete re-caulking is a major enterprise that may not solve the problem and can yield even more bad news. Deck leaks can cause water to be trapped between the deck laminates resulting in God-knows-what problems.

Cruising in the tropics is usually done barefooted. Teak decks can be hot on the tootsies. The heat absorbed by teak decks may also raise the temperature inside the boat. If teak decks are desired or the boat selected has teak decks, check them over very carefully. Even if they look great and don't currently have leaks, unless they aren't fastened with screws the leaks will come.

2.3.4 Electrical system

In North America our homes are "built to code." Anyone who thinks *boat electrical systems* are installed or maintained with that or better standards is living in La-La land. We have known and helped cruisers with electrical problems that were so bad they could barely continue their cruises. Hidden behind nice looking electrical panels there can be incomprehensible wiring rats nests. When looking to buy a boat, take more than a peek at the evil that lurks therein. If you can't rework the rat's nest, think about how many 60 to 80 dollar-hours an electrician will absorb. On *Francesca*, it took a personal effort of a couple hundred hours to sort it all out. Hmmm!

2.3.5 Steering system

Hydraulic steering is mostly favored these days, but don't disqualify a vessel just because it has chain and shaft steering. This older type of steering can have very low steering resistance and is easy to maintain. Also, a good autopilot, having a rudder position sensor mounted at the quadrant, will ignore the slack in the chain system and work nearly as well as hydraulic steering.

2.3.6 Fuel tanks

Deck leaks, whether associated with teak or not, can become an oh-mi-gosh nightmarish adventure. If there is or has been a history of water getting to the tops of the fuel tanks, seriously expensive problems can occur. Replacement of fuel tanks is so difficult that at times a section of the hull has to be cut out to do the job. In other cases the old tank(s) has to be cut into pieces to be removed and a series of smaller tanks installed. Bladders have been tried, but have not been found to be a satisfactory solution for this problem. Sometimes fuel tanks can be repaired with an excellent product called POR-15. There is more on that in the chapter on maintenance.

The object is to go cruising, not spend a lifetime correcting deficiencies. In the buying process, unless your surveyor is specifically asked to check for this, it is almost a certainty that it will not be done. Insist on it.

2.3.7 Hull blisters

Oh my, this is a good one and the answers are unclear. Of course, no one wants hull blisters, but do a few small blisters qualify for a no-go boat purchase decision? That's a tough question. It is best answered with a lot of research and dialogue with experts. The problem for the boat buyer is that the answers can be ambiguous or even contradictory and *real* experts are hard to find or recognize when you do find them. So, not being an "expert," I disqualify myself from offering advice except for the following.

There is an often quoted cliché, "all boats are sinking; it is just a matter of time." Given enough time a fiberglass hull will eventually absorb water, delaminate and fail structurally. There are lots of 25 year-old fiberglass vessels, which hulls are in very fine condition. There are also some 5 year-old poorly built vessels that are in alarmingly poor condition.

The hull condition depends upon the manufacturing methods, age of the boat, whether it has been kept in fresh or salt water, how it was maintained, yada, yada. A full blister repair job can cost $10,000 to $30,000. Just as bad, there is rarely a guarantee that the repair job will last.

However, minor blisters can be spot repaired. If regularly watched and repaired

These deck fills are highly suspect. They may be sealed to the teak deck, but if water gets between the teak deck and the fiberglass, it will flow through to the tops of the tanks. The deck fills should have been sealed directly to the fiberglass structure beneath the teak. This problem is common to many trawlers.

they need not be much of a threat. The bigger threat to an otherwise good hull is that an uninformed, ham-handed boatyard worker can easily damage the barrier coat and create very costly problems.

Major blister repair work can be done at Trinidad, Puerto La Cruz, VE, and Cartagena, Colombia at a fraction of the cost of that in the U.S. A little homework is needed before venturing into this minefield. There are large differences in the quality of the work and available materials at the various yards.

2.3.8 Marina queens

Marina queens can be a good buy or not. They often have low engine hours, lack equipment and have had questionable maintenance. Depending upon one's capabilities and pocketbook, these can be good or not so good attributes. Project boats require a lot of time and cash to set straight and equip. If your interest doesn't lie in that direction look for a boat that has been recently cruised. There aren't many that will be equipped well enough for extended cruising, but try to find one that has done something besides sit in a marina. Also, try to determine if the previous owner was personally interested in the care and maintenance of the boat. Often their only concerns have been to keep the icemaker running and have a marina worker wash the exterior. In the best-case scenario, find a boat with good maintenance documentation, well-kept equipment manuals, and an owner that had pride in keeping the entire vessel in apple pie order.

2.3.9 The surveyor

Boat surveys are necessary for insurance and boat loan purposes. It would therefore logically follow that surveyors are qualified, certified and regulated much like home appraisers. Such is not the case, however. No governmental body certifies or regulates that enterprise and anyone with a business card qualifies to do business as a marine surveyor. Thus, the terms honest and qualified come under question. Fortunately, it isn't quite that bad. There are associations that help to educate and aid in self-regulating boat surveyors. Also, banks and insurance companies may require certain known qualified surveyors to be involved.

For the boat buyer, however, uncertainties may remain. The bank or insurance company may not be local and they may not have a preferred surveyor. Remember also that it is never prudent to ask the yacht broker for a recommendation.

Surveys come in all sizes, colors, and verbosity. Don't be fooled by the number of pages, color pictures, or seeming thoroughness; the bad stuff may have been overlooked or perhaps buried within otherwise innocuous text. It is best to be personally on sight and do the survey with the surveyor. If the surveyor doesn't want to do it that way, find another. Surveys can cost many hundreds of dollars. Get your moneys worth and make sure the surveyor is interested in protecting you from a bad deal and not just helping the broker consummate the deal. There are lots of good and honest surveyors; take the time to find one.

2.4 SUMMARIZING

In this book it would be unreasonable to try and cover the problems of boat buying in any detail. Only the headline buying issues have been given. In the boat buying process take plenty of time, try to understand what your needs are, look around and don't just fall for a pretty face with a Jacuzzi, ice maker and bar. If the plan is to do serious cruising, a serious boat is needed. Early in the chapter on *Outfitting* there is a list of expensive goodies; most of which will be needed for cruising. Keep the list in mind when looking for or negotiating the price of a boat.

One last thought. It isn't universally true, but many boats are not really the product of thoroughly thoughtful design. With those vessels, it may be obvious that the boat designers had never been exposed to live-aboard cruising. Without such experience, the designer is a poor judge of design features. Therefore, it is unreasonable for you to be obsessive about keeping a newly acquired vessel "as designed." Obviously, care must be taken not to degrade structurally important elements, but after gaining some cruising experience, if a feature isn't found to be suitable, fix it, change it or throw it out.

Chapter 3
Dinghies, Dinghy Retrieval, Engines and Security

FOLKS WHO LIVE ON A FARM OFTEN DRIVE A PICKUP TRUCK IN ADDITION to the family van or SUV. In Alaska, a four-wheel drive vehicle would be needed for sure. Landlubbers need different vehicles for different environments and activities. A cruiser's dinghy needs to be versatile as well. It will be used as a towboat, water taxi, supplies carrier, dive boat, fishing boat, touring boat and more. It will need to be reliable, safe, reasonably dry, have modest speed, and carry the expected loads. Sort of like the tail wagging the dog, dinghy requirements may even influence the selection of a cruising boat. The criteria for selection are little complicated and compromises are always required. If the larger vessel is already owned, this chapter may be helpful in defining useful upgrades or modifications.

3.1 DINGHIES AND DINGHY LAUNCH/RECOVERY

Until the advent of the "RIB" (rigid bottom inflatable boat) hard bottom dinghies, dinghy rides were often *wet butt* experiences. A good RIB has a high bow, large tubes, can handle plenty of horsepower and satisfies a variety of requirements. Among cruisers, the most popular RIBs are made by AB and Carib.

A *hard* dinghy such as a skiff, may also be practical, but they are more difficult to stow and cruisers are never happy having visitors' hard dinghies bash their boats. A

RIB, or other inflatable, will save friends and paint jobs.

If a currently owned cruising boat has davits, that may be good or bad depending upon their characteristics. But, if one is still in the market for a cruising boat, the dinghy stowing system is certainly one of the criteria for selection. The best system will be capable of safely handling the dinghy, with engine, quickly, easily, and in a variety of weather and sea conditions. That's a tall order and one that only a few cruising powerboats and even fewer sailboats have really sorted out.

It may come as a surprise that at many or even most anchorages, for security and other reasons, it will be necessary to raise the dinghy every night. Inadequate recovery equipment will quickly become a serious aggravation. Here are three examples to help clarify this.

> *After a long night*, a cruiser arrives at a new port where it is known that the officials have little patience with captains who arrive and check-in hours later. It's a chore to launch the dinghy and even more so when tired. Groan!

> *A cruiser is anchored* in a harbor where dinghy theft is a known hazard. The captain and mate return to their boat after an evening of festivities. They are tired and have slightly impaired faculties. The decision is made to leave the dinghy in the water for the night. The next morning, no surprise, no dinghy! There will be more about dinghy security later in this chapter.

> *Anchored behind a reef* in Belize the captain and mate returned to their boat after a long day of diving. No one was around for miles so there weren't any security issues. However, the wind was up and there was about a 2-foot chop. During attempts to raise the dinghy, the jamming and banging on lifting points threatened damage. The captain decided it would be safer to leave the dinghy in the water. His decision was also influenced by fatigue. That night, torrential tropical rains fell and the captain had to get up and bail out the dinghy twice during the night. The captain was then exposed to more risk, wet twice, and everyone aboard got a poor nights sleep.

There is a general lack of availability of good dinghy recovery systems. For instance, most reasonably sized after market bolt on stern mounted davits cannot handle the load of dinghy and engine together. Having to frequently remove/replace the outboard motor, often under difficult conditions, can be an unreasonably difficult and risky chore.

As an alternative and popular with many powerboats, a single davit may be used to raise the dinghy to an upper deck cradle. For trawlers with an elevated sun deck, there aren't many options. But, this system has several deficiencies. Raising a dinghy to an upper deck in rolly conditions can be challenging and there is a risk of damage to the boat, dinghy, and participants. Another undesired feature is that an electric winch is usually employed. If the winch fails, then what? A yet further disadvantage is that mounting a dinghy high can adversely affect the roll characteristics of the cruise boat.

When applicable, well-designed stern mounted davits can be a better system. Dinghy launch and retrieval is quicker, safer, and when done manually, very reliable. Handling the dinghy in rolly/windy conditions may be difficult, but it is far less risky than with the single davit system.

As mentioned earlier, the strength of stern mounted davits is a primary concern. If the outboard is to remain mounted, the davit system must be capable of restraining the dinghy in all the wind and sea conditions your vessel is likely to encounter. For example, one of the worst sea conditions for stressing the dinghy and davits is a steep chop. The cruising boat's bow tends to drop off the waves causing the stern to pitch up. The dinghy is accelerated vertically and tends to float with slack cables. Then, as the stern moves back down, severe peak loads acting upon the davits and the dinghy hard points follow the momentary slack in the bridles. An ideal, but rarely seen system, is one where a dinghy that is hung on two davits, has cross connected cables to prevent shifting with roll and is also *tied down* to a low point to prevent the float/jerk problem.

These davits are much too large for the boat, lack strength at the attachment points and have no lateral stabilization.

A system frequently seen on the Intra-coastal Waterway is one in which the dinghy is flipped on its side, beyond vertical, using a hinge-like fastener on the swim platform. The dinghy rests against and is secure to the stern of the boat. This system is unsatisfactory for extended cruising and should not be considered.

Compared with others, the davits on *Francesca* may appear to be under-designed. Yet, in any position they easily support a person standing in the dinghy. The outboard motor is always left on the dinghy. Years of trouble free use in all encountered sea conditions have proven the design. Unfortunately, at present, they must be custom made. Note the dinghy cover in some of the photos.

3.2 TOWING A DINGHY

We've all seen cruising boats towing their dinghies in the waterway. So, what's wrong with that? Plenty. Towing a dinghy except briefly is not a good idea. A couple of examples will best illustrate the problems.

> For the sake of time and energy the captain decides to tow his dinghy to the next island just 5 miles away. Arriving at the next anchorage, the captain and mate are distracted by something or other. The captain drops anchor and backs down. Unsurprisingly the dinghy painter gets wrapped in the props. The result is the dinghy is jammed under the swim platform, with damage to both, and the cruising boat is temporarily disabled. Were that in tight quarters with the wind blowing, things could get exciting.

> Or, while towing the dinghy at sea, conditions deteriorate and the painter, experiencing extreme loads, chafes and parts. The dinghy may then capsize. Sea conditions would likely be too bad to attempt a recovery.

But realistically there are times when, for short distances, it is more convenient to tow astern. In those cases, a painter that floats or has floats on it should be used. Anti-chafing precautions may be needed and, if the sea conditions worsen, adjust the painter length for the best ride and to minimize shock loads. The use of a bridle may be helpful in controlling fishtailing and to reduce line and point loads. However, before anchoring, avoid problems by bringing the dinghy alongside and tying it off on a relatively short painter. More preferably, for short distances in calm conditions, a side tow is best.

3.3 DINGHY COVERS

A few hundred dollars spent on a dinghy cover is a good investment. In the tropics, the heat and sun's ultraviolet will degrade dinghy material badly within 5 or 6 years. A dinghy cover also provides protection against abrasion during all kinds of activities.

3.4 SELECTING AN OUTBOARD MOTOR

Everyone has their favorites, but in the Caribbean, parts and services are generally assured for just two types of outboard motor, Honda and Yamaha.

The single davit is sometimes a good selection. This steel vessel has good roll stability for safe dinghy recovery and stowage.

The davits on Francesca are small, lightweight, stable and very strong. In the raised position, forked keepers provide additional lateral stability.

And, until recently, it has been difficult to get service on four-cycle outboards. The latter situation is improving.

How much power is enough? New cruisers often make the mistake of not having enough power. In most areas there will be frequent trips of a mile or more and snorkeling/diving/river trips may be all day excursions covering much greater distances. Yet, carrying large quantities of gasoline aboard, perhaps on deck, is not a great idea either. Most cruisers have found that 10 or 15 horsepower is a good compromise. Their dinghies are reasonably quick and the fuel consumption is manageable. Four-cycle engines are more expensive and heavier than two cycle engines, yet they have much better fuel economy, are quieter, and less malodorous.

Today's small outboard motors are very reliable, but they all fall short of having adequately sized fuel filters. In most cases, outboard motor failures are associated with fuel contaminants getting into the carburetor. It isn't often that freshly purchased fuel is bad, but, after many refills, fuel tanks accumulate dirt, water and rust. Therefore, the first thing to do after buying a new or used outboard motor is to replace the small in-line filter with a larger one. In addition, inspect and thoroughly clean the fuel tank as necessary.

3.5 OUTBOARD MOTOR FUEL STORAGE ABOARD THE CRUISING BOAT

This is a difficult issue and one for which there is no easy answer. On the

The assembly is raised and lowered using a single hand cranked boat winch located in the lazarette. The low pivot point allows the dinghy to clear the swim platform.

The center post has within it a pulley that guides the cable into the lazarette and to the boat winch.

Cross-tied cables provide stability and have quick disconnect terminations.

Intra-coastal Waterway, jerry jugs are often seen mounted on the swim platform of trawlers. That may be fine in the waterway, but it's no good at sea. Most cruisers keep jerry jugs of gasoline in the open air, tied to a rail or otherwise secured. We all know that fuel jugs need to be vented for expansion, and to avoid evaporation, they should be kept as cool as possible. But, in sloppy sea conditions, fuel may weep from the vent. A few drops of gasoline not only smell bad; they also create a slipping and fire hazard. Closing the vents during these conditions is justified, but that requires assurance that the jugs remain cool and the vents reopened when it is safe to do so. These are common sense issues, but yet one more thing to remember to do.

3.6 DINGHY SECURITY

No matter where you go in the Caribbean, dinghy theft is a hot topic of discussion with the cruisers. While there are exceptions, dinghies are most often stolen at night and when left on the painter at a dock or tied to the cruise boat. The thieves are mainly interested in the outboard motors. One might suppose that a dinghy secured with a cable or chain would be an adequate deterrent, however, the thieves everywhere have dandy-fine cable cutters. Padlocked cables or chains may be adequate for daytime security, but can't be depended upon at night. It is advisable to use the largest diameter cable or chain that can comfortably be managed and secure the cable or chain to both the outboard motor and dinghy.

Francesca in the Rio Orinoco, Venezuela

Francesca under Spanish Guns at Portobelo, Panama

For overnight dinghy security and while at anchor, there is only one good solution. Raise the dinghy out of the water. On one occasion, we have even had thieves try to take the engine off the dinghy while it was on davits and we were aboard. We did not hear them, but the job apparently proved to be too difficult and risky. The thieves only managed to get the outboard loosened on the transom.

In nearly everyone's cruising life there will be times when, against all wishes and better judgment, the dinghy must be left in the water overnight. The reasons may be weather, broken davit part, broken dinghy lifting point, bridle or whatever. It will happen and when it does there are just a few options. First, try to make sure it doesn't happen two nights in a row. Thieves don't usually go for stuff the first night, but don't count on that either. The next thing is to tie fishing line from a rod and reel to the dinghy or outboard motor and set the "clicker" on. Finally, the best deterrent is to take turns standing watch. Be prepared to turn on the spreader lights and have a spotlight or flashlight handy too.

Fortunately, almost all marinas in the Caribbean have security guards. Even then, however, there are occasional reports of dinghies being stolen at night that were cabled or chained to the dock. Ask around before taking such risks.

Chapter 4
Vessel Tax and Insurance Issues

4.1 PERSONAL PROPERTY TAX

Everyone knows that tax evasion is a crime. It is also a crime to give advice on how to evade taxes. Tax avoidance, however, is legal and fair game. What's the difference? Tax evasion is not reporting and paying taxes that are owed. Tax avoidance is using legitimate means not to owe taxes in the first place.

One's state of residence in the U.S. makes a big difference in the amount of sales tax and other on-going local taxes that will have to be paid while owning a cruising boat. For a few people, especially those who have divested themselves of a land based home place, the choice of a new state residence can be made. Some states have established a maximum amount of sales tax that can be levied on boats. For instance, in South Carolina the maximum is $300. It doesn't matter if the vessel is a dinghy or a large yacht. Rhode Island has no boat sales tax and many boat owners in nearby states buy and maintain their boats there. In most other states, sales tax is levied as a percentage of the purchase price.

Another way to avoid a high sales tax is to buy a boat owned by a corporation. That is, a boat owned by a corporation that was created only for the purpose of owning it under a corporate umbrella. Thus, when buying a corporation boat one doesn't buy the boat, one buys the corporation. There is no sales tax on a corporation. Then, later when selling your corporation-boat, the sales tax avoidance may be an attractive selling point.

Corporation boats can be documented in states such as Delaware where there is no sales tax, property tax or stock transfer tax. In fact, it may be to a boat owner's advantage to change a boat currently owned as personal property to a corporate owned vessel. A number of companies specialize in setting up corporations for this purpose. They also maintain a mailing address for the vessel documentation and for the renewal process. The initial and ongoing fees are very reasonable. Owning a boat under a corporation may also provide personal protection against some lawsuits.

Then, why would anyone not want his or her vessel under corporate ownership? There are several reasons. First, a small annual fee must be paid to a registered agent. There is also a small annual franchise tax. These generally add up to less than $150. But, if the vessel stays in one location in the States for more than a few months, the local tax officials may levy a user tax or equivalent. Finally, owning a boat under a corporation is a level of complication many people don't want to be bothered with.

Another means to avoid local taxes in the U.S. is through foreign vessel documentation. Here again, if the vessel remains in U.S. waters for any length of time, local taxes can be levied.

Let's get back to extended cruising and what that means in terms of taxes. In many states, local property taxes are levied because a vessel owner has a mailing address or the vessel's documented homeport is at that locality. Taxes may also be levied if a visiting vessel remains at a location for more than some minimum amount of time, three months for example. In other states, vessel owners are taxed if the vessel is at a location on some date, e.g., January first. It does not matter that the vessel is federally documented and not state registered. States are getting tough on this point and local governments often have workers walk the docks periodically taking pictures, making notes and establishing the basis for taxes. In another era, they were called revenuers.

We cruisers, however, spend most of our time outside of the U.S. As such, we do not use any U.S. state or local public services. Local governments may levy a tax, but they should not be entitled to collect it. To make your case, be sure to retain all foreign customs documents and a collection of receipts such as for fuel, marinas, and boat yards.

One way to avoid being billed every year and having to repeatedly prove that the vessel has been out of the country is to document your vessel's home port and mailing address at an inland city. Inland county governments don't usually check on federally documented vessels. A trusted relative can then send you the yearly documentation renewal notice. This advice is offered only for vessels and owners that spend most of their time outside of U.S. territorial waters.

There is yet another aspect of taxation that may be useful. Full time liveaboards can claim their boat as their primary residence. In such cases, the local tax officials may allow a vessel to be taxed at a lower rate such as for a mobile home. Some states also have exemptions for senior citizens. For example, the first $100,000 of a home's value is exempt in South Carolina. Local officials aren't often helpful with these suggestions, so it would be wise to do some research before going to make your case.

We've spent our entire lives working and paying taxes. Now, as cruisers, we want to be free of as much of that as possible. Take the time to think about the issues. Weigh the cost and inconvenience of the various tax avoidance methods against the possibility of having to pay some taxes. As cruisers, we are a fringe group. We have little representation and standard forms rarely apply.

4.2 INSURANCE ISSUES

Finding good insurance for your vessel can be a problem. Most popular stateside insurers don't cover trips to the Caribbean, especially to Colombia and Nicaragua. They often even have a rider charge to cover the Bahamas. There may be exceptions, but it appears that to get complete coverage for the Caribbean the best sources are, at present, European Insurers.

One Dutch insurance broker, Commandeur Assurantien b.v., provides coverage for everywhere in the Caribbean, including Cuba, Colombia and Nicaragua. There are no riders, even for going through the Panama Canal. That insurer specifies that the policy will not cover damage to vessels in war zones or from a named storm in the hurricane box. The policy appears to provide excellent coverage and at a reasonable price. Many Caribbean cruisers have this type of policy. However, we have no testimonials regarding claims. This information as well as information on other companies providing Caribbean coverage is posted on our website.

Take the time to check around for the desired coverage for your vessel. Once locked in, it is time consuming, frustrating and expensive to change policies.

Chapter 5
Gaining Confidence

*E*XTENDED CRUISING IS VERY DIFFERENT FROM SOLELY CRUISING the inland and coastal waters of North America. The differences lie not only in the exposure to more varied conditions, but also in how the owner regards his or her vessel, the crew and potential problems. Sailboaters seem to make the transition more easily than those with powerboats. Perhaps this is true because sailboats are traditionally thought of as open ocean cruisers. However, many trawlers have the legs and seaworthiness to safely make long passages. In fact, trawlers have advantages over sailboats for moderate crossings. We think a change from traditional thinking is needed.

The idea that trawlers have questionable seaworthiness is probably a carryover from experiences with lesser powerboats. Let's look at some of the reasons for this. First, small boats are disposable craft and maintenance is often only marginally effective. These craft weren't designed for long-term reliability. Larger vessels used for weekend cruising, while perhaps better designed, still suffer from maintenance ills. For any boat used intermittently, poor reliability is an inherent problem because the frequency of equipment failure is inversely related to regularity with which the equipment is used. The lack of ventilation, loss of lubrication, moisture and salt buildup, discharged batteries, marine growth, etc. are all responsible for this. Other weekend boating problems can be blamed on the crew's lack of experience. Their mistakes are manifest in groundings, bent props and shafts, flooding, collisions, dock rash, etc.

Thus, even though the weekend boater may spend lots of money on maintenance, his or her experiences are predestined to have frequent breakdowns and only brief hours of enjoyment. Considering those factors, it is not the least surprising that the general attitude toward powerboats is that they are not to be trusted beyond the range of a local towing company.

A good trawler can be quite a different story. The diesel engines were designed for long service, the hulls are strong, equipment is protected from salt spray and, as a system, trawlers are designed to last. Used frequently and with proper maintenance a trawler can be remarkably trouble free for long periods.

So, how does a new cruiser make the transition from the understanding that boats are inherently unreliable to a position of placing great trust in himself and his boat for long voyages? The simple answer is that it does not happen overnight, nor should it. Experience needs to be gained and trust has to be deserved. One might say that a crew and boat make up a complex system that is in the continuous process of attempting to maintain a stable condition. When one or the other fails to do their job, the system breaks down. It takes time, an open mind, and patience to learn how best to keep the system stable.

For full time cruisers, the boat is their primary home. As such, maintenance is like that with any home. But, instead of mowing, mulching, trimming and painting, there is varnishing, polishing, hull cleaning and oil changes to be done routinely. These activities help keep both the boat and crew healthy, reliable and ready to go.

In the process of preparing a boat, every new cruiser goes through extensive personal and vessel teething problems. At times the list of work items may seem interminable. Pre-cruise equipment problems run the gamut of engineering, manufacturing and material defects, insufficient prior routine maintenance, improper installation and incompetent maintenance services. Yet with some diligence, and of course money, a new boat, used boat and even a marina queen (like *Francesca* was) can be tamed and brought up to a high standard of reliability.

To begin the learning process there should be clarification of all of the various vessel subsystems. Most people are shocked at the scope of the list. However, a cruising boat is the miniature equivalent of a small town. The cruising boat's system includes various combinations of the following:

Air conditioning, fans and filters
Appliances
    Stove, refrigerator, freezer, microwave, video, stereo, and intercom
Batteries, small, chargers
Bilge pumps
Cabin integrity
    Doors, windows, locks, fastenings, trim, seals, furniture,
Cleaning and other maintenance items
Clothing and storage
Communications
    VHF, VHF handheld, SSB, satellite telephone, email, hailer
Dinghy stowage, dinghy fuel storage
Dinghy Engine, fuel filter and tank
Dinghy security cable & locks
Documentation of vessel components
Electrical
    Gensets, solar panels, wind generators, inverters, AC & DC power distribution, batteries
Electronics
    Radar, depth sounders, GPS, autopilot, wind instruments
Engine control panel(s) and mechanical controls

Engine water intakes, filter/strainers, exhaust
Fire extinguishers
Fresh water system
    Tanks, pumps, filters, pressure system, hot water heater
Fuel system
    Tankage, pumps, polishers, filters
Galvanic protection
    Plates, zincs, electrical bonding
Ground tackle
    Windlass, anchors, chain & rode, bridles/snubbers
Hull and deck fittings
    Thru hull fittings, sea cocks, screens, transponders, deck fills, cleats, dock lines, fenders
Hull barrier coat and antifouling protection
Lighting
    Running, anchor, spreader, interior, deck, spot
Maintenance stores,
    Paint, primer, sandpaper, caulk, fasteners
Medical supplies and books
Navigation
    Computer, software, charts
Propulsion
    Engine(s), transmission(s), shaft(s), seal(s), propeller(s), mast(s), sails, rigging
Personal storage
    Clothing, books, shoes, etc.
Provision storage
    Canned goods, frozen food, paper towels, toilet paper, etc.
Safety equipment
    Flares, flare gun, life jackets, lifeboat, EPIRB, safety lines, non-skid surfaces, strobes
Sanitary system
    Toilets, holding tank, Y valves, macerator, pump out
Spare parts storage
Steering and stabilizers
    Mechanics/hydraulics, dual station
Tools
Wash down system
Watermaker

This is quite a list and each of the items needs to be *examined, understood* and *documented* as well as possible. The goal is to be reasonably comfortable in your knowledge of the vessel's condition, strengths and needs.

Examine everything, everywhere, top to bottom, fore and aft, and especially the hard to get to places that have been ignored since the vessel was commissioned. It may be necessary to cut holes in panels for adequate inspection. Establish a baseline with every area clean and easy to inspect. The reasons are simple. A dirty, cluttered space is less likely to be regularly inspected than a clean organized one. A dirty engine room and bilge can hide all kinds of problems that can become serious later. Consider that failures at sea rarely happen in pleasant calm, daylight conditions with lots of time to work out a solution. Plan for the likelihood of having to make expedient repairs in an uncomfortable, rolling, pitching, hot, smelly, noisy, potentially dangerous environment. Having done the homework, that eventuality is far less likely to occur.

Understand as much as possible. If one lacks technical background then it would be well to be prepared with as much information and involvement as time allows. Before a cruise, there are always knowledgeable people around to consult with. Most boaters are eager to share their hands on knowledge. But before relying on any one person's advice or help, try to understand their level of competence. There is much to be lost by following poor advice.

If repair/installation services are necessary, try to get testimonials from *knowledgeable*, satisfied customers before doing so. Everyone likes to think they have been treated fairly and paid for the services of competent technical help. But as regards marine services, competent service may be the exception, not the rule.

When it is necessary to contract with a marine service technician, stay involved as much as possible. The contractor may grumble or say something like, "it costs more when the boat owner helps," but try not to be put off (perhaps choose another contractor). Being involved helps weed out excessive, even fraudulent charges and can yield valuable learning experiences. Later, after achieving a reasonable understanding of the various onboard systems, the boat owner will be less dependent upon others, enjoy reduced costs, and gain confidence regarding the management of problems that might occur at sea.

During the familiarization process, practice thinking defensively in terms of potential critical failures and back-up strategies. For example, consider the implications of a generator failure. There should be a work-around strategy for handling that and most other situations without canceling cruise plans or being exposed to a maintenance fleecing.

Documentation should be more than just a box of randomly stacked papers. The documentation system can be file folders, binder volumes, or the information can be scanned and put on CDs. On *Francesca*, we have eleven volumes of three-ring binders. They are completely full of pertinent data. Some might think this is overkill, but on the many occasions it was needed, it was invaluable.

Documentation should include information on equipment manufacturers, model and serial numbers, parts catalogs, service centers, maintenance schedules, diagrams, pictures, good contacts, and servicing articles. When modifications are made, they should be recorded and dated. Lack of this data can have far reaching consequences.

The experience the captain and mate gain while cleaning, inspecting, repairing documenting and installing will be invaluable in the future. When there is any kind of equipment failure, even a cursory understanding of the various systems will help to minimize anxiety and resolve the problem.

So, what can be expected of a well maintained trawler? Let's first define equipment failures as being unexpected, non-trivial (e.g. burned out light bulbs) and not related to normal life expectancy or wear and tear. In eight years, the following equipment failures have occurred on *Francesca*:

Cutlass bearing (damaged by fishing line)
Mechanical fuel pump leak (cracked at a fitting)
Transmission bearing (probable manufacturing defect)
Inverter (unknown)
Fly bridge VHF radio (died of old age and internal corrosion)
Raw water pump (obsolete version, broken shaft)
Engine fresh water coolant pump (old pump, seal failure)

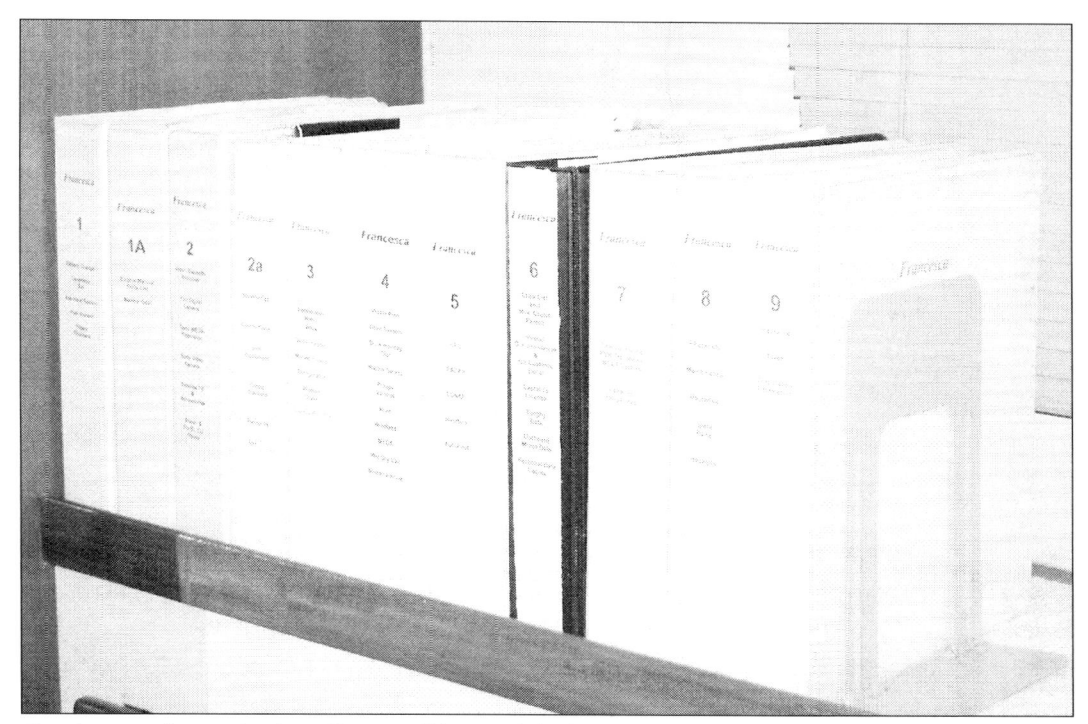

Keeping a well organized, easily accessible set of the boat's records is invaluable. As new equipment or modifications are installed, it's easy to keep up with the changes. As repairs are needed, maintenance data, part numbers and service center information can be found without a hassle. Three ring binders with tabbed dividers work well, however, if space is a problem, scan all the data and store it on CD.

Of these, the transmission problem was the only failure that caused more than a one-day delay. Serendipitously, the cutlass bearing failure coincided with a regularly scheduled haulout. Otherwise, redundancy and an adequate spare parts inventory took care of the rest.

That does not suggest that there aren't other unexpected maintenance issues such as window leaks, computer glitches or washing machine hiccups. But they are infrequent and most often easily managed.

Chapter 6
Building Range

WE HAVE MET A FEW COUPLES WHO, WITH LITTLE OR NO EXPERIENCE, bought their boat and within weeks, set out for foreign shores. In those exceptional cases, the crews successfully learned the boat and worked out the problems while underway. However, with all the uncertainties of boat reliability, weather, and inexperience, it was probably their lack of knowledge that helped keep them sane. We never asked if they would recommend that course for anyone else.

The great majority of us, who are not as impulsive, will take months to prepare for serious cruising. Each experience and trial will add to the individual's and vessel's tested capability. We build our range a step at a time.

Building range is about feeling the boat, having confidence in its reliability, understanding the crew apprehensions (captain included), developing routines and generally making oneself at home on the water. Because of the highly diverse backgrounds of cruisers, it is not reasonable to suggest a preferred method of building range. But here are some ways that have worked well for us.

In the beginning make frequent engine room inspections. Get to know the sounds of the engine(s), shaft(s) and propeller(s), hull creaks and groans. It won't be long before comfort will be found in those *normal* sounds. Also, get to know where the unfixable oil drips come from as well as the normal rate of oil consumption at different power settings. A clean engine will help with this.

To do offshore cruising, good data about engine rpm, boat speed and fuel consumption are needed. Review the suggestions in Chapter 13. But before spending a lot of time making those graphs or tables, be sure the vessel's prop(s) and hull are clean of barnacles and other growth. Just a few barneys on the prop(s) make a big difference.

There is also a substantial chapter on anchoring later in the book, but the main points are briefly summarized here. To gain experience, anchor in as many different settings as possible. Become familiar how the vessel's anchors work with the various bottoms and shifting currents. Here are a few keys items that really count.

Use a large enough anchor.
(Manufacturer specs are always optimistic, get the next size up.)
Use the right anchor for the bottom.
Use plenty of scope.
(Chain or rode in the locker does nothing but hold the bow down.)
Consistently set the anchor.
(About 800 to 1000 lbs of force works well.)
Whenever possible, stay well away from other boats.
(They may be draggers.)
Never use two when one will do.

Don't be too concerned about having limited anchoring experience. Just know the rules, apply them diligently and be alert to changing conditions.

The best open sea experience is gained through exposure to varying conditions. There's no point in going to sea in extreme conditions, (that's always to be avoided), but neither should excursions be limited to only the "pretty days." Instead, work up to increased sea conditions. In a controlled way that will test the boat for: how well things are stowed, fuel tank contamination and autopilot performance. It will also be valuable to experience how, in some sea conditions, it is easier on both the boat and crew to throttle back, go slower and/or tack.

To make crossings in many parts of the Caribbean, the wait for a good weather window and calm seas need not be long. But it would not be fair to say that is the case everywhere. Sometimes it is necessary to begin a crossing in 6 to 8 foot seas (that may be as good as it gets). However, for those conditions, the forecast direction and period of the waves as well as the weather forecast are critical in making a go/no go decision. With light winds, six to eight foot swells having a period of eight seconds or more can be nicely acceptable for a trawler; especially if they are not smack on the nose.

Conditions with short period (4 to 6 second) waves on the bow can make for a real slog. If they are on the beam, without stabilizers, it can be intolerable. The same conditions, as a following sea, can make a comfortable passage if the autopilot is happy.

Few people need prompting to be cautious, yet there are times when patience may wear thin. A bad judgment call regarding weather or sea conditions can result in an overly long, difficult passage. That adds up to an unhappy crew, little or no sleep, extra fuel costs, boat punishment and a variety of other risks. With experience, one's judgment improves. Be patient.

Because we are always asked about storms at sea, here are a few words about them. Our worst storm experiences have all been at anchor; there's more about that in the chapter on anchoring. With weather fax and virtual buoy data there's no reason to be caught at sea in an area wide storm. Squalls are, however, a

Approaching Squall, Panama

different matter. These storms are usually fast moving. They can have high winds and torrential rain, but because they are transient, the seas don't often have time to build. That doesn't mean they can't be dangerous. High winds, poor visibility and lightning are a bad mix. Use radar to avoid squalls when possible. In a squall, a well-adjusted radar is needed for collision avoidance and general navigation.

Crew competence is not internalized like riding a bicycle; it needs to be regularly reinforced. Similarly, vessel reliability degrades with time in port. Thus, even long time cruisers, who have been in port a few months, can have minor feelings of insecurity when the sight of land first drops below the horizon. The more current and well prepared the crew and vessel are, the more confident and comfortable the cruise will be.

Chapter 7
Outfitting

T HE BEST CRUISING ENVIRONMENT IS ONE in which the participants enjoy a lifestyle with few inconvenient compromises. The achievement of creating such an environment requires time, money and a large measure of thoughtful, perhaps artful integration into the available space. Outfitting is a complicated subject and logical progression through the subject matter is needed. Thus, this chapter is broken into three parts. Part I deals with costs and reliability. Part II is an overview of energy production, storage, conversion and use. Part III discusses equipment and special needs.

7.1 COSTS OF OUTFITTING

Cruise ready boats are rarely found on the market. Even recently cruised boats will need replacement upgrades and personalization. More commonly, boats are not so well equipped and, to be made cruise ready, need significant improvements.

The costs of outfitting a boat can be surprisingly high. For instance, a relatively bare trawler may need fifty thousand dollars or more to prepare it for extended cruising. A new boat owner's unbridled enthusiasm to get on with outfitting can increase that costs by 20 to 40 percent. How come? With the convenience of comparison-shopping at local marine stores, Internet sales, eBay, etc, where's the problem? To answer that question, let's review some of the possible expenditures. These expenses are only approximations and range from used equipment (do-it-yourself installations) to new equipment turnkey installations.

Dinghy and outboard	3000–7000
Dinghy davits	2000–4000
Single Sideband Radio	1500–3500
Autopilot	1000–6000
Radar	1000–4000
Upper helm electronics	1000–4000
Computer and TNC	1500–3000
Software and charts	500–2500
House batteries	500–1000

Fenders/dock lines	200–500
Second Anchor/chain	1000–1500
Bow pulpit modifications	0–4000
Inverter(s)	1000–3000
Books & cruising guides	500–1000
Spare parts	3000–10000
Misc. caulk, paint, tools	1000–3000
Storage space mods.	500–2000
Watermaker	3000–5000
Upgrade fuel filtration	0–1500
Solar Panels	0–3000

On the low side this may be about $20,000, but on the high side $70,000 or more. If this is a little shocking, remember this list only covers major items and the expenses don't begin to address the probable need to improve or repair existing equipment, structure or the cosmetics of a used boat.

For those kinds of expenditures, it will be prudent to get an account with a marine wholesaler(s). The wholesaler may require, as a minimum, purchases of $5000 to open an account, but the item discounts will range from 30 to 50 percent below the local retail store. Perhaps the account will only be needed for one year, but even the short-term savings can be whopping.

If there is a problem working directly with a marine wholesaler, find someone who has an account. Fish boat owners, marina workers, marine contractors, and others will often be happy to work with you so that their wholesale account purchases can be maintained above the yearly minimum.

It may not be possible to buy items, such as electronics, through a marine wholesaler, but most of the marine retailers will offer discounts if there is an agreement for electronics outfitting in advance. Electronics usually have a small retail markup. Therefore the savings won't be as great as with other equipment.

7.2 OUTFITTING FOR RELIABILITY

Clearly all of the onboard equipment needs to be as reliable as can be reasonably achieved. But all equipment eventually fails and sometimes there are even infant failures.

When one piece of equipment fails it can usually be worked around without too much difficulty. Yet, when a second and third item fails, albeit non-critical equipment, the situation becomes more difficult. It is well to note that when equipment reliability degrades, the captain and crew's confidence also fades. Take for instance a vessel making a two-day Gulf crossing.

Early in a crossing, an electric toilet chokes. It leaves the cabin smelly and it's inconvenient, but the vessel has a second head and there's always the low-tech bucket solution. With spare parts aboard, the captain can fix the problem at the next port.

Then, a second failure occurs; the autopilot becomes unreliable. Hand steering at night, in anything other than calm water, is taxing. The captain and crew are not only aggravated by the failed toilet, but now also have to work harder. They reduce the shift times to adjust to the situation.

> On the fly bridge sometime later that night a soft drink is spilled on the control console. The sticky fluid runs into the old style non-water-resistant VHF radio causing another failure. Their hand-held short-range radio must then be used for communications and they worry about its battery charge level. Yet, if needed, another functional VHF radio is mounted at the lower helm station.
>
> The captain and mate become anxious about what might next befall them, but they are far from being seriously handicapped. Even though the increased workload of hand steering makes it more difficult for one person to track ships, the frequent use of a hand-bearing compass and the radar keeps them out of trouble. The rest of the crossing is less than enjoyable, but they manage well.

That kind of scenario is not so unusual, especially early in a cruise. But, the ease with which the captain and mate work-a-round and recover from these conditions can make a very big difference in how well the rest of the cruise goes. Work-a-rounds require some level of real-time redundancy and full recovery often requires spare parts. With regard to outfitting, redundancy and a good stock of spares should be of special concern.

But, redundancy doesn't necessarily mean having two of everything. What it does suggest is that there are two and three means to accomplish some function or at a minimum avoid the need for that function. Thoughtfully prepared, a cruise need not be aborted because of peripheral equipment problems. A few additional examples may be useful here.

True redundancy is not often practical for refrigeration equipment; therefore, a work-a-round strategy is needed. For example, the empty spaces in the refrigerator or freezer are detrimental and only show what is not there. Those spaces can be beneficially filled with containers of water. After the equilibrium temperature is reached, the increased thermal mass will cause the unit to cycle less frequently and save energy. Also, should there be a power or refrigeration unit failure, the cold water or ice will extend the time before perishables begin to spoil. If there are both a refrigerator and freezer aboard, ice from the freezer can be used to keep the refrigerator cold.

Throughout the vessel, consider each piece of equipment and what will be done when it fails.

7.3 OUTFITTING POWER CONSIDERATIONS AND POWER SYSTEMS

This section presents information for the new cruiser to better understand the conflict between equipment wants and energy capability. Taken to the extreme, a captain may want to run air-conditioning and an icemaker full time. Of course it can be done, but running an 8 to 10 kilowatt generator continuously will consume 20 to 25 gallons of diesel fuel per day. Over 30 days, that's 600 gallons consumed without going anywhere. Fuel capacity, price and availability mostly preclude this from normal extended power cruising.

Powerboats are usually equipped with and depend upon a generator for the gross power needs. But, what is to be done *when* the genset fails. Alternative power sources are needed to keep the refrigeration and other critical systems running. The captain with the A/C, icemaker and a failed generator is clearly out of business, but to appreciate more practical problems, it is necessary to understand a few things about energy production, storage, conversion and use.

7.3.1 Power generation

Cruising boats energy requirements and the means to generate power vary significantly depending upon how they are operated.

Typical trawler power generation:

Underway
1 or 2, 12-VDC alternators capable of 50 to 100 Amps output. These are sufficient to maintain all batteries in their fully charged condition while at the same time operating the vessel's lights and other equipment needed for cruising. Battery combiners or battery isolators are suggested such that all of the vessel's batteries can be charged by this means.

At anchor
5 to 15 kW diesel generator. The daily operating time required to maintain the house batteries charge should be in the range of 3–4 hours. Without a genset, 4–6 hours daily operation of main engine(s) with high output alternator(s) will be needed to maintain the house batteries charge.

For the best efficiency, generator manufacturers suggest that the installed power generation capacity should be scaled such that normal operation is done at about 50 percent of the maximum load. That's nice, but not very helpful. From that point of view it would be great to have a 2 or 3 kW diesel genset just for charging batteries and another larger unit for cooking, running the watermaker, and everything else. The fuel savings could be significant. Practically, however, we don't need more stuff to maintain, stock parts for, and have failures of. One genset will do fine for most folks. The generators most commonly found on trawlers are capable of 8 to 10 kilowatts output power.

A good genset installation should offer quiet and reliable operation while being easy to maintain. Twenty years ago generators were so noisy that boxes were routinely needed. Even today, some generator manufacturers put their noisy machines in sound boxes to give "quiet" operation. But sound boxes tend to make maintenance more difficult and often hide problems. Worst case they can be a fire hazard. It may be better to select an inherently less noisy, unboxed machine and let the engine room soundproofing do the job.

With greatly increased fuel costs, trawler owners have a new challenge to think about. The diesel generator no longer has an economic advantage over alternate systems. Here are some cost numbers to think about. A $7000, 8 kW generator, amortized over a life of 20,000 hours has a capital cost of $0.35 per hour to run. The genset uses approximately 1 gallon per hour, thus at a fuel cost of $3.00 per gallon, that's an additional $3.00 per hour. If the generator is run at an average 40 percent of maximum load (optimistic), then the cost per kilowatt-hour is about $1.00. (Considering most of us won't be around to use a generator

20,000 hours, the cost per kilowatt-hour is a bit more.)

Alternatively, solar panels, amortized over a life of 7 years (just a guess), and estimating the time at anchor at 30 percent, the cost per kilowatt-hour will be about $1.00. That cost is further reduced (slightly) by the fact that less energy may be consumed when dockside. For a trawler, that is at anchor much of the time, the fuel savings will pay for the cost of solar panels in a year or two.

Since trawlers have enough space for solar panels to provide for all the house energy needs, is there any reason not to do so? The answer is not simply yes or no. Compared with a diesel generator, the initial installed cost of solar panels is low. But, because of the daily 12 hours of darkness and varying degrees of daytime cloud cover, total dependence on solar panels would not be recommended. Yet, with a few additional batteries to help support periods of lean sunlight, it is probable that solar energy could provide the largest portion of energy needs.

On overcast days, sailboats with solar panels must run their main engines to charge batteries. Without a generator, a trawler could do the same, but the run time and economics don't make a lot of sense.

Were we again beginning to outfit *Francesca* today, I think a good system would be to install a small (4 kW) diesel generator and four 100 watt solar panels. The generator would supply adequate power for periods of heavy load and during overcast periods. But, on average, the fuel requirement would be a fraction of that used by an 8 kW generator run three to four hours a day. The lower cost of a small generator would help offset the cost of solar panels.

Thus, the advantages of solar power augmentation sum up to: energy source redundancy, fuel savings, reduced generator wear, reduced maintenance and extended vessel range.

Wind powered generators are less advantageous. They require 15 knots or more to provide useful charging current. However, the combination of solar and wind power has been found to be useful on sailboats and as fuel costs rise, trawlers will be outfitted that way as well.

7.3.2 Energy storage (house batteries)

The normally used unit of energy is the watt-hour or kilowatt-hour. Home electric bills are based upon kilowatt-hours. Cruisers, however, most often use Amp-hours when discussing energy consumption. They do this because the daily energy needs are drawn from batteries. But Amp-hours by itself is not a correct unit of energy. That nomenclature can only correctly convey energy consumption when the associated voltage is included. For example, 225 Amp-hours @ 12 VDC adequately describes energy. From this the watt-hour energy equivalent can easily be calculated as Amps × volts × hours or, for kilowatt-hours, divide that product by 1000.

A typical 6-volt golf-cart battery stores about 200 Amp-hours of charge. When put in series with a second 6-volt battery the combination stores 200 Amp-hours at 12-volts. Series battery pairs may then be connected in parallel to provide 12 volts at corresponding Amp-hour multiples. For example, 8 golf-cart batteries, installed in series-parallel, have 800 Amp-hours of 12-volt storage capacity. Most cruising vessels will have at least six or preferably more golf cart or equivalent deep cycle batteries for house batteries.

Batteries used for engine starting have the capacity for providing high cranking current, however, they are not very tolerant of being repeatedly discharged and should not be used for house batteries. Deep cycle batteries are designed to be tolerant of being routinely discharged to a low level and as house batteries they will last 4 to 8 times longer than starting batteries. But, as a rule, it is best not to discharge any batteries below about 50 percent of capacity. To do so increases the charging time and charging cycle temperature extremes, cooks out more water (for wet cells) and shortens the life of most batteries.

Several different types of deep cycle batteries are on the market. Most notably these are wet cell (golf cart), gel-cell and AGM (absorbed glass matt) batteries. The gel-cell and AGM batteries are more expensive, but they are maintenance free and have other advantages as well. If cost weren't the governing factor why then would Gel or AGM not be the best choice? The answer is that when a battery fails the same battery type must replace it. Although the situation is improving, Gel or AGM batteries are not often available in the Caribbean. Golf-cart batteries are available almost everywhere.

Batteries of any type need to be installed securely and convenient for servicing, inspection and replacement. The fulfillment of those requirements can be difficult given the space limitations on a boat. Structure may have to be added to accommodate the battery banks. See the chapter on Maintenance for more information regarding house batteries.

7.3.3 Energy conversion (inverters)

The next modest space eater and equipment expense is the inverter. These devices need space for free air circulation, but have been known to operate reliably in not too hot engine rooms so long as they are kept well away from the engine(s). If your refrigeration runs on 12 VDC then it is likely that you can get by with a small unit. However, to power up a 110 VAC ¾ size or full size home type refrigerator or freezer, the starting currents are large and a 2000-watt unit is required. The best choice of high power inverter is to install a combination inverter-charger. Most 2kW (and larger) combination units have a quality 100-Amp battery charger for quick charging using the genset or shore power. (The switchover to genset or shore power is transparent and automatic.)

Modern inverters and chargers are designed to be energy efficient. However, motors powered by inverters that produce a "modified sine wave" tend to run somewhat less efficiently than with a pure sine wave. In years past, pure sine wave inverters had been very expensive and the efficiency penalty for using the modified sine wave inverters was not all that serious. But in recent years the argument is closer to a toss up. The price premium for a comparable performance pure sine wave inverter is only 25 to 50 percent more than for a modified sine wave unit. Still, for the dollars, it might be better to have the redundancy of two modified sine wave inverters than a single pure sine wave inverter.

A second inverter will provide redundancy as well as to help reduce the battery charging time. It is also a good idea to divide the boat's AC circuits. For instance, have one inverter dedicated to refrigeration equipment and the other to TVs, computer, lighting, etc. If either of the inverters fails, a switch or simple jumper wire can connect the two circuits after the bad unit has been disconnected.

7.4 ENERGY USE

Somewhere in the vessel's documentation, there should be data sheets for each electrical appliance found aboard. The data sheets for most electrical appliances will list the electrical current requirements. If a unit is to be operated on 110 VAC using an inverter, then multiply the 110 VAC operating current by 10 to determine the approximate 12 VDC current requirements. The ×10 multiplier roughly takes the inverter's inefficiency into account.

The following table exemplifies the 12-hour energy consumption of a typical trawler. Twelve hours is used because it is normal to run the genset in the morning and late afternoon/evening. The reasons for this will be apparent later.

Table I

Appliance	DC Operating Current (Amps)	Anticipated Duty Cycle	Total 12-hour Energy Consumption (Amp-hours)
Refrigerator (¾ size)	15.0	0.3	54
Freezer (home type)	10.0	0.15	18
Watermaker, 8 gph	12.0	0.15	22
Microwave oven	100.0	0.01	1
Lighting (internal & anchor)	5.0	0.2	12
*Entertainment (TV, etc.)	8.0	0.13	13
SSB	2.0	0.1	3
VHF radio	0.2	0.7	2
Computer (lap top)	3.0	0.3	11
GPS	0.5	1.0	6
Fans and Misc.	1.5	0.5	9
Pumps, various	10.0	0.05	6
Toilets	12.0	0.02	6

Total (12 volt) energy used in 12 hours   163 Amp-hours

Or in keeping with proper convention the 12-hour energy consumption is:
(162 Amp-hours) × (12 volts) / (1000) = 1.9 kilowatt-hours

*Most television sets (picture tube type) have instant on capability. These sets draw significant power even when turned off (quiescent power). When they are not in use, be sure to unplug or otherwise disconnect these units whenever battery power is being used. Also, check other consumer type equipment, e.g. microwave oven, VCR, DVD player, for quiescent power to avoid unexpected energy consumption.

Note: A convention is used for batteries which states: the Amp-hour capacity is the total amount of energy a battery can deliver at a constant rate of discharge for 20 hours (before the battery voltage falls below 10.5 volts).

In Table 1, if the appliance is inverter operated on 110 VAC the current requirements have been converted as if 12 VDC powered it. The duty cycle is the proportion of time the equipment will be on and operating and the 12-hour energy consumption is calculated by (Operating current) x (Duty Cycle) x (12 hours). The numbers used are only approximations.

Using the earlier example of 8 golf cart batteries having 800 Amp-hours @ 12 VDC of storage capacity, the equipment needs in Table 1 would easily satisfy the desire not to discharge the batteries below 50 percent of full charge even if they were not charged more than once per day. However, battery charging has another limiting factor. Inverter/chargers usually deliver a maximum charging rate of 100 to 150 Amps and then only when the batteries are sufficiently discharged to accept that high rate. As batteries approach full charge the charging current drops to a lower rate. In this example, the *average* charging rate over three hours would be in the range of 50 to 70 Amps. Thus, twice daily, it would require two to three hours of genset operation to charge the 8 batteries back to their fully charged state. That would consume 3 to 5 gallons of fuel per day.

There are ways to reduce the time and fuel needed to charge batteries. For example, the more batteries installed the better. More batteries equate to less energy drain per battery, higher overall charging current (less charging time), less water cook off and longer battery life. A second way to reduce the charging time is to install a higher current charging source(s). Both methods will apply a higher load to the generator (improve the generator operating efficiency) and reduce generator run time.

7.5 EQUIPMENT SELECTION FOR EXTENDED CRUISING

This section assumes that a vessel is already minimally equipped with VHF radio, depth sounders, refrigerator, radar, adequate fuel filtration, etc.

7.5.1 Communications systems

The chapter on *Communications* covers this subject in terms of the use of equipment, frequencies, times and various modalities. In this chapter the equipment needs are considered, but there is necessarily some overlap of the two chapters for clarity.

7.5.1.1 High Frequency (HF) Single sideband (SSB) radio

The two main types of equipment available are Marine and Ham radios.

Marine radios *are restricted* to operation on only the marine frequencies. This is a disadvantage for those who want to be able to monitor or participate in Ham radio nets, Winlink email or listen to the BBC and other news sources.

Ham radios from the factory *are normally* restricted to transmitting on only the Ham frequencies. They do, however, have general coverage receivers.

The best choice for an SSB transceiver is a Ham unit that has been modified to enable transmission on *both the Marine and Ham radio frequencies*. The modification is simple and well known in the marine radio service industry.

For email communications at sea or at anchor there are several options. The first means uses a high frequency (HF) single sideband (SSB) radio in combination with a terminal node connection

(TNC) unit. The TNC may be thought of as a smart modem. When selecting an SSB radio make sure that it is compatible with a TNC. Older units may not work well or at all with TNCs.

There are a number of TNCs available on the market. However, those capable of communicating using the Pactor II and Pactor III protocols are by far the most popular. TNCs usually cost between $600 and $800.

The two most used SSB/TNC email systems are *Sailmail* and *Winlink*. *Sailmail* is a subscription service using marine radio frequencies and *Winlink* uses the Ham radio frequencies and is a free service to all licensed radio amateurs. *Winlink* may not be used for business communications.

Weatherfax transmissions are a free service of the U.S. Coast Guard (USCG) and the National Weather Service (NWS). The equipment needed for WeFax reception can be of two types. The first is a dedicated WeFax receiver/plotter system. These units are effectively SSB receivers/printers with limited capabilities and which require a dedicated antenna. With a big equipment budget it might be nice to have such a system. Just punch a couple of buttons and, bingo-, weatherfax.

For the rest of us a satisfactory alternative is to use the SSB communications transceiver to receive weatherfax transmissions. When operated in conjunction with a computer this system offers the same capability as a dedicated WeFax receiver. Some WeFax software systems require only software and use the microphone input on the computer. Other systems additionally require a small demodulator that plugs into one of the communications ports on the computer. Compared to the dedicated WeFax receiver, the software systems are quite inexpensive. It may sound complicated, but it is not difficult to use once the few wires are connected and software is installed.

7.5.1.2 Satellite communications

There are a variety of systems available. Most are expensive, but new generations of satellite services are bringing the costs down. The services offer combinations of voice, email and weatherfax data. See the chapter on Communications for more details.

7.5.2 GPS, Computer and Navigation Software

These days virtually everyone relies upon his or her electronic systems. Occasionally there will be a disgruntled gob who decries the need for electronics, but they are going the way of the dodo. Still, dependence upon electronics needs to be thoughtfully hedged.

The GPS or GPS chartplotter are fundamental to easy, precise navigation. Having a backup unit is highly recommended. Some cruisers like the expensive chartplotter chart chips, but at present, most cruisers rely upon their computer navigation software and CD charts.

7.5.3 Computer System

Cruising extensively around the Caribbean requires far too many paper charts to be practical. That quantity of charts would cost more than a good computer system. Several excellent and friendly computer navigation programs are available, e.g. Captain®, Nobeltec® and others. Check with other cruisers on the pros and cons and try each of them before making a decision about which software to choose.

As standard operating procedure before departing on a cruising leg, we print the *Route Report* and necessary charts on 8½" × 11" paper. The charts are then easily handled on the fly bridge and the captain can have as much or little detail as desired. If the computer should pack it in, there won't be a crisis.

Most cruisers have laptop computers. Some even have spare laptops aboard. Be forewarned, however. When laptops fail, local computer repair services seldom have the needed parts and a dead laptop may need to be sent away for repairs. Sometimes this can take weeks. It is also likely that the programs and stored data will need to be resurrected from backup CDs (oh-oh).

On most power cruising boats, there is sufficient room and power to accommodate a full size computer system. For these, parts and service are available almost everywhere.

Whatever the system it's a good idea to have a CD burner to archive your programs, photos, adventures, charts, etc. The system should also be able to play DVDs in case the vessel's TV decides to go south.

A four-in-one, printer/copier/FAX/scanner, is also an excellent addition to the vessel's capabilities. They are very inexpensive and every time an official asks for multiple document copies or you want to share some document or other with a friend, it is great to have one aboard.

WiFi Internet access is popping up at marinas all over the Caribbean; even at some anchorages. Check on the Internet and with local computer stores for a good moderate range WiFi card or USB plug in device. A range of a mile or so will be adequate at most locations. The longer range, more expensive, devices are better, but not necessary at most locations.

7.5.4 Other navigation and collision avoidance equipment

Hand steering during long passages, even in modest sea conditions and especially during overnighters, can be difficult and mind-numbing. A good functioning autopilot can make passages a heck of a lot safer, more enjoyable, and fuel efficient. Without the steering workload the crew has more time to mind-the-store and mind the traffic. Also, during adverse sea and weather conditions the crew's stress levels will be greatly reduced. But, that doesn't mean it's necessary to buy the most expensive autopilot either. Clearly, modern digital autopilots will perform better than the old analog systems. If an old system is troublesome it may be less expensive to upgrade than repair and repair and repair. It's a good bet, however, that the old system's drive unit will be compatible with a new autopilot control unit and that may cover about half the expense. But, with any autopilot, the quality of the installation is at least as important as the quality of the equipment and a poorly installed unit can be less than useless. So, here's just one more bit of homework to be done.

The need for and most uses of radar are obvious and power cruising boats are usually thusly equipped. Some uses a new cruiser may not have considered for radar include anchor watches and weather avoidance.

Binoculars are also helpful for finding range markers, landmarks and other vessels. Binoculars having a built in compass are very helpful for collision avoidance navigation.

7.5.5 Watermakers

Reverse osmosis (RO) watermakers are expensive to buy, operate, have high maintenance requirements and can be easily damaged. On the other hand, properly cared for they offer the convenience of providing excellent drinking water in quantities that allow you to take real showers, wash clothes, dishes, etc. in ways that are a reasonable approximation of land based living. Many serious cruisers have them.

After deciding that a watermaker is justified, don't be too conservative in choosing the size. On first blush it would seem that a 6-gallon per hour watermaker should satisfy most needs. After all, while underway the unit can be run full time and in 10 hours it will make 60 gallons. Well, sort of.

Operating the watermaker while underway does indeed produce good quantities of water. But at anchor and because of the high-energy requirement, a watermaker can only reasonably be run while the generator or main engine is operating. If that's only 4 hours a day, then considering some lack of personal diligence plus the watermaker's startup overhead, a realistic expectation would be only about 12 or 14 gallons per day. Therefore, an 8-gallon per hour watermaker should be considered as the minimum useful size.

Most people think of using watermakers only at sea or at anchor away from polluted harbors. Indeed, the only place to operate a watermaker is in very clean water. A small amount of fuel-saturated water will not be cleaned by the filters and will ruin the RO membrane(s). But, there is another application where using a watermaker makes a lot of sense.

In many third world countries the tap water is of questionable purity or not potable. The water may have been chlorinated at some central facility, yet that is no guarantee it is potable at a dock considering the age and maintenance standards of the water distribution systems. At some marinas, they use well water, but that is clearly no guarantee of safety. With a little care, your watermaker can take that city or well water and process it into very good drinking water.

The instructions for all watermakers include fresh water flushing. Sometimes they describe the method of making battery quality water from fresh water. They also state that, to avoid poisoning the membrane with chlorinated water, you must process the water through a carbon block filter prior to routing it through the RO membrane. Check with the watermaker manufacturer for the best procedure to do this.

There is another benefit of making drinking water from city or well water. Running fresh water through the system every week or two will keep the watermaker fresh and ready to go. Otherwise, for long stays at the dock, the alternative to fresh water processing/flushing is to pickle the watermaker.

Watermakers are expensive and require frequent attention, but they can also add significant comfort to a long cruise.

With a watermaker aboard, a vessel's water tankage can be reduced. *Francesca* originally had 4 tanks totaling about 300 gallons. We removed the two tanks in the lazarette and gained valued storage space. If the watermaker fails, 150 gallons of water tankage is easily adequate (with a little practice) for two people for a month or more. Spartan Sailboaters get by with a whole lot less than that.

Here's a final suggestion on watermakers that some will find to be all around advantageous. A few hours of research will . bought for a fraction of the retail watermaker system prices. For those who have the time and inclination, a 20 or 40 gph watermaker can be built from new components found on the Internet; even on eBay. Along with a bit of PVC pipe and valves, the assembly time won't be much more than the installation time of a purchased complete system.

7.5.6 Freezers

Freezers are not heavy power users and if space is available, it can make a lot of sense to have one aboard. In the U.S. and Canada we are fortunate to have reasonably high standards for meat quality, freshness and cleanliness. In other parts of the world, that is often not the case. Stocking a freezer before leaving North America can provide meats throughout an extended cruise. Other things like the fish catch of the day, berries, ice cream, hard cheeses, eggs (see provisioning) and other special goodies will satisfy basic needs, occasional cravings and help make dinner parties special.

A freezer also provides refrigeration redundancy. If the refrigerator fails, frozen jugs of water from the freezer (filling the empty spaces) can be used to keep the refrigerator cold. Thankfully, freezer failures are rare, but in such an event call upon fellow cruisers to help store supplies until a new unit can be installed.

If space is available, a small dormitory type refrigerator can be a good backup refrigerator or when turned up to maximum, they work well as a freezer. Even the otherwise relatively dormant icemaker can be used as a freezer in a pinch.

7.5.7 Washing machine

Many vessels simply don't have the room for a washing machine. But if one can be squeezed in, it will provide a lot of convenience and savings, even if there is no watermaker aboard and can only be used while at the dock. In some ports, laundry can be done using marina equipment, or other laundry services. Laundry services can be very expensive and charges need to be clearly understood up front. We have known cruisers who have been charged up to 10 times a reasonable fee.

Because of the space limitations, full size home washers are not often an option. There are a few popular small models available in the U.S. They work well and consume only 12 to 15 gallons of water per wash, but they are also quite expensive. One particular machine ($900) has critical internal components that will fail irreparably in 3 to 5 years. A good alternative is to buy a washing machine while in the Caribbean. In Central and South America, small machines are available for $125 to $350. They may not be miserly with water, but our experience and reports from others have been mostly positive. Many of the small machines will run just fine with inverter (modified sine wave) power.

7.5.8 Pressure water system

Almost all trawlers have a pressurized water system, but they usually depend upon the pressure pump cycling whenever water is used. Too frequent cycling causes the little pump switches (integral to most marine pressure pumps) to fail in a short time. To make the system reliable, add a small ballast (accumulator) tank, a common well pump pressure switch and a water pressure gauge. Mount the well pump switch at or near the ballast tank, not at the pump (unless the distance to the tank is very short). The little integral pump switch, which can now be bypassed, will be there if it's ever needed. The cost of the tank and well pump switch is about the same as buying two of the little marine pump switches, but they will last years and years.

Set the ballast tank air pressure with the pump turned off (no water pressure on the system), and at least one faucet open. The air pressure should be adjusted to 50% of the highest water pressure set point to have the least pump cycling. Most boat pressure systems run at 40 to 45 psi. The well pump pressure switch can be adjusted for the minimum and maximum pressures, usually 20 to 45 psi respectively.

Also, most marine water pumps use neoprene diaphragms that can be easily damaged by bits of grit in the system. Install a small screen ahead of the pump to avoid early pump failure.

7.5.9 Television and movies

There are so many types and sizes of TV sets available that the right equipment can be found given almost any space and energy consideration. An alternative is to use your computer system, but dependence on one piece of equipment for navigation and entertainment may be begging for problems.

Below about 23°. North Lat. U.S. satellite TV reception with a small dish is not possible. The U.S. standard 18" dish does not have the signal collecting capacity needed for the fringes. But, if a cruiser plans to be dockside for an extended period, a 2 meter dish will work well down to about 15 or 16° North Lat. At lower latitudes it is possible to get a Latin American satellite TV subscription using a one-meter dish.

The next issue, therefore, is program/movie storage media. Up until recently most cruisers had VCRs aboard and storage of a quantity of movies required a lot of volume. Now, with DVDs, the amount of space required is greatly diminished. Swapping movies is a feature of cruising that many of us relish. Boats are often stocked with a hundred or more movies.

Everyone knows the FBI warning at the beginning of VHS and DVD movies. Briefly restated it says that copying and selling the movies is a federal offense. You can moralize about buying pirate recordings, but the fact is they are available everywhere outside of the U.S. They are sold at department stores, malls, flea markets and on the streets. Some recordings are VCDs and the quality can be poor. They are marked as VCD and generally sell for $2 to $3. Other recordings are good quality DVDs with all the subtitle options. They often cost $3 to $4 each. This information is not an endorsement of the pirate movie business.

7.5.10 Scuba and hooka equipment

A large proportion of cruisers are also divers and where better to have scuba gear aboard than the Caribbean. Occasionally cruising boats are equipped with small compressors or hooka compressors; otherwise scuba tanks can be filled anywhere there is good diving. But, diving gear can be very useful for other things too.

In many bays and harbors marine growth on props, rudders, through hull fittings, engine cooling water intakes and the hull can be a problem. After only a week or two, propeller(s) may need to be cleaned to avoid excess fuel consumption. Generally snorkeling is the best means of cleaning the props. Yet, with extended inland trips or flights back to the U.S., time may slip away and the vessel's bottom growth excessive. A diver can almost always be hired to do the job, but many cruisers prefer to keep up with it themselves. For that purpose, scuba gear is cumbersome under the hull. A good alternative is to dedicate a regulator for use as a hooka rig. To do this, plumb 50 feet of ⅜" reinforced plastic hose between first and second regulator stages. Then, with a tank on the deck and wearing only mask, fins, weight belt and the second stage regulator, it is easy to inspect, clean, and make repairs to the boat's bottom. The hooka rig is also convenient for shallow dives from the dinghy.

7.5.11 Anchor windlass

A rugged, reliable, fast anchor windlass is a great ally. Anchoring and anchor retrieval are easier and the odd dragging event can be better kept under control.

A rule of thumb for selecting a windlass is that it should be sized to be able to lift twice the combined weight of the anchor and all the chain in the locker. There are obvious compromises to be considered here since too much heavy chain in the bow can affect the vessel's trim. Perhaps the best tradeoff is to use lower weight high tensile chain (having the same strength as the next larger size BBB chain) and a large anchor.

Anchor, chain and rode selection information may be found in Chapter 18, *Anchoring and Anchorages*.

7.6 SAFETY EQUIPMENT

Beyond the standard Coast Guard requirements of fire extinguishers, flares, horn, etc., cruisers have to decide about the need for and expense of an EPIRB and life raft. Aside from the expense, there is little controversy regarding the advantages of having an EPIRB aboard. The need for a life raft is not as clear. For ocean crossings, where heavy weather and drifting for long periods is possible, they are basic equipment. They are expensive and require periodic service and inspection. Get the facts on each life raft system that might be considered. In the Caribbean, the vessel's dinghy may be a reasonable alternative if an emergency means of launching has been worked out.

A ditch bag is a waterproof bag or container in which survival gear is stored in the unlikely event of a sinking. It should be maintained and kept where it is readily accessible. Contents of the bag should include packaged food, water, flashlight, and spare batteries, horn or whistle, some cash, credit card(s) and copies of all credit cards, current passports, drivers license, vessel documentation, telephone list and the vessel's insurance covernote.

7.7 TOOLS

The need for a good tool selection aboard is obvious and each boat will have its own peculiar needs. However, here are a few items that may not have been considered.

Few cruising vessels seem to be prepared with a wrench large enough for the propeller nut or have aboard a propeller puller. Given time, they will both likely be needed. Even at boatyards, it can be difficult to find a puller that will fit your propeller. Effective yet simple propeller pullers can be fabricated from two steel plates and several lengths of all-thread with washers and nuts. They can be made from scratch or purchased for under $200.

A Saws-all is not often needed, but can be an invaluable asset. The long blade may be the only good means and method for removing a cutlass bearing.

Another often-overlooked tool is a strap wrench. They are useful for all kinds of oddball needs.

A Brother's electronic label maker or an equivalent is invaluable in labeling plastic food containers, tool containers, wiring, terminal strips, breakers, meters, stock bins, CDs (not DVDs), valves, dating installed components, on and on.

7.8 SOME FLUFF

During the summer, only a few countries around the Caribbean use daylight savings time. There's little point in it since, in the lower latitudes, the sun rises and sets very nearly the same time every day regardless of season. But, there are also Atlantic, Eastern and Central times to deal with. Having two clocks aboard, one for local time and one for UTC may seem a little frivolous, but for us old timers, it saves mental processes and possible error.

7.9 ONE LAST COMMENT ABOUT OUTFITTING TO AVOID AN OOPS

Outfitting a vessel usually takes several months. At the same time, your mate may be working on provisioning. Let's see now-, the boat has never been cruised, you've added: 400 lbs of chain a second anchor, new windlass, 750 lbs of house batteries, two inverters, a full freezer, watermaker and hundreds of smaller items. Provisioning has also added quite a few hundred pounds and all the live-aboard personal gear is aboard. Hmmm, the boat's painted waterline is below the surface.

Most cruisers have to raise the painted waterline a time or two. That's not normally a problem except for the pocketbook and yard work. But, there may be thru-hull fittings in the water that were originally intended to be above the waterline. The plumbing to these thru-hull fittings should have anti-siphon devices installed, but since they've never been needed, they may never have been checked. What this means is that siphoning could take place in any number of pump-out lines. That could be real bad.

Anti-siphon devices easily fail from dirt contamination or material degradation and aren't very trustworthy. There are several solutions. A short term fix is to back the loops up with an appropriate check valve and put them on the pre-cruise checklist for inspection. The long-term solution is to raise the pump-out ports. The abandoned port can then be valved off (and plugged) or removed and faired over.

Chapter 8
Communications and Supporting Electronics

NOT MANY YEARS AGO, before the Internet, communications was a significant problem for cruisers. At sea, scheduled voice communications or expensive ship-to-shore telephone were the primary means to stay in touch. Even landline telephone calls from foreign ports were costly and often unreliable. Thankfully, today we have many communications options. Older systems continue to evolve and new ones are introduced every year. We can now keep in touch with our family and friends frequently, reliably, conveniently and inexpensively. This chapter introduces the basics of cruiser communications.

8.1 LICENSING

The U.S. domestic rules for licensing are a little complicated. To make it as simple as possible, we shall consider that our vessels are to be operated *internationally*. In that event, a Radio Station Licensing is required for all transmitting equipment. In the marine environment, that includes marine HF-SSB, VHF, satellite telephone, RADAR, and EPIRB. If requested, a single marine station license can cover all of these categories on the license application. Like all government functions, the license application has a fair dose of alphabet soup to wade through, but it is not too daunting. The cost for a U.S. Station License is $145 and the license is valid for 10 years.

The Operator's Permit. For international travel, U.S. citizens must also obtain a Restricted Radiotelephone Operator's Permit. There's not much to the form, just name, address, signature and $50 please. The permit is also good for 10 years.

Licensing information and forms may be found at the U.S. Federal Communications Commission website at: http://www.fcc.gov/formpage.html or call (800) 418-3676.

A second type of radio license is the Amateur Radio (Ham) license. The requirements for this type of license have recently been relaxed considerably. Up until February 23, 2007, the General Class license required passing both a technical examination and a Morse Code competency test. The Code requirement has now been dropped. Those with a very modest understanding of electronics can acquire this license which is good for and renewable after 10 years.

Amateur frequencies may not be transmitted upon without having this license *except* in an emergency. For more information regarding testing and licensing visit the Amateur Radio Relay League (ARRL) website at: http://www.arrl.org and for Canadian citizens, The Radio Amateurs of Canada (RAC) website at: http://www.rac.ca

8.2 VHF COMMUNICATIONS

Very High Frequency (VHF) communications is limited to line of sight operation. VHF channel 16 is the international emergency and hailing frequency. Near a coastline, Coast Guard stations (U.S. and foreign) may be called on this frequency. Ships often call other nearby transiting vessels on channel 16 to clarify their intentions during close encounters. It is the most often used vessel-to-vessel hailing frequency. However, for vessels (usually only ships) equipped with a Global Marine Distress Safety System (GMDSS), a continuous watch on VHF channel 16 is no longer mandatory. The GMDSS system relies upon Digital Selective Communications (DSC) to establish communications. That being the case, without having DSC capability, communications with ships on the high seas using channel 16 cannot be depended upon.

Outside of the U.S., cruisers will find that at nearly every harbor there is a preferred boat to boat hailing frequency that is not usually channel 16. Regional cruising guides may specify which channel is preferred for calling. Also, in many of the more popular anchorages, there may be local VHF nets where weather and local information are shared.

On marine VHF radio, there are significant differences in frequency (channel) allocations for Canada, the U.S. and International. However, in the Caribbean, the U.S. channelized frequencies are most often used.

For cruisers, the most used channels are:

CHANNEL	U.S. DESIGNATED USES
06	Intership safety
09	Calling, comm'l and non-comm'l
13	Intership (bridge to bridge) safety
16	International distress, safety, calling
17	State Control, (low power only)
18A	Commercial
19A	Commercial
22A	Coast Guard liaison and marine safety broadcasts
67	Commercial (Intership)

(continued)

CHANNEL	U.S. DESIGNATED USES
68	Non-commercial (intership)
69	Non-commercial (intership)
71	Non-commercial (intership)
72	Non-commercial (intership)
78A	Non-commercial (intership)
79A	Commercial
80A	Commercial
81A	U.S. Gov't only– Environmental Protection ops.
82A	U.S. Gov"t only
83A	U.S. Coast Guard only
88A	Commercial (intership)

In the table above, the "A" or alpha designation is used in U.S. waters to avoid confusion with International channels. The designator is seldom displayed on the radio's panel. In the Caribbean, there is no need to say the alpha designator.

The reason for including commercial, State and U.S. Government-only channels is that, beyond VHF communication range with the U.S., they are often used by cruisers for boat-to-boat communications. As communications is line-of-sight, no interference with U.S. communications is possible. In all foreign ports one must listen and become aware of how the channels are used locally. For instance, dive-shops, hotels or taxis may use normally non-commercial channels. Be courteous and avoid interfering with those operations.

8.3 HIGH FREQUENCY SINGLE SIDE BAND (HF-SSB) COMMUNICATIONS

HF-SSB radio is a roughly 60-year-old technology. Yet, today ongoing evolutionary changes continue to enhance performance and capability. Much like computers, powerful transceivers that were once large are now compact, simple to operate units of only a few pounds.

For those new to long range cruising or unfamiliar with Ham radio, it is unlikely that there has been a need to have a single sideband radio aboard. But, for *extended cruising*, SSB radio should be an important part of the daily routine in a variety of ways. These include: gathering weather information, routine long distance communications with other vessels or shore stations, emergency communications, email, ham radio and for keeping abreast of world news events. These facets can only be introduced here. Other sources are presented for further information. Ham radio applications are briefly mentioned, but for the non-technical user, Ham radio may not be an option.

8.3.1 SSB Email

The two most popular systems are *SailMail* and *Winlink*. These systems both require a Terminal Node Controller (TNC) linking the SSB transceiver to a computer. The TNC can be thought of as a specialized modem for single sideband. They must be compatible with the Pactor II or Pactor III communications protocol. The cost of these small-specialized units is in the range of $600 to $900.

To use either the *SailMail* or *Winlink* systems, *Airmail* software needs to be installed in the computer. The software is free and available for download at: http://www.airmail2000.com

SailMail is a subscription service available to all licensed marine radio stations. The annual fee in 2005 was $250. This covers any quantity of email communications, but *SailMail* requires that use by any one station be limited (on average) to 10 minutes per day. That limit is strictly enforced. The system is effective throughout the Caribbean. Information regarding *SailMail* can be obtained online at: http://www.sailmail.com

The *Winlink-2000* system is similar to *Sailmail* in software and hardware, but is limited to those having Ham licenses. The service was originated and is maintained by amateur radio volunteers. It is FREE and effective throughout the Caribbean. It may be used for private noncommercial vessel support needs, but it is limited to non-business related communications. Information about the *Winlink-2000* system can also be found online at: http://www.winlink.org

8.3.2 SSB Voice Communications

The marine frequencies provide a broad capability for communicating with friends, the Coast Guard and area nets. For every cruising region, daily networks are conducted on both marine and Ham frequencies. The many aids these nets provide include: assistance for medical emergencies, safety and security information, weather information, vessel progress reports, and other boat-to-boat communications.

There are many nets and they are all important. For the purposes of this chapter, however, only the most commonly used Marine Nets are listed. All of the marine frequencies use upper sideband (USB). On the Ham bands, lower sideband (LSB) is used on the 3 and 7 MHz frequencies. Upper sideband is used on all of the higher frequencies.

NETS	TIME (UTC)	FREQUENCY (MHz)
Carib. Safety & Security	1215	8.104
Cruiseheimer's (east coast U.S.)	1330	8.152
NW Caribbean	1400	8.188
Panama Pacific	1400	8.143
Panama Connection (Carib.)	1330	8.107

8.3.3 Weather Information

To avoid repetition and possible confusion, all of the information regarding equipment and weather reception may be found in the chapter on weather.

8.3.4 The World News

The World News can best be found on BBC World Service broadcasts. Reception of amplitude modulated (AM) broadcasts require only a general-purpose short-wave receiver. An SSB receiver can be switched to the AM mode for reception of the BBC and other AM broadcasts such as the Voice of America (VOA), CBC, Radio Netherlands, etc. Throughout the Caribbean, the BBC broadcasts have fair to good signal strength. The service provides excellent world news information.

The BBC transmitting schedule (2005) that can be received in the Caribbean is as follows:

TIME (UTC)		FREQUENCY (MHz)
0100 – 0200	Daily	12.095
0200 – 0300	Daily	5.975, 9.825
0300 – 0400	Daily	5.975, 9.750, 9.410
0400 – 0600	Daily	6.195, 9.410
0600 – 0700	Daily	9.410, 12.095
1000 – 1100	Daily	6.195
1100 – 1300	Daily	11.865*
1200 – 1300	Daily	9.605
1300 – 1400	Daily	15.190
1900 – 2100	Daily	9.140, 12.095
2100 – 2200	Daily	15.390*
2100 – 2130	M-F	11.675*

* With Caribbean news.

Voices of America AM broadcasts in English are directed toward Africa and can be heard in the Caribbean, but reception is spotty. Frequencies (MHz) on which the VOA may be heard are: 5.995, 6.130, 7.405, 9.445, 9.590.

8.4 SATELLITE COMMUNICATIONS

A number of systems are now available offering better communications reliability, convenience and capabilities than the alternatives. They provide a variety of capabilities including: voice only, data only, voice/data, and weather products.

8.5 EMERGENCY COMMUNICATIONS

Older VHF EPIRBs are not very effective because of the high rate of false alarms. More recent UHF EPIRBs are great for mid-ocean emergency announcements and provide vessel identification. The satellite system helps to locate the vessel within a reasonably small search area. Models having built in GPS receivers and automatic position reporting are available. But, dependence upon an EPIRB of any vintage is unlikely to provide immediate local assistance. For that, communications with nearby vessels and/or land-based stations is needed.

Calling for assistance is not as straightforward as it historically has been. Commercial vessels *within U.S. territorial waters* are required to monitor 2.182 MHz and VHF channel 16. But, outside of U.S. territory, that is no longer a requirement for commercial vessels that comply with the Safety of Life at Sea (SOLAS) regulations. They now have Global Marine Distress Safety System (GMDSS) equipment aboard that uses digital selective calling. Thus, a *Mayday* broadcast on the SSB emergency frequency 2.182 MHz will likely yield no results and the VHF radio range may be too short to be effective.

For the Caribbean area, the Coast Guard Radio Stations of interest are NMF (Boston, MA), NMN (Portsmouth, VA), NMA (Miami, FL) and NMG (New Orleans, LA). Effective January 1, 2005 the following emergency frequencies are monitored by these stations.

TIME (UTC)	FREQUENCY (MHz) UPPER SIDEBAND
Discontinued	*2.182*
2300 – 1100	4.125
24 hours	6.215
24 hours	8.291
24 hours	12.290

These are simplex communications channels where the transmission and reception alternately use the same frequency.

Formal emergency calling procedures may be found in any number of documents. The classifications for emergencies are PAN and MAYDAY. PAN is used for a *very urgent message concerning the safety of a ship or person.* MAYDAY is used when there is *grave and imminent danger*.

If the Coast Guard cannot be contacted, here are a few suggestions for making emergency calls. This information is especially relevant for cruisers in international or foreign waters.

First, determine your location on the GPS. Alternatively, a dead reckoned position or other understandable relative position might have to suffice.

Begin by making PAN or MAYDAY calls on VHF channel 16. Be sure to use high power. A nearby vessel or shore station may provide the quickest response to a problem.

Failing that, if the vessel is equipped with a satellite telephone (or in range cell phone), call the emergency numbers that have been conveniently listed beside the handset. (Yes, of course they are posted there.)

If there is no satphone (or cell phone) and if no one is within VHF range, the following may speed the process of getting assistance.

If the time of the emergency approximately coincides with that of any single sideband net, one call should generate a flurry of assistance activity. Although there is only a small hope of coincidental timing, keep in mind that cruisers often use those same frequencies for other scheduled communications. Put out an emergency call on each of the commonly used marine net frequencies.

Next, be aware that any radio frequency can be used in case of an emergency. For instance, If the SSB radio is equipped to give access to the Ham (amateur radio) frequencies, calls can be made on 14.300 megahertz (USB) to the Maritime Mobile Net, the Transcontinental Net or any ham that might be heard. The nets are active during much of the daylight hours. The Maritime Mobile Net has a volunteer medical doctor on call for emergencies. Lower sideband (LSB) is used on all amateur frequencies at or below the 7 megahertz band and upper sideband (USB) is used on all the higher frequencies.

If the SSB radio is functionally restricted to the marine frequencies, then the options are limited. One must then try to find someone conversing on any channel and "break" in. (By common convention, such contacts are made by making a "break, break" call between transmissions.)

Once contact has been established, clearly state and repeat as conditions require:

- the name of the vessel, call sign and home port,
- the position (lat./long.) of the vessel,
- the nature of the emergency,
- the number of people on board,
- the type and color of the vessel and the sea state, weather and vessel conditions.

All other information is of secondary importance. Only after the above information has been successfully transmitted and acknowledged should other details be communicated.

If communication is reliable on whatever frequency it has been established, do not change frequency without very good reason. For instance, if the contacted station wants the distressed vessel to change frequency just as a matter of procedure, do not do so. Once communication is lost, it may not be possible to be regained. A vessel declaring an emergency has priority over other communications.

Interference or weak signal strength may make it prudent to change to a different frequency. No matter which side of the communications you are on, clearly establish that the current frequency will be returned to should contact not be made on the new frequency.

Also, as repeated elsewhere in this book, *in an emergency situation, any radio frequency may be used to gain assistance.*

8.6 COMPUTER SYSTEM

For many of the communications requirements a computer, software and other peripherals are needed. Computer equipment is covered in the chapters on outfitting and weather.

Chapter 9
Provisioning

THIS CHAPTER COVERS A SUBJECT FOR WHICH CRUISERS HAVE A GOOD DEAL OF PERSONAL CHOICE. Some may prefer to stock only specialty items and others the whole enchilada. What is offered here is a provisioning system and other tips about consumables that will help save money, time and inconvenience throughout the cruise.

Thankfully, powerboats and many sailboats have a good bit of storage space. But, where do you start, how much is enough and when is it too much?

The first issue to be decided is where food storage spaces are to be. Here are some things to consider. If the boat has never been cruised or at sea, some storage areas may never have been tested for integrity. By that we mean there may be a chance of saltwater intrusion or condensation. Over time, just a few drops of water can destroy a large number of canned goods. Similarly, storage of bulk foods in hot spaces like the engine room will considerably shorten the shelf life.

9.1 STORAGE SPACE

While there may be many spaces to store materials on a cruising vessel there are also competing needs for the space. Maintenance items such as tools, materials and spare parts necessarily get first priority. It is possible to do without cake mixes, but not the equipment and materials necessary to keep the boat up and running. Maintenance items need to be kept in locations appropriate to the need and frequency of use. Fortunately some spaces that are not useful for foodstuffs, such as the engine room, lazarette and deck boxes are often sufficient for these items.

Foodstuff storage locations need to be carefully considered for dryness, temperature and accessibility. The spaces should be such that the items can be organized, periodically inventoried and restocked. For instance, a well organized canned goods space might be shelved such that each type of vegetable or meat is grouped

Sealable plastic containers are available in all shapes and sizes from laboratory and industrial supply houses. They are excellent for long-term storage of flour, pastas, mixes, sugar, etc. Selecting the best sizes to fit the spaces will result in good storage density and stowage that won't move about in rough conditions.

together. The cans can then be dated on the tops with a magic marker and arranged for first in/first out consumption. Sound like a lot of busy work to you and is it really necessary? The answer is that some cruisers prefer to shop as they go, pay more and sometimes do without. However, this chapter's complete provisioning system will begin paying off at the grocery store and continue throughout the extended cruise.

Before bringing cart loads of provisions aboard there should be an evaluation of the available space and how best to utilize it. In some closets there may be dead spaces wherein shelves can be installed. Similarly, that old icemaker, an item of questionable need, might be removed and replaced with shelves or modified to become a freezer. Take a careful look around. If the intention is to have a well-stocked cruising vessel, every cubbyhole will be treasured.

9.2 CRUISE DURATION

Cruisers, who have done their homework, have a well-prepared vessel and reasonable expectations, may well go on a 12–18 month first cruise. However, six to eight months may be a more reasonable choice for most. During the initial excursion there is more than a good chance of finding a long list of vessel shortcomings. Minor issues can be taken care of while cruising, but more often the cruiser will be glad to be back where parts and services can be readily obtained.

Even on a perfect trip there are times of anxiety. But trying to bull through with a series of nagging problems makes it tough on everyone aboard. If the experience gets bad enough there may not be a second cruise.

But let's say everything does go perfectly. There are still other factors that affect the provisioning stock levels. Some folks like to stay at marinas and eat out a lot. For them there could be a problem of overstocking and spoilage. Other cruisers may ride at anchor for months, rarely visiting restaurants. For them there is the risk of being under-stocked. As a beginning point try to figure out what your expectations are and make some guesses. Then, if records are reasonably well-kept, stock levels for subsequent cruises will be close to the real need.

9.3 BUYING IN QUANTITY AND SHELF LIFE

Vessel preparations such as outfitting, repairs and modifications take months, so there should be plenty of time for the provisioner to shop-the-sales and otherwise look for good deals. Buying bulk lots of canned goods, paper products and boxed foods can also produce good savings. These types of items may be brought aboard at any time during the provisioning process. The overall savings for foods and other provisions can be very significant.

The saving from buying and stocking in quantity can be negated if shelf life is not taken into account. For instance diet soft drinks have a shelf life of only a few months and after six months in the tropics they are tasteless or worse. Thus, frozen foods, beer, and soft drinks should not be purchased until the last month or so before beginning the cruise.

Non-diet drinks like Coke, Pepsi, orange and lemon drinks are always available and often less expensive outside of North America. Tonic water can be found in most, but not all areas and it can be pricey.

About 1 year is all you can expect for many items to remain palatable. Boxed food items like hamburger helper, cake mixes, etc., are almost inedible after a year in the tropics. Flour and corn meal products, unless stored in Ziploc® (or equivalent) bags with several bay leaves, will almost always have weevils after about 6 months. For all dry foods stored in canisters and bags, a few bay leaves will help keep the bugs out without affecting the food's flavor.

Canned foods have expiration dates that should be checked when they are purchased. These items are often just fine a bit beyond the expiration date, but watch out for bulging cans, which of course must be discarded. Mark the date of purchase on each can with a magic marker, then consume the oldest first.

Eggs are always available, but having a good stock in the freezer will take care of those times when the cruiser doesn't go to the dock for a month or more. What? Frozen eggs? Yes indeed! Here's how.

> Break the eggs into a bowl. Break the egg yolks and lightly stir the batch to mix the yellow and white evenly together. Do not entrain air or create froth. Then stir in 1/2 teaspoon of salt for each group of eight eggs. Package the mixed eggs in zip-lock bags (with no air) in meal-sized quantities.

Eggs frozen and stored by this means can be kept for up to nine months. Another advantage of freezing eggs is that some countries have been known to confiscate fresh eggs. They apparently do this to reduce the spread of diseases.

Hard cheeses may also be frozen and have a good storage life when wrapped well in aluminum foil, (double wrapping is recommended). Buy your favorite cheeses in bulk, then cut, package and freeze them in week-sized portions. Most cheeses, except cheddar, are available in the Caribbean.

At sea, your catch of the day should be filleted and all of the reddish colored flesh removed. Then, store the meal-sized portions of fillets in Ziplock® bags. The fish should be covered with fresh water and the air squeezed out of the bag before sealing. The fresh water covering will prevent freezer burn and, with the exception of tuna, months old frozen fish will be just as good as fresh caught fish. Tuna, even the best of it, changes flavor with freezing, but is still fine for chowders.

For the maximum storage density, buy only boneless meats. They can be packaged for maximum storage density in individual meal-sized storage bags. Vacuum sealing is ideal, but otherwise squeeze the air out as much as possible.

For many frozen foods, a vacuum sealer can increase the shelf life and help eliminate freezer burn. For some produce, the bags can go straight from the freezer into boiling water or the microwave.

Labeled storage containers, such as Rubbermaid®, make excellent dividers for various bagged meats and other frozen produce. The containers mold the bagged foods nicely into the available space and help to prevent frost from making solid frozen blocks of groups of bagged foods. When defrosting is necessary, the foods are removed and replaced without damage or disorder.

9.4 WHAT TO BUY IN THE U.S. AND CANADA

Most of your favorite food items, toothpaste, cosmetics, shaving products, packaged meats and paper products can be found at population centers around the Caribbean, but the prices may be several times that found in North America, e.g. $3.00 for a roll of Bounty® paper towels or $15.00 for a small bag of cat food.

But wait just a darn minute! How can that be when the Caribbean countries all have much lower average incomes? The answer is that items like canned foods, paper towels and pet foods are mostly imports and not a big part of the average Caribbean citizens weekly buying habits. They mostly buy abundant fresh fruits and vegetables and other local products. So, unless the cruiser has no budget issues and doesn't mind inconvenience and uncertainty it is best to buy these things in North America. Provisioning special items in the north and traveling in the tropics provides the unique opportunity to have the best of both worlds. Have what you want, when you want it, at the price you are willing to pay.

Here is a list of things to stock in North America:

> boxed foods such as hamburger helper and cake mixes,
> pet foods,
> paper products,
> canned foods,
> meats and other frozen foods,
> pastas, various,
> tortilla chips, potato chips, nuts and other snack food,
> cosmetics, soaps and other personal hygiene products,

brand name hot dogs and packaged meat products,
insect repellents,
ice cream and frozen yogurt,
the Christmas or Thanksgiving turkey,
horseradish.

With the exception of the eastern Caribbean Islands, items that can often be purchased less expensively outside of North America include:

boxed milk, e.g. Parmalat
beer, wine and liquors . (note, bourbon is rarely found)
fresh fruits and vegetables
dried beans, rice
meats, occasionally less
soft drinks
some cheeses

Other items that are priced equivalent to that found in North American include:

eggs
chicken
bread
mayonnaise
margarine
cereals, slightly more expensive in the Carib.
some cheeses

9.5 PROVISIONING OUTSIDE OF NORTH AMERICA

In the Caribbean, there are great places, not so good places and terrible places to re-provision and make repairs. There are also places where it is advantageous to get some types of products but not others. Here are some standout recommendations.

The very best buys can be made at the italicized locations. If no italics are shown, then for various reasons, the locations roughly are equal but still have good prices.

Non-U.S. made liquors only,
    Nassau, Bahamas
Non-U.S. made beer, wine and liquors
    Puerto La Cruz, Venezuela
    Colon, Panama
    Cartagena, Colombia
Duty free, all products including beer, wine and liquors,
    Isla de Margarita, Venezuela
    Isla de San Andres, Colombia
    Colon, Panama (in the duty free zone)
        (some effort required - good for quantity purchases.)
Produce, good and at reasonable prices
    Puerto Rico
    Trinidad
Produce, excellent quality and low cost
    Puerto La Cruz, Venezuela
    Isla de Margarita, Venezuela
    Fronteras, Guatemala (Rio Dulce)
    La Ceiba, Honduras
    Panama, spotty
    Cartagena, Colombia
Appliances and electronics
    Isla de Margarita, Venezuela
    Cartagena, Colombia
    Puerto La Cruz, Venezuela
    Isla de San Andres, Colombia
    Colon, Panama
Marine supplies
    Puerto Rico
    Chagaramus, Trinidad

    Puerto La Cruz, Venezuela
    Cartagena, Colombia
Dinghies, new at reduced cost
    Puerto La Cruz, Venezuela
    (Caribe® manufactured in Caracas)
Marine repairs with large capacity travel lifts at reasonable costs
    Puerto Rico
    Chagaramus, Trinidad
    La Ceiba, Honduras
    Puerto La Cruz, Venezuela
Marine repairs as above, but with bargain labor rates
(more supervision needed also).
    Cartagena, Colombia

If cruisers plan their needs and stops well, there can be big savings with quality service and products.

9.6 MAINTAINING A STOCK INVENTORY

You might think that using spreadsheets to keep track of the provisions inventory is taking the whole affair one step too far. That may be a fair criticism. On the other hand, in the following spreadsheet pages, take special note of the number and diversity of items and quantities. Yup, you can wing it, but isn't it nicer to know what, where and when to buy. Also, because of the range and quantities of the goods, knowing where it is on board saves time and purchasing mistakes.

Of course, everyone will have different preferences, but when starting from scratch it is difficult to estimate the actual needs. These lists should be helpful in that regard. Obviously, the prices will vary greatly, but with randomized errors, one can get a fair idea as to the quantities and cost for a year's supply of stocked foodstuffs.

The spreadsheets we have prepared are for a 12-month cruise duration with two people aboard full time. They have evolved over 6 major cruises. In some, mostly obvious cases, items have *not* been stocked for the cruise duration. These would include soft drinks, beer, margarine, and other large volume, short shelf life items. Other items, only partially stocked, included those that can be purchase abroad at lower costs.

The location legend on the spreadsheet is an entirely arbitrary code. For instance, G stands for galley and the numbers for specific locations within the galley. S is for Salon and so on.

For your specific cruise, decide which items are relevant for you, add some, take some away, make quantity changes favoring specific appetites and make a cruise duration decision. From that point on it is relatively easy to buy in quantity, buy-the-sales, have a fully stocked boat and save a bundle to boot. You get happy shopping while provisioning and happy, easy shopping from your provisions when at sea.

The provisioning, spare parts and pre-cruise checklist Excel® spreadsheets can be downloaded from our website at: www.cruisingfrancesca.org

After downloading, they can be quickly modified for your needs.

9.7 SOME LEFTOVER BITS

With foreign ports on the itinerary, it is necessary to have a quarantine flag (Q flag) and the proper courtesy flags aboard. Buying the whole complement of courtesy flags from outlets in the U.S. can be surprisingly expensive, particularly if each island nation is covered. For sure, some flags must be acquired in the U.S., but as your cruise proceeds, the needed flags can be picked up at the marina swap meets, from other cruisers and local stores with big savings. Some cruisers even prefer to make their own. For many of the island nations, a British, French, or Dutch flag will suffice.

Cruising is never boring, but evenings often provide ample time for reading. So, after having little time for recreational reading during our working lives, we can at last be indulgent. Fortunately, nearly every marina around the Caribbean has a book exchange and most don't worry about the exchange part. But, the book exchanges do need a steady stream of recently published books. In some areas, where mildew is bad, older books become unreadable, even untouchable. Thus, before leaving North America, load up on books and help keep the supply current. One good source for volume purchases is eBay where used books can be obtained very reasonably.

Provision List 1

Nov. 1, 2004

ITEM DESCRIPTION	Source	Size	Quantity	Location	Unit Cost	Total Cost
Canned Foods: Vegetables						
Tomatoes	Kroger	14.5 oz	45	G1	0.33	14.85
Peas	Bi-Lo	14.5 oz	30	S2	0.40	12.00
Corn, Whole Kernel	Kroger	14.5 oz	30	S2	0.33	9.90
Corn, Cream	Bi-Lo	14.5 oz	10	S2	0.50	5.00
Green Beans, Cut	Kroger	14.5 oz	15	P3	0.33	4.95
Green Beans, French Style	Kroger	14.5 oz	12	P3	0.33	3.96
Kidney Beans	Walmart	15.5 oz	12	G2	0.38	4.56
Mixed Vegetables	Walmart	15.5 oz	5	G2	0.50	2.50
Pork & Beans	IGA	15.5 oz	5	G2	0.25	1.25
Refried Beans	Walmart	15.5 oz	6	G2	0.50	3.00
Mushrooms	Walmart	5 oz	25	P3	0.50	12.50
Beets	Kroger	14.5 oz	4	P3	0.33	1.32
Artichote Hearts	Bi-Lo	14.5 oz	6	1P1, 1G2	2.97	17.82
Canned & Packaged Soups:						
Tomato	Food Lion	10.5 oz	45	G1	0.40	18.00
Chicken Noodle	Food Lion	10.5 oz	10	P1	0.40	4.00
Cream of Celery	Food Lion	10.5 oz	8	P4	0.82	6.56
Cream of Chicken	Food Lion	10.5 oz	12	P4	0.82	9.84
Cream of Mushroom	Walmart	10.5 oz	30	S2	0.66	19.80
Cream of Broccoli	Walmart	10.5 oz	6	S2	0.92	5.52
Vegetable	Walmart	10.5 oz	38	S2	0.57	21.66
Clam Chowder, New England	Food Lion	18.8 oz	30	P3	1.33	39.90
Ramen, Packages	Food Lion	pkg.	30	12G4, 5G3	0.10	3.00
Onion, Box	Walmart	box w/2	6	G4	0.77	4.62
Canned Fruits:						
Crushed Pineapple	Bi-Lo	15.5 oz.	24	P2	0.99	23.76
Pineapple Chunks	Bi-Lo	15.5 oz.	4	P2	0.99	3.96
Peaches	Bi-Lo	15.5 oz.	8	P2	0.89	7.12
Fruit Cocktail	Kroger	15.5 oz.	10	P2	0.89	8.90
Pears	Kroger	15.5 oz.	6	P2	0.89	5.34
Mandarin Oranges	Kroger	15.5 oz.	4	P3	0.50	2.00
Applesauce	Walmart	15.5 oz.	6	P1	0.89	5.34
Canned Pie Filling:						
Apple	Walmart	15.5 oz.	4	P2	1.50	6.00
Cherry	Walmart	15.5 oz.	8	P2	1.50	12.00
Pumpkin	Walmart	15.5 oz.	2	G2	0.69	1.38
Canned Meats:						
Tuna	Walmart	can	48	P4	0.25	12.00
Sardines	Walmart	can	12	G6	0.44	5.28
Dinty Moore Stew	Food Lion	24 oz	20	S2	1.50	30.00
Chili Sauce	Walmart	can	4	G2	0.50	2.00
Page Total						351.59

Provision List 2

Nov. 1, 2004

ITEM DESCRIPTION	Source	Size	Quantity	Location	Unit Cost	Total Cost
Juices:						
Apple Juice (concentrate)	Walmart	can	10	VB-P	0.88	8.80
Grape Juice (concentrate)	Walmart	can	10	VB-P	1.28	12.80
Grapefruit Juice	Walmart	1/2 gal.	10	S2	1.99	19.90
Tomato Juice	Walmart	1/2 gal.	10	S2	1.50	15.00
Orange Juice (concentrate)	Walmart	can	10	VB-P	0.88	8.80
Coffee:						
Coffee	Food Lion	13 oz bags	14	P1	1.50	21.00
Coffee	Food Lion	3 lb cans	5	2S4,2VB-S	4.50	22.50
note: Coffees in Latin America are expensive, but many brands are outstanding.						
Milk Products:						
Permalat	Mexico	1 liter box	20	S1	0.75	15.00
Store Brand Box Milk	Venezuela	1 liter box	30	S1	0.72	21.60
Canned Milk, Carnation	Walmart	can	6	P1	0.54	3.24
Condensed Milk	Walmart	can	4	G1	0.97	3.88
Creamers	Walmart	12 oz. jar	15	5P1,10BR flr	1.27	19.05
Hot Chocolate Mix, Carnation	Walmart	can	2	G3	2.18	4.36
Dry Milk	Walmart	pkg.	44	S4	0.45	19.80
Dry Stuffing Mixes:						
Chicken	Walmart	box	8	VB-P	0.96	7.68
Turkey	Walmart	box	8	S1	0.96	7.68
Crackers:						
Ritz	Sams	box	2	GalleyCounter	4.99	9.98
Club	Bi-Lo	box	4	2S1, 1VB-S	1.64	6.56
Triscuts, Garden Herb	Walmart	box	6	G3	1.97	11.82
Lances Peanut Butter	Walmart	pkg.	2	G7	1.97	3.94
Honey Graham	Bi-Lo	box	2	VB-S	1.50	3.00
Club Socials (similar to Club and can buy anywhere outside of U.S. for less than $1.00 for 9 pkgs of 3 individually wrapped crackers)						
Hamburger Helper:						
Potato Stroganoff	Walmart	box	6	S1	1.50	9.00
Lasagne, Four Cheese	Walmart	box	4	S1	1.50	6.00
Stroganoff w/sour cream	Walmart	box	6	S1	1.50	9.00
Stroganoff	Walmart	box	8	VB-S	1.50	12.00
Cheesy Enchilada	Food Lion	box	6	VB-S	1.50	9.00
Tuna Helper:						
Creamy Pasta	Walmart	box	6	S1	1.50	9.00
Futtucini Alfredo	Walmart	box	6	S1	1.50	9.00
Creamy Parmesan	Walmart	box	6	S1	1.50	9.00
Page Total						318.39

Provision List 3

Nov. 1, 2004

ITEM DESCRIPTION	Source	Size	Quantity	Location	Unit Cost	Total Cost
Salad Fixings						
Croutons	Sams	lg. bag	2	G6	3.99	7.98
Bacon Bits	Walmart	bottle	2	G5	1.46	2.92
Blue Cheese Dressing	Food Lion	bottle	6	P1	1.50	9.00
French Dressing	Bi-Lo	bottle	6	P1	1.25	7.50
Ranch Dressing	Bi-Lo	bottle	6	P1	1.25	7.50
Italian Dressing	Bi-Lo	bottle	4	P1	1.25	5.00
Honey Dijon Dressing	Bi-Lo	bottle	3	P1	1.25	3.75
Rice:						
Long Grain Rice	Walmart	3 lb. pkg.	2	1G3, 1G7	1.44	2.88
Yellow Rice	Walmart	5 oz. pkg.	15	G4	0.36	5.40
Spanish Rice	Walmart	5 oz. pkg.	6	G4	0.54	3.24
Beans:						
Black Beans	Walmart	1 lb. bag	10	5G4, 5G7	0.74	7.40
Lima Beans	Walmart	1 lb. bag	2	G7	0.72	1.44
Cereals:						
Great Grains	Walmart	box	6	1G3,1G4,4VBS	2.74	16.44
Raisin Bran	Walmart	box	6	3G3, 3G4	1.87	11.22
Oatmeal	Walmart	box	2	S1	1.77	3.54
Pasta:						
Elbow Macaroni	Kroger	1 lb. pkg.	17	15S4, 1G4, 1G7	0.25	4.25
Spaghetti	Kroger	1 lb. pkg.	14	13S4, 1G4	0.25	3.50
Lasagne	Walmart	box	2	G3	0.88	1.76
Egg Noodles	Sams	bag	2	S1	2.65	5.30
Penne Rigate	Walmart	box	1	G7	1.50	1.50
Bow Ties	Walmart	box	1	G7	0.67	0.67
Macaroni & Cheese	Walmart	box	12	G4	0.50	6.00
Sauces in Packages:						
Alfredo	Walmart	pkg.	8	G7	0.69	5.52
Bernaise	Walmart	pkg.	6	G7	0.69	4.14
Brown Gravy	Dollar General	pkg.	2	G7	0.33	0.66
Page Total						128.51

Provision List 4						Nov. 1, 2004
ITEM DESCRIPTION	Source	Size	Quantity	Location	Unit Cost	Total Cost
Baking Needs:						
Bread Flour	Walmart	5 lb. bag	7	3S1, 4S2	1.12	7.84
All Purpose Flour	Walmart	5 lb. bag	2	1G7, 1S1	0.98	1.96
Self-Rising Flour	Walmart	5 lb. bag	2	1G7, 1S1	0.98	1.96
Sugar	Walmart	5 lb. bag	3	2S2, 1G7	1.50	4.50
Confectioners Sugar	Walmart	1 lb. bag	2	G4	0.98	1.96
Brown Sugar	Walmart	1 lb. bag	2	G4	0.98	1.96
Corn Meal	Walmart	2 lb. bag	2	1G3, 1S2	1.50	3.00
Corn Starch	Walmart	1 lb. box	1	G4	0.77	0.77
Baking Soda	Walmart	box	6	G4	0.25	1.50
Baking Powder	Walmart	box	1	G4	0.73	0.73
Graham Cracker Pie Crusts	Walmart	ea.	4	G4		
Cake Mixes & Frostings:						
Yellow Cake Mix	Food Lion	box	4	2S1, 2VB-S	0.75	3.00
White Cake Mix	Food Lion	box	6	4S1, 2VB-S	0.75	4.50
Chocolate Cake Mix	Food Lion	box	4	S1	0.75	3.00
German Chocolate Cake Mix	Food Lion	box	4	S1	0.75	3.00
Devils Food Cake Mix	Food Lion	box	2	VB-S	0.69	1.38
Cheesecake Mix	Walmart	box	6	G3	1.37	8.22
German Chocolate Frosting	Walmart	can	2	G3	1.00	2.00
Chocolate Frosting	Walmart	can	2	G3	1.00	2.00
Vanilla Frosting	Walmart	can	2	G3	1.00	2.00
Dried Fruits						
Coconut	Walmart	1 lb. bag	3	G3	1.50	4.50
Raisins	Sams	1 lb. bag	4	VB-S	5.29	21.16
Prunes	Sams	48 oz. bag	1	VB-S	3.99	3.99
Puddings:						
Vanilla	Dollar General	box	12	VB-S	0.33	3.96
Chocolate	Walmart	box	6	VB-S	0.33	1.98
Pistachio	Bi-Lo	box	4	VB-S	0.50	2.00
Tapioca	Walmart	box	2	G4	1.50	3.00
Orange	Walmart	box	2	VB-S	0.33	0.66
Jello:						
Lime	Walmart	box	20	VB-S	0.30	6.00
Strawberry	Walmart	box	20	VB-S	0.30	6.00
Cookies:						
Vanilla Wafers	Walmart	box	6	S2	1.00	6.00
Ginger Snaps	Dollar General	box	4	2VB-S, 2G7	1.00	4.00
Vanilla & Chocolate Mix	Walmart	box	4	VB-S	1.50	6.00
Chips & Snacks:						
Potato Chips	Food Lion	bag	4	VB-S	3.00	12.00
Tortilla Chips	Sams	box of 2	2	G2. VB-S	3.99	7.98
Scoops Chips	Food Lion	bag	10	VB-S	2.29	22.90
Chex Mix	Sams	bag	4	VB-P	5.89	23.56
Doritos	Food Lion	bag	4	VB-S	2.00	8.00
Cheetos	Food Lion	bag	2	VB-S	2.00	4.00
Trail Mix	Walmart	bag	2	VB-S	3.00	6.00
Popcorn, Pop Secret	Food Lion	pkg.	87	15G2, 72S2	0.33	28.71
Sunflower Seeds	Walmart	jar	1	G6	1.38	1.38
Page Total						239.06

Provision List 5

Nov. 1, 2004

ITEM DESCRIPTION	Source	Size	Quantity	Location	Unit Cost	Total Cost
Zip Locks, Foil, Etc.						
Zip Locks	Family Dollar	gal. size	6	S1	3.00	18.00
Zip Locks	Sams	qt. 63 ea.	5	S4	2.38	11.90
Zip Locks	Food Lion	pint, 20 ea.	8	S1	2.59	20.72
Zip Locks	Food Lion	mini, 50 ea.	2	S1	1.50	3.00
Sandwich	Walmart	50 ea.	2	G1	1.00	2.00
Saran Wrap	Dollar General	box	2	G1	1.00	2.00
Wax Paper	Dollar General	75 sq.ft.ea.	1	S1	1.00	1.00
Aluminum Foil, Heavy Duty	Sams	150 sq. ft.	2	S1	5.50	11.00
Aluminum Foil, Small, Heavy Duty	Sams	250 sq. ft.	3	S1	5.50	16.50
Trash Bags, Kitchen	Food Lion	13 gal.	4	S4	3.00	12.00
Grocery Store Bags for Trash	Walmart	for sml trash	200	G	Free	
Paper Products:						
Toilet Paper, Northern	Kroger	roll	150	VB	0.19	28.50
Paper Towels, Bounty	Various Stores	roll	150	Fbridge&VB	0.62	93.00
Paper Plates, dinner size	Family Dollar	bundle (200)	4	320S4	2.00	8.00
Paper Plates, small	Walmart	bundle (100)	3	VB-S	1.00	3.00
Napkins	Walmart	bundle	1	Galley Counter	1.00	1.00
Coffee Filters	Walmart	pkg.	365	VB	0.01	3.65
Plastic Cups	Food Lion	9 oz. pkg.	100	VB-S	0.04	4.00
Kitchen, Laundry & Cleaning Items:						
Tide Liquid	Eckerds	100 oz.	2	Stateroom	5.00	10.00
Clorox	IGA	1 gal.	4	2BR,2VB-S	0.99	3.96
Oxi-Clean	Walmart	6 lb.	1	BR	10.93	10.93
Downey Liquid Softener	Dollar General	60 oz.	1	BR		
Bounce	Walmart	box of 60	1	Stateroom	2.19	2.19
Febreeze	Family Dollar	bottle	1	BR	5.00	5.00
Pine Sol	Family Dollar	bottle	1	Galley Sink	2.00	2.00
Windex Refill	Family Dollar	bottle	1	BR	1.00	1.00
Fantastic	Dollar General	bottle	2	BR	2.00	4.00
Purple Stuff	Walmart	bottle	1	BR	4.00	4.00
Toilet Bowl Cleaner	Family Dollar	bottle	3	BR	2.00	6.00
Toilet Bowl Tablets	Food Lion	box of 4	2	BR	1.19	2.38
Dishwashing Soap, Joy	Family Dollar	bottle	2	Under Sink	1.50	3.00
Aerosol Sprays						
Off Insect Repellent	Food Lion	can	4	Salon AC Cab.	4.39	17.56
Hot Shot (spray for mosquitos)	Food Lion	can	4	Salon AC Cab.	3.87	15.48
Scotchgard	Home Depot	can	1	Flybridge	5.96	5.96
Page Total						332.73

Provision List 6

Nov. 1, 2004

ITEM DESCRIPTION	Source	Size	Quantity	Location	Unit Cost	Total Cost
Spices:						
Seasoned Salt	Walmart	bottle	2	1G3, 1G6	0.97	1.94
Sea Salt	Walmart	box	1	1G3	1.08	1.08
Regular Iodized Salt	Walmart	box	1	1G3	0.38	0.38
Pepper	Walmart	can	2	G5, G6	0.50	1.00
Meat Tenderizer				G6		
Cilantro, dry				G6		
Curry				G6		
Thyme, ground				G5		
Thyme, leaves				G6		
Allspice				G6		
Garlic Powder	Walmart	bottle	2	G5, G6	2.98	5.96
Chicken Bouillon				G5		
Beef Bouillon				G5		
Tarragon	Bi-Lo	bottle	2	G5, G6	3.66	7.32
Oregano				G5		
Kitchen Bouquet				G5		
Cinnamon				G5		
Chili Powder				G5		
Basil				G5		
Parsley				G5		
Pumpkin Spice				G5		
Celery Seeds				G5		
Mustard Seeds				G5		
Poultry Seasoning				G5		
Paprika				G5		
Bay Leaves	Walmart	jar	2	G5	1.57	3.14
Wasaba				G7		
Cajun Seasoning	Walmart	Box	1	G7	1.19	1.19
Nuts:						
Mixed	General Dollar	can	10	G3	2.00	20.00
Mixed, large jar	Cosco	2 lb. jar	4	VB	8.00	32.00
Cashews	General Dollar	can	3	G3	3.00	9.00
Honey Roasted	General Dollar	can	4	G3	1.00	4.00
Walnuts	Sams	bag	3	G3	6.47	19.41
Page Total						106.42

Provision List 7

Nov. 1, 2002

ITEM DESCRIPTION	Source	Size	Quantity	Location	Unit Cost	Total Cost
Miscellaneous food items:						
Catsup, Heinz	Walmart	bottle	5	P1	1.25	6.25
Mustard	Walmart	bottle	3	P1	1.08	3.24
Mayonnaise, Dukes	Kroger	jar	6	2S1,2G3,2VBS	1.19	7.14
Horseradish Sauce	Walmart	jar	5	4P1, 1Frig.	1.08	5.40
Salsa	Walmart	jar	3	P1	1.50	4.50
Cocktail Sauce	Walmart	bottle	3	P1	2.00	6.00
Hot Sauce, Cholula	Walmart	5 oz. bottle	3	P1	2.44	7.32
Hot Sauce, Louisiana	Walmart	5 oz. bottle	1	P1	1.50	1.50
Tabasco Sauce	Walmart	5 oz. bottle	1	G3	0.98	0.98
A-1 Steak Sauce	Walmart	sm. bottle	1	Frig.	0.99	0.99
Potato Topping Mix	Walmart	pkg.	3	G7		
Bacon Bits	Walmart	bottle	2	G5, P1	1.46	2.92
Vanilla Flavoring	Honduras	bottle	1	G6		
Molasses	Walmart	16 oz. bottle	1	G6		
Maple Pancake Syrup	Walmart	jar	1	G8, G5		
White Corn Syrup	Walmart	bottle	1	P1	0.97	0.97
Pam	Walmart	can	2	G8 & P1	1.50	3.00
Olive Oil	Sams	jug	1	G8	3.97	3.97
Canola & Vegetable Oil	Food Lion	jug	15	S4	0.99	14.85
Vinegar	Walmart	1/2 gal.	1	G8	1.67	1.67
Peanut Butter	Bi-Lo	jar	5	P1	1.68	8.40
Honey	Walmart	jar	1	G8, G5		
Strawberry Preserves	Walmart	jar	1	P1	1.50	1.50
Blackberry Preserves	Walmart	jar	1	P1	1.50	1.50
Apricot Preserves	Walmart	jar	1	P1	1.50	1.50
Butter	Walmart	1 lb.	3	1Frig.,2FR	1.98	5.94
Margarine	Walmart	squeeze btl.	11	Frig.	0.93	10.23
Ripe Olives	Walmart	can	10	2P1,4G2,4S2	0.69	6.90
Green Olives	Walmart	jar	4	G1	0.98	3.92
Dill Pickles	Walmart	jar	1	P1	2.27	2.27
Sweet Gerkins Pickles	Dollar General	.7 liter bottle	4	P1	0.99	3.96
Relish	Food Lion	jar	5	P1	1.39	6.95
Jalapenos	Walmart	jar	4	P1	1.50	6.00
Corn Muffin Mix	Walmart	box	2	G3		
Pancake Mix	Walmart	box	2	G7, VB-S	1.50	3.00
Hushpuppy Mix	Walmart	bag	1	G7		
Shake & Bake	Walmart	box	2	G3		
Dream Whip	Walmart	box	1	G4		
Page Total						132.77

Provision List 8

Nov. 1, 2004

ITEM DESCRIPTION	Source	Size	Quantity	Location	Unit Cost	Total Cost
Sodas & Teas:						
Pepsi	Eckerds	can	48	S3	0.16	7.68
Twist Ups	Walmart	can	36	S3	0.16	5.76
7 Ups	Eckerds	can	24	S3	0.16	3.84
Sunkist Orange	Eckerds	can	24	S3	0.16	3.84
Ginger Ale, Canada Dry	Eckerds	can	24	S3	0.16	3.84
Gatorade, Lime or Orange	Sams	can	1	G3	4.00	4.00
Nestea	Walmart	jar	3	G3	2.50	7.50
Green Tea	Bi-Lo	box	1	Galley	1.50	1.50
Mango, Passion Fruit, etc. powder	Venezuela	15/box	4	VB	1.75	7.00
Cocktail Mixers:						
Tonic Water	South Carolina	12 oz. bottle	24		0.50	12.00
Tonic Water	Venezuela	can	24		0.50	12.00
Page Total (supply as needed locally)						68.96

For price comparison only

Liquor:						
Tequila	Mexico	1.75 liter	1		12.00	12.00
Kahlua	Mexico	1.75 liter	1		10.00	10.00
Baileys	Mex. or Hond.	1.75 liter	1		10.00	10.00
Rum	Honduras	.75 liter	1		3.00	3.00
Rum, Santa Thereisa	Venezuela	.75 liter	1		2.66	2.66
Rum, Anniversario	Venezueal	.75 liter	1		5.60	5.60
Scotch, Clan McGregor	Venezuela	.75 liter	1		3.77	3.77
Beer:						
Coors Lite	South Carolina	can	24		0.55	13.20
Gallo	Guatemala	can	24		0.55	13.20
Brahma or Polar	Venezuela	can	24		0.19	4.56
Wine:						
Cab. Sauv. Castillo Diablo (2004)	South Carolina	bottle reg.	1		12.00	12.00
Cab. Sauv. Castillo Diablo (2004)	Venezuela	bottle reg.	1		6.00	6.00
Page totals						

Provision List 9

Nov. 1, 2004

ITEM DESCRIPTION	Source	Size	Quantity	Location	Unit Cost	Total Cost
Dental Care:						
Toothpaste	Flea Market	tube	4	BR	1.00	4.00
Toothbrushes	Flea Market	ea.	4	BR	1.00	4.00
Dental Floss	Walmart	ea.	2	BR	2.66	5.32
Dental Tape	Walmart	ea.	2	BR	3.78	7.56
Toothpicks	Walmart	box	1	G6		
Medical items:						
Neosporin	Sams	tube	1	BR	4.00	4.00
Benadryl	Sams	tablets	1	BR	5.00	5.00
Liquid Bandaid	CVS	box	1	BR	6.97	6.97
Echinacea	CVS	bottle	2	Galley	3.00	6.00
Theraflu, lemon flavor	Walmart	box	3	BR	4.00	12.00
Bengay	Walmart	tube	1	BR	5.97	5.97
Cotton Balls	Dollar General	bag	1	BR	1.00	1.00
Q tips	Walmart	box	1	BR	1.00	1.00
Cosmetics and Cremes						
Oil of Olay	Walmart	ea.	2	BR	8.37	16.74
Hand Creams	Walmart	ea.	3	BR	2.97	8.91
Mascara	Walmart	ea.	1	BR	3.47	3.47
Eyebrow Pencil	Flea Market	ea.	2	BR	1.00	2.00
Lipstick	Walmart	tube	2	BR		
Lip Balm	Eckerds	tube	6	BR	1.50	9.00
Personal Hygene Products:						
Bar Soap, Dial	Dollar General	bar	16	BR	0.50	8.00
Bar Soap, Dove	Dollar General	bar	8	BR	0.50	4.00
Liquid Hand Soap, Antibacterial	Dollar General	bottle	1	BR	2.00	2.00
Deodorant	Flea Market	ea.	4	BR	2.00	8.00
Shampoo	Walmart	bottle	2	BR	1.84	3.68
Computer, Misc. Supplies						
Printer Paper	Sams	case	1	BR	16.93	16.93
Labeler Tapes, Brothers	Office Max	box	2	S4	5.00	10.00
Printer Cartridge (Black)		ea.	2			
Printer Cartridge (Color)		ea.	2			
CDs R,		pkg.	50			
Printer Cartridge Refill Kit		kit	1			
Flashlight Bulbs	Walmart	ea.	5	S4	2.00	10.00
AA NiMh Batteries	Walmart	ea.	12			
AAA NiMh Batteries			8			
DVDs -R			50			
Page Total						122.70

Provision List 10

Nov. 1, 2004

ITEM DESCRIPTION	Source	Size	Quantity	Location	Unit Cost	Total Cost
Freezer Foods:						
Chicken, boneless	Various	2 per pkg.	30	FR	2.50	75.00
Chicken, Cut-up	Various	2 per pkg.	6	FR	4.00	24.00
Pork Chops	Various	2 per pkg.	30	FR	2.00	60.00
Steak	IGA	1 per pkg.	40	FR	4.00	160.00
Hamburger	IGA	2 per pkg.	40	FR	1.00	40.00
Hot Dogs, Oscar Mayer Beef	Various	8 pkg.	6	FR	2.00	12.00
Shrimp	at Dock	24 per pkg.	12	FR	3.00	36.00
Kielbasa	Walmart	ring	3	FR	2.00	6.00
Bacon	Food Lion	lb.	6	FR	3.00	18.00
Sausage	Food Lion	lb.	3	FR	1.50	4.50
Eggs	Bi-Lo	doz.	4	FR	1.00	4.00
Bell Pepper	Food Lion	pkg.	3	FR	1.00	3.00
Beef Roasts	Various	2 lb.	3	FR	4.50	13.50
Limeade	Food Lion	sm.	2	FR	0.69	1.38
Ice Cream	Food Lion	1/2 gal.	2	FR	2.50	5.00
Butter	Walmart	1 lb.	4	FR	2.50	10.00
Cheese, Cheddar	Food Lion	1lb.	3	FR	1.65	4.95
Blueberries	Free	2 cup pkg.	15	FR		
Ham slices	Kroger	1/4" slices	6	FR	2.00	12.00
Strawberries	Free	pkg.	6	FR		
Page Total (food)						489.33
Pet Needs (sm. dog):						
Health Certificate			1		35.00	35.00
Heartworm Antigen Test			1		24.00	24.00
Distemper/Parvo Vaccine			1		27.00	27.00
Topspot Plus (frontline)		3 per box	6		32.50	195.00
Interceptor (green)		6 per box	3		16.34	49.02
Shampoo, Relief			3		10.00	30.00
Greenies			2		15.99	31.98
Carrot Bones			3		2.49	7.47
Nutro food (chicken meal & rice)		5 lbs.	2		5.80	11.60
Page Total (pet supplies)						411.07

Chapter 10
Spare Parts

As one would expect, the degree to which spare parts are stocked depends upon the time and distance of the intended cruise as well as the availability and price of parts along the way. After that, the selection of parts for inventory can be boiled down to factors of, critical spares, non-critical spares and consumables. Finally, the approximate stock level for each part can be deduced from the quantity (e.g. two engines), age and maintenance history of the boat's equipment.

Some examples may be helpful.

- Critical spares are parts which malfunction can prevent a vessel from making way. They include, but are not limited to:
  - raw water pump(s) and impellers
  - fresh water pump(s)
  - belts, hoses
  - heat exchangers, various
  - alternator(s), regulators
  - starter(s), solenoid(s)
- Non-critical spares include:
  - toilet repair kit(s),
  - macerator or repair kit,
  - house batteries,
  - genset parts
  - radio equipment

Consumable spares include:
- oil and fuel filters,
- zincs,
- raw water pump impellers,
- motor oil,
- water filters
- fuses, light bulbs, wire ties
- O-rings, hose clamps, tapes

10.1 CRITICAL SPARES

These components should be aboard for nearly all offshore trips. While it is true that a twin-engine vessel can make it to a port on a single engine, without adequate spare parts the best-case scenario for repairs will be one of delays. Receiving parts in foreign ports can be frustrating and costly. For example, shipping is expensive, parts can be lost in transit, there may be customs delays or the wrong part may be sent. Added to that, a vessel may be stuck in a place not of the crews liking. Spare parts are expensive, but not having a stock of critical parts aboard adds a significant risk of delays and economic uncertainty to any extended cruise.

10.2 NON-CRITICAL SPARES

These parts aren't showstoppers, but the lack thereof can be very inconvenient. Imagine having all of the toilets inoperable. No one will be pleased with a malodorous vessel or the problems associated with the need of a porta-bucket. Similarly irritating, a genset failure can require seeming endless hours of main engine operation to keep the house batteries up. These spares aren't often as individually expensive as critical spares, but they are likely to be more numerous in type and quantity.

10.3 CONSUMABLE SPARES

The decision to stock high levels of consumable spares can save a lot of time and money, but it is mostly a matter of convenience. For instance, engine heat exchanger zincs can be purchased in the States, from a catalog, in small bulk packages and at a reasonable price. In foreign ports the correct size may take time to locate and when found, have to be purchased piecemeal at a higher price. In that regard, fuel filters and raw water impellers can be an even bigger problem.

10.4 SPARE PARTS INVENTORY

The following spreadsheets are examples of an effective means of maintaining a spares inventory. Cross-referenced part numbers should be included when possible. The listing of spare part's locations on the boat may be particularly helpful in time critical situations.

The spare parts, provisioning and pre-cruise checklist spreadsheets can be downloaded from our website at: www.cruisingfrancesca.org

After downloading, they can be tailored for your needs.

Spare Parts and Consummables Inventory   12/15/2005

	Type & model number	Location	Desired Stock Level	Qty on hand
Ford Lehman Engines	Oil Filter PH8A or Napa 1515	Eng. Rm.	6	6
	Fuel Filter, Racor			
	2 micron element - 2040SM-OR	Eng. Rm.	5	4
	10 micron element - 2040TM-OR	Eng. Rm.	5	4
	Raw Water Pump (complete)	Laz.	1	1
	Raw Water Pump Impellers	Salon	6	4
	Jabsco 1210-0001 or Globe model 075			
	Raw Water Pump Rebuild Kits (wear plates)	Laz.	2	1
	Engine Heat Exchanger	Laz.	1 used	1 used
	Engine Oil Cooler	Laz	2 used	2 used
	Transmission Oil Cooler	Laz.	1	0
	Damper Plates	Laz.	2	2 used
	Belts	Laz.	2	2
	Alternator	Laz.	1	2 used
	Engine Mechanical Fuel Pump	Laz.	1	1 new, 1 used
	Fresh Water Coolant Pump	Laz.	2	2
	Exhaust Elbow	Laz.	1 new, 1 used	1 new, 1 used
	Water Hose Kit	Salon	1 set	1 set
Genset	Bando Belt FM 37.6	Salon	1	1
	Kubota " Raw Water Pump Impeller	Salon	2	1
	Kubota Fresh Water Coolant Pump	Salon	2	1
	Primary Fuel Filter - Racor R20P	Eng. Rm.	1	1
	Secondary Fuel Filter - Luber-finer FP-591-F	Eng. Rm.	2	1
	Oil Filter Kubota 16271-32090	Eng. Rm	2	1
	Car Quest 85064, Purolator L24458			
Outboard Motor	Outboard Motor, Fuel Filter, GF61A	Eng. Rm.	0	1
	Outboard Motor, Oil Filter	Eng. Rm.		
	Fram PH6017A, Yam. 3FV-13440-00	Eng. Rm.	2	3

Spare Parts Inventory, page 2

	Type & model number	Location	Desired Stock Level	Qty on hand
Pump Repair Kits				
	Macerator Repair Kit, Jabsco 18598-1000	Salon	1	2
	Electric Toilet Repair Kit, Jabsco 37040-000	Salon	2	0
	FW Pump Repair Kit for Jabsco 30620-0012	Salon	0	0
Zincs				
	Engine Heat Exchanger	Eng. Rm.	16	10
	Genset Heat Exchanger	Eng. Rm.	10	6
	Rudder 5" dia.	Eng. Rm.	2	4
	Shaft 1 3/4"	Eng. Rm.	6	2
Oil				
	Rotella 40 wt.	Eng. Rm.	10	6
	OB Motor Oil, 20W40	Aft cabin floor	2 qts	2 qts
	Lower End Lubricant, Hypoid 90	Eng. Rm.	2-10 oz tubes	1 tube
Dinghy				
	Battery	Aft Dock Box	1	1
	Propeller (9 1/4" x 10 1/2"- J)	Lazarette	1	2 for repair
Biobor	Fuel Biocide	Salon Step	1 pint	1 pint
Watermaker	10u Prefilter	Laz.	8	12
	Carbon Block Filter	Laz.	2	2
	Pump Oil	Laz.	1 quart	1 quart
	Cleaner Chemical #1	Laz.	1 pint	1 pint
	Cleaner Chemical #2	Laz.	1 pint	1 pint
	Pickling Chemical	Laz.	1 pint	1 pint
House Batteries				
	Golf Cart Battery	Eng. Rm.	1	0
Computer				
	Black Ink Cartridge, Lexmark 70	Comp. shelf	2	2
	Color Ink Cartridge, Lexmark 15M0120	Comp. shelf	2	1
	Refill Ink, Black	Comp. shelf	1 pt	1 pt
	Refill Ink, Color	Comp. shelf	1/3 pint each	1/3 pint each
	Paper	Aft stateroom	1 case	1 case
	DVD-R disks	Comp. Shelf	50	14
	CD-R disks	Comp. Shelf	50	32
	Diskettes	Comp. Shelf	10	2
	Bus. Card Stock, Avery 8571	V-berth	1 pkg	1/4 pkg
Label Maker				
	Tape, White w/1/2" Black Letters, TZ-231	Salon	2 cartridges	1/2 cartridge
Batteries				
	D cells	Salon	8	6
	C cells	Salon	4	2
	AA cells, NiMH	Salon	12 rchrgble	12 rchrgble
	AAA cells	Salon	12	6 rchrgble

Chapter 11
Preparing For Foreign Destinations

Your vessel is well stocked with provisions, the cruising plan and route are complete, the necessary courtesy flags and quarantine flag are aboard and the fuel tanks topped off. The next stop is some foreign port. You are all prepared. Well, maybe -.

Depending upon the cruise duration, it may be a good idea to get the U.S. Customs Decal before leaving the states. It will be necessary to have or get one upon your return. Information regarding the purchase of a Customs Decal sticker can be obtained by email through *Decal Help Desk* at decals@dhs.gov. The cost is $25 per year.

If you are away for a lengthy period, your vessel documentation renewal may come due. It is a simple matter of signing the *Renewal Certification* form and sending it in, but if the due date is missed, it will cost about $100. If you don't receive a renewal form by mail, they can be obtained through the Internet at www.uscg.mil. On the main USCG screen, click on services. Then, under the heading Marine Safety & Environment Protection, click on Vessel Documentation Forms.

Most cruisers carry current cruising guides and other pertinent reference material. These are needed and very helpful, but even current guides are not truly current. They offer general guidance, but for check-in/out procedures, nothing beats talking with fellow cruisers on VHF before going through the process.

Checking in and out of foreign ports is always a little wearing, even when it has been done a hundred times before. The reason for this is that every foreign port has a different way of doing things. At some ports, it is necessary to check-in first with the Port Captain, then immigration, customs, and sometimes agriculture and health officials. In others, only visits to the Port Captain and immigration are necessary. At yet others, an agent is required. In some ports of entry, only the captain is allowed off the vessel until cleared in, while in others, all crewmembers and passengers must go to immigration. To make matters more confusing, sometimes these characteristics change from year to year. What's a captain to do?

Here's a little story.

> A bright nicely outfitted ketch entered a foreign harbor after a two night crossing and dropped the hook sometime just at daybreak. The captain, Bill, and mate, Jean, very reasonably slept until 10:00 AM before arousing. After a shower, the captain gathered up all of his papers, stuffed them in a plastic bag, launched the dinghy and went ashore.
>
> Finding the Port Captain, Bill is quickly on the defensive because the Port Captain wants to know why he didn't check-in immediately when the office opened at 8:00 AM. After some discussion, that issue is settled, but not before Bill has been reprimanded.
>
> Then Bill offers his pile of papers. The Port Captain is not at all impressed. He wants things neat and tidy. After ruffling through them, he tells Bill to go and get multiple photocopies of several documents. The photocopy shop is 4 blocks away.
>
> Three quarters of an hour later and after returning with the copies, the Port Captains tells Bill to first go to the clinic, second to immigration, third to customs and then return to the Port Captain's office.
>
> Eight blocks away, the clinic check-in goes well. Only a few papers need to be stamped and there is no charge. Bill is showing some signs of stress and impatience, not to mention the perspiration circles under his arms. He's tired, a little intimidated and doesn't like it one bit. He says to himself that in the USA this process would be more organized and efficient.
>
> At the immigration office the official is unhappy that Bill's spouse has not accompanied him. He is directed to go back to the boat and bring her to the office. This results in another long walk, a dinghy ride, and another long walk. Returning they find that the immigration office has been closed for the two hour lunchtime. A quick check also reveals that the customs office is closed.
>
> Well hell, it's time for lunch anyway so Bill and Jean find a nice little restaurant to relax with a beer or three, some chips, salsa and four tired feet. They discuss how awful and stupid this procedure is and feed upon each other's frustrations.
>
> Finally, the immigration office opens. The official says that they must go to the bank to pay the immigrations fee. The bank is only a block away. After payment and back at immigration, they get their 30-day visas and passports stamped. Next stop, customs-, but the office still isn't open. So, Bill and Jean sit on the steps waiting for the official to return. After a half-hour in the hot sun, Bill's patience is at an all time low. He and Jean storm down to the Port Captain's office.

> The Port Captain is not impressed with Bill's demeanor. He says simply that the customs office is only infrequently open and not to worry about it. Bill fumes. Fortunately, the Port Captain has been at his job for several years and has some understanding of the nature of a captain's first exposure to the process. When Bill begins to show his anger the Port Captain will have none of it and with a few choice words Bill wilts like a damp rag. It is a fool's errand to argue with the officials unless they are being unreasonable – and know it.
>
> At last the Port Captain has Bill sign some papers, hands him a few documents and explains that the procedure to checkout of the port must be followed precisely. They are finally checked in. It only took 5 hours, elevated blood pressure, sweat, some choice words and, oh yeah-, 155 USD, (Isla Mujeres, Mex.).
>
> That is how NOT to check in to a foreign port. Understand that with a little more stress and less friendly officials there could have been bogus fines, fees, lost papers, delays and. . . . End of little story.
>
> (It has been reported that Mexico now requires an agent for check-in/out.)

Admittedly, the preceding little story is an extreme case, but it has happened.

Now here is how to go through check-in / out with the least upset. Upon entering the port, fly the courtesy flag (right side up if you please) above the quarantine (Q) flag. Try to schedule your arrival for the early morning during a weekday and drop the hook in the anchorage. Rarely are cruising boats allowed to go to a marina before checking in. In many ports overtime will be charged for weekends, holidays and arrivals outside normal business hours. Refer to the cruising guide for the check-in procedure, but also ask other cruisers in the anchorage on VHF radio if there have been any changes. You may be caught off guard by arriving during a holiday. You can't win 'em all, but then again there's no point in trying to check in near the lunch hour or late in the day.

Then, have all the personal and boat papers neatly secured in a binder or file folder. Be prepared with copies of the crew list, vessel documentation, passports, zarpe (if checking in from foreign port other than the USA), pet health certificate, pet rabies vaccination certificate and vessel insurance policy cover note (rarely requested). Multiple copies may be required of several of the items and as many as 5 copies of the crew list may be needed.

> Note: the zarpe is a document prepared at the previous Port Captain's office. In essence, the zarpe is the official clearance for traveling from one port to another. The document is recognition that all of the paper work was completed, there have been no reported complaints, unpaid bills or criminal behavior against the crew and the crew has been properly accounted for.

With the convenience of scanners and computers, a really good way to present your crew list may be seen in the following example pages. One side of the page is printed in Spanish while the other is in English. That crew list is seldom an accepted format, but all of the information can be clearly understood and the officials often appreciate it, especially when there is a language problem.

Vessel Specification for motor vessel <u>vessel name</u>

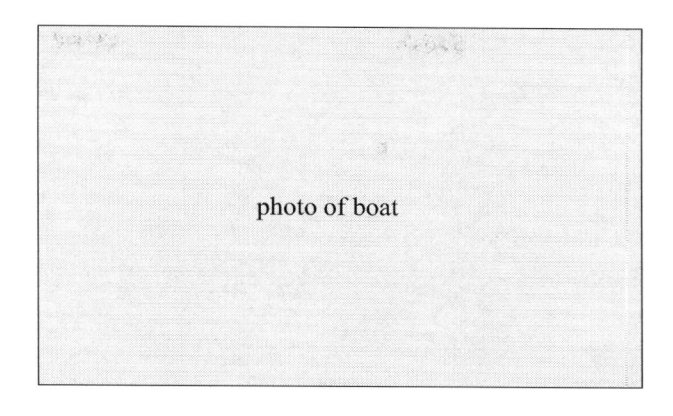

[photo of boat]

Vessel Name:
Flag: Country
Registration: Reg. Number and home port
Owner:
Type: Trawler, sport fish, etc.
Hull matl.:   Steel, fiberglass etc.
Length: feet & inches
Beam: feet & inches
Draft: feet & inches
Gross Tonnage: tons
Net Tonnage: tons
Color: hull and trim
Motor(s):   make
HP: each engine
Dinghy: Make, year & hull ID number
Dinghy OB: Make, year, hp and serial number

Crew list for motor vessel <u>vessel name</u>

[photo of captain]   [photo of crew member]

_____, Captain   _____, Mate
Nationality: Nationality:
Passport No: (and place of origin)   Passport No:
DOB: DOB:

Informacion del embarcacion <u>vessel name</u>

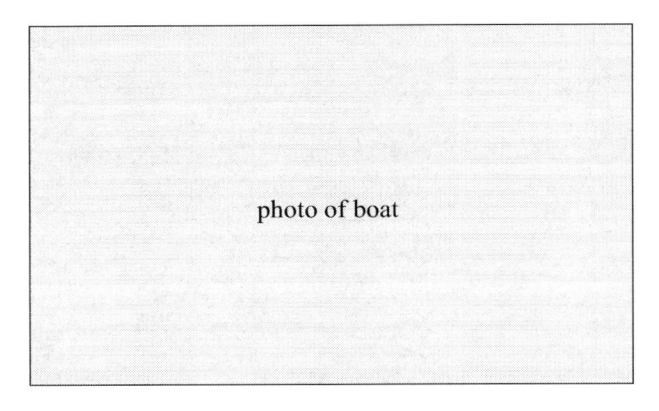

[photo of boat]

Nombre:	vessel name
Bandera:	country e.g. Estados Unidos
Marticula:	registration e.g. Estados Unidos numero registration number
Proprietario:	owners name
Tipo:	vessel type e.g. Motor Yate
Hull:	Hull material e.g. Fibra
Eslora:	length in meters
Manga:	beam in meters
Calado:	draft in meters
Tonnelada:	tunage e.g. 34 tonnes gross, 27 tonnes net
Color:	e.g. Blanco con rojo
Motor(s):	e.g. 2 - Ford Lehman, 6 cylindros diesel
HP:	e.g. 120 caballos poder
Dinghy:	Make, length, year & hull ID number
Dinghy OB:	Make, year, hp and serial number

Lista tripulacion para <u>vessel name</u>

[photo of captain]   [photo of crew member]

_____, Capitano   _____, Tripulante
Nacionalidad: Nacionalidad:
Pasaporte numero: Pasaporte numero:
Nacido: DOB   Nacido: DOB

11.1 BOARDING INSPECTIONS

Often there must be an official visit to the arriving vessel. In some ports the inspection may be made soon after the vessel has been anchored. In other ports the inspections will be made after the Port Captain's office has been visited. There can be as many as five departments represented for the inspection tour(s). Most often only one to three officials will visit. When being visited by various officials be pleasant, patient, respectful and help the officials through the process. You might wish to offer them soft drinks, water or even beer to provide a friendly climate.

The inspections are simple but there can be concerns about fresh fruits, vegetables, meats and even eggs. Confiscations are rare, but an extreme case happened in Belize where an "official" confiscated all of a vessels fruits and vegetables that had just been provisioned in Guatemala. In some other instances, there have even been bogus fines. Check the cruiser's nets on VHF and SSB for the current scuttlebutt. Foolishness such as this may often be avoided by changing to a different port of entry.

11.2 THE CHECK-IN

Next, take a few minutes to freshen up, dress respectfully and have breakfast. Then, launch the dinghy, gather up your papers, put your mind and impatient nature in neutral, and with a smile, head for the Port Captain's office.

Well informed and prepared, the check-in procedure most often can be completed in one to two hours, sometimes less. But occasionally and no matter how well you're prepared, the "officials" can be uncooperative. We have experienced officials who dragged out the process with personal phone calls, chats with other office workers or fiddled with other paperwork and other delaying ploys. It may seem they do it just to annoy you. Be patient and don't get riled. Act as though you have all the time in the world.

Only rarely, these days, does a cruiser run afoul of an official who tries to charge a bogus fee or asks for a "tip." Hopefully those bad old days are gone forever. But just in case, have witnesses around when dealing with officials where there might be a question regarding their integrity. Always ask for a receipt for unusual charges. That alone may change their need for a fee.

At a few ports, an agent is required for both check-in and checkout. Using an agent is always a little more expensive, but makes it easier for the captain and crew. However, before using an agent, first determine that an agent is necessary and then what the charges are to be. Make certain that the agents fees are in line with *normal* charges. A few years ago, in Honduras, where check-in is simple, normally done by the captain and costs less than five dollars, a captain was charged, and actually paid, $250 to an *agent*.

Clearing in and out of foreign ports is rarely enjoyable and can be tedious. We have had many more good check-ins than bad. Scams and rip-offs are exceptions and can be avoided by getting up to date information from fellow cruisers. So, be prepared, respectful, relax, smile and make the best of it. During the process, get the information needed for the eventual, generally less stressful, checkout. Once your vessel is cleared in, take down the Q flag and begin enjoying the neighborhood.

11.3 TRAVELING BY AIR BACK TO NORTH AMERICA

Often cruisers have to fly home for some reason or other. There is a pitfall to be avoided.

A cruiser needing to fly home has properly purchased a round trip ticket to the U.S. or Canada. But when the traveler later attempts to return using the second half of the round trip ticket, they are told that they must have a round trip ticket to the foreign country or they won't be allowed to enter that country. Well, nuts, it's a catch-22. The airline folks should then tell the traveler that they can later get a refund for the second leg of the trip, but a good bit of cash will be tied up, perhaps for several months. It's even more difficult if it's a foreign airline.

To avoid that trap, the traveler should have carried along copies of the boat's papers and all the check-in paperwork. A letter from the marina, stating your vessel is at their facility, may also be helpful. Those documents would have been sufficient to avoid having to buy a second round trip ticket. The documents will also be necessary to avoid customs charges if any parts or equipment are being hand carried back to the boat.

PART TWO
CRUISING

Chapter 12
Cruise Planning and Operating Costs

AFTER OUTFITTING AND PROVISIONING THERE IS A LOT MORE TO CRUISE preparation than just getting charts and topping off the fuel and water tanks. Continuing with the organized approach to cruise preparations, the main topics of a grand plan are:

estimate a desired departure date, cruise duration and general route,
evaluate the vessels readiness and capability,
outfit and provision accordingly,
organize personal obligations for a long-term absence,
gather and review detailed guides, charts and other information,
then fuel up and go.

Many of the line items above are covered in detail in respective chapters. This chapter will fill in some of the blanks and help to order the preparations process chronologically.

12.1 CRUISING START DATE, DURATION AND ROUTE

The time for beginning any cruise route is far from arbitrary. The major seasonal factors for cruise timing are obvious, but new cruisers may be surprised at how closely bracketed within the seasons cruise timing really is. Thus, from the first moment of planning to the day the extended cruise begins, the primary goal is to have all of the preparations timely completed for the beginning of the best seasonal weather conditions.

The following paragraphs describe the timing constraints of a U.S. East Coast cruise departure toward Mexico and south and to the Bahamas and south.

The summertime Gulf of Mexico and Caribbean waters are warm and very often placid. But hurricane season, July to November, is not a real good time to be meandering through much of the tropics. In the first place, vessel insurance coverage won't be in effect and in the second, well-, it's obvious isn't it. Yet, every year we hear rationalizations by boat owners (not often cruisers) who have kept or keep their boats in the islands during the tropical storm season. The reasons range from the absurd to business necessity. And, nearly every year acquaintances, or friends of friends, have severe damage or lose their boats during tropical storm-hurricane season. Let's just skip hurricane season, OK? Then from the east coast, a prudent wintertime departure date should be no earlier than late November with the further need to be back home in North America or south of 12 degrees North before the first of July.

A further constraint is that in December, the northers start cranking up. Fortunately, they usually aren't too severe before January. So, from late November to the end of December cruisers hang about in Florida waiting for good weather windows to make their crossings.

January, February and March are bad for the northers and March often has generally blustery conditions. That leaves April, May and June as good springtime crossing months. But let's not forget that in May and June the tropical waves begin their periodic passages having been driven by the trades from the eastern Atlantic and every now and again, a hurricane is spawned in June.

So, is it a good plan to join the snowbirds heading south on the ICW in October or November? Generally yes, but it also depends on the planned destination and how quickly the vessel can transit.

12.2 EASTERN CRUISING, THE BAHAMAS

If the grand plan is to spend the winter in the Bahamas, reflect on this. Northers (cold fronts) blast through the Bahamas during January, February and March. During those months, cruisers spend much of their time looking for protection or hunkered down. In some areas, the holding is bad and the anchorages crowded. The seawater temperature in winter is cool and most people will want to wear a wetsuit for comfort.

There are regional differences in the Bahamas also. For instance, Andros Island makes its own weather. One year, during February and March, we were able to get out in the dinghy only a few days because of nearly continuous high wind and rain. Just 50 miles away, in the Exuma Islands, it is usually very dry. Added to all this is the Bahamas entry fee, a whopping $300, the highest anywhere. The only good news about the north and central Bahamas during winter is that cruisers often get to practice their dragging techniques. Still, be optimistic, maybe you'll catch that, one chance in four, good year.

Further south at Georgetown, Exumas, there is a large community of boaters who spend much of the year there. They have organized activities and the town is geared for boaters. The Georgetown area has ample anchorages with generally good holding.

But the best time to be in the Bahamas is April through June when the water is warming up and calming down. When late June rolls around and hurricane season begins, it will be hard to leave the gin clear water, light breezes, peace and beauty of the Bahamas. Also, beginning in May, fishing in the Tongue of the Ocean is outstanding with abundant large Dorado and other species.

12.3 SOUTH OF THE BAHAMAS

During the winter months, it may be best to continue right through the Bahamas. Unless there are plans to hang out in the Bahamas, fly the Q flag *only*, continue through the Bahamas and avoid the $300 check-in fee. Overnight anchoring has not been a problem, but as you are quarantined, you may not go ashore.

South of the Turks and Caicos Islands there are fewer northers or when encountered, they don't usually have as much punch. The whole of the Eastern Caribbean island chain is then open to good cruising. Be prepared to have lots of company. By late May or early June it will be time to begin the trip north.

But if you really want to get away from it all, continue down the island chain all the way to Trinidad and Venezuela. This puts cruisers below the hurricane belt, in mostly benign weather conditions, where the cost of fuel and living are low and the cruising is great. Be aware, however, that the "Christmas Winds," somewhat elevated trade winds (15–25 knots), begin in late December and last several months. For making passages, there are lulls in these conditions every few days but the swell height may be large. Also, the distance between islands and lee protection is usually not far.

If the grand Caribbean tour is planned, then cruisers often leave Venezuela in the fall, visit the Venezuelan islands, then the ABC islands (Aruba, Bonaire, Curacao) and continue to Cartagena, Colombia and Panama where they may spend the next hurricane season or go north and hide out in the Rio Dulce of Guatemala. There is more on this in the next section.

12.4 CRUISING WEST

Even considering the approximately 400 nm crossing from the Florida Keys to Isla Mujeres, Mexico, this may be easier, more rewarding wintertime cruising than the eastern route. Often in November and December, there are weeklong windows of calm wind and seas. Even if the wind is up a bit, going downwind with a following sea makes a fair passage. There may be times during the crossing when the Gulf Stream current will slow the cruisers progress. But regions of strong current are usually localized. A good track for making the passage west is to angle across toward Cuba and follow the coast closely. Often the Gulf Stream current can be avoided or the coastal counter current can be ridden to advantage. Some may find it uncomfortable being within 5 or 10 miles of the Cuban coast, but we know of no incidents in that regard. It may be good to have a cruising guidebook for Cuba just in case sea conditions force a landfall. Maritime law provides for emergency access to any safe harbor and historically the Cubans have been very accommodating. For weather problems, no check-in will be required so long as the stay is brief.

Another good route is a direct rhumb line from Isla Mujeres to the Dry Tortugas. Very often, the current on this path is light and localized.

From Isla Mujeres south to Belize, Guatemala, and Honduras, the cruising can be done in day trips. However, the midstream Straits of Yucatan current off the Mexican coast can be tough, sometimes 2 to 3 knots on the nose. When practical, stay in tight with the coast (½ mile or less) and ride the coastal counter current. The day cruises along the Mexican coast southbound mostly crowd the daylight hours at both ends. An alternative is an overnighter from Isla Mujeres to Cayo Norte at the Chinchorro Banks. From there all the way to Honduras the day trips are of more reasonable lengths. No matter how you go from Isla Mujeres, it is best to both check-in and out of the country there. Historically there has been no problem staying in bays or at the Banks in coastal Mexico even though you have been checked out.

To avoid the cool weather and northers of January and February it may be well to spend those months in the Rio Dulce of Guatemala. The Rio is a great cruisers haunt with very pleasant weather during the winter. During April and May, however, forest fires and field burning can make it unpleasantly smoky. But, they are good months to be on the reef in Belize.

In late May, early June, as in the eastern Caribbean, a decision needs to be made about where to spend hurricane season. Cruisers either return to the States, stay in the Rio Dulce (no hurricane wind or sea risk), or go south to Panama and Colombia.

12.5 THE GRAND PLAN

We have now seen that the characteristics that govern cruise planning are timing, duration, distance and region. A seeming contradiction is that open-ended cruising or cruises of unplanned duration require even more planning than one that is well defined. This is true because the open-ended cruise plan must account for many more cruise contingencies and longer personal absence from the main stream.

For short cruises, e.g. three to six months in the Bahamas, it may be reasonable to stay tuned in to the old life with a cell or satellite telephone. But, the same kinds of control, finagling, and access are just the ticket to really screw up a long cruise. Cruisers caught between worlds are neither cruisers nor businessmen. They are always juggling time, destinations, taking chances with weather, missing maintenance schedules, frustrated, upset and suffer unreasonable expenses.

Folks who have never thought about being away for many months at a time may be surprised at how difficult it is to drop out. The inability to be regularly personally involved in matters concerning family, finance, taxes, etc. requires compromise planning and is never without sacrifice. Where do you start?

Very few cruisers totally drop out. They are the ones who don't require a driver's license, health insurance, vessel insurance and bank account. They may even ignore filing taxes and have few family ties. We have met a few like this and it remains a mystery how they get by. Most of us don't seek that kind of isolation and realize that the cruising life is one that will continue only so long as we are healthy and enjoy it.

Around the Caribbean, mail services have spotty reputations for delays, loss and theft. Package delivery services such as DHL and FedEx, while more prompt and trustworthy, are expensive. A small package containing only mail might cost over $100. Also, cruisers can't often predict where they will be at a given time to receive a package. Thus, for cruisers to maintain the essentials, there should be a trusted-someone, perhaps with *Power of Attorney*, who will look after one's mail, make bank deposits, pay a few bills and sign yearly renewal documents.

If the bills are set up to be automatically paid through a bank or other means then the workload for the trusted-someone can be minimized. But, even with the best planning, a trip back to North America may be needed yearly for such matters as tax preparation and payment. It is especially problematic for Canadian cruisers who may have to return to Canada six months out of each year in order to maintain their National Health Insurance.

For those cruisers who no longer own property in North America there is another frustrating problem. Everyone needs a home address and must declare a location in a state or province as a permanent residence. You cannot simply be a citizen of the United States or Canada. Driver's licenses, vessel documentation and insurance, health insurance, banking, tax and income related matters all require a home address. In some cases services like *Mail Boxes, etc.* will help, but it may be more practical to use the trusted-someone's address. Other concerns regarding a resident address are also covered in the chapter on *Tax Issues*.

12.6 EVALUATING THE CREW AND VESSEL'S READINESS AND CAPABILITY

Having made large time and cash investments in preparing a vessel, this section's function is important as closure to the project work.

Review all of the things-to-do lists. There may yet be items to do, but which have been deferred because of their relative importance. Are any of the previously deferred items critical to the newly formed or forming cruise plan? Are any items missing from the lists that are critical to that plan? Will all of the unfinished projects be complete in time?

Are all of the necessary charts and guides aboard or planned for?

Have all of the boat's systems been tested? You can decide whether sea time is needed for testing or if the waterway trip south will suffice.

Next, review the pre-cruise maintenance check-list for completeness. Make sure that all of the vessel documents, insurance policy and communications licenses are up-to-date and aboard.

Remember also that all vessels must have a copy of *Navigation Rules* aboard. The vessel's documentation number must be stenciled or otherwise permanently affixed somewhere within the boat. The safety equipment, flares, etc. must be within the expiration date and otherwise in good condition.

Now for the crew. After months at the dock sorting through all of the projects and problems, there hasn't been much time or opportunity to taking the boat out. If the plan calls for cruising a few hundred or more miles down the ICW before venturing out from Florida, that may be adequate to ring out the systems, work out routines, become proficient with new equipment, etc. But if the plan is to jump off from New Jersey and run offshore only ducking in when necessary, that's a big leap of faith for an untested boat and crew. Don't let time pressures govern actions. If a weather window is missed, there will be another and another. Also, remember that equipment failures most often occur during the first hours or few days after a vessel has set up for a few months. As such, more frequent instrument scans, as well as engine room and bilge inspections, are necessary to avoid unfortunate, perhaps untimely incidents.

12.7 COSTS OF CRUISING

Every boat and budget will be different, but let's go through a little exercise everyone can tailor to their needs. We shall assume that there is a stock of spare parts and that the main provisioning was done before the cruise began. All costs are then broken down to average monthly amounts. Taken one at a time, each item needs explanation.

Health insurance. For those on Medicare there are a variety of relatively inexpensive plans. Otherwise, the cost of private major medical health insurance begins at about $800 per month for two people.   _____

Health insurance is, of course, optional and some cruisers choose to self insure. If a serious health condition should occur, foreign healthcare may be their best option.

Health and dental care abroad including medicines. This is tough to call, but for seniors, it is hard to get by for less than about $50 per person per month.   _____

Boat (home) mortgage   _____

Provisioning. For stocked foodstuff, try $2500 per year or $210 per month.   _____

Fresh produce and eating out. In much of the southern and Western Caribbean, produce and eating out is inexpensive. But to consider the eastern Caribbean as well, start with an estimate of $150 per month. Remember, there may be months at anchor with little opportunity to eat out.   _____

Beverages. In all but the eastern Caribbean, liquor, beer and wine are a bargain. You're on your own on this one, but try starting with your U.S. beverage budget.   _____

Entertainment. To each his own. Include DVDs, movies, books, inland travel, etc. Try budgeting $150 per month and see what happens.

Vessel insurance. The yearly premium can be conservatively estimated at 2 percent of the hull value. Thus, the monthly Cost is 0.017 percent of the hull value.

Spare parts. This includes all of the parts that will be needed to maintain the vessel reliably. Assuming a stock of spares already exists, then for twin engines a reasonable estimate to maintain the spares stock will be around $1500 per year or $125 per month.

Fuel and oil. Estimating an average annual cruising mileage at 3,500 nautical miles, with fuel economy at 2 nmpg and fuel cost at $3.00 per gallon, the monthly fuel cost will be about $435.

Dockage, water and electricity. Unless your vessel is especially large, dockage rates at favorite cruiser haunts can be as low as $200 per month (Guatemala), but the average will be around $600 per month. Electricity and water can be no additional charge or as high as $100 per month.

Check in/out costs. This expense will average about $50 per country (a few a lot more and some a lot less). If you cruise 3,500 nm per year that will add up to about 6 to 10 countries per year or perhaps $30 per month.

Maintenance. This includes haul out, bottom paint, occasional bottom scraping, oil changes, other paints, sand paper, etc. Assuming the boat is in good condition, this may be as low as $200 per month.

Repairs (other than covered by spares). This is anybody's guess, but for a well maintained vessel, it may be as little as $50 per month.

Communications. Include expected landline phone calls, Sailmail, satellite telephone, satellite TV, cable, etc. Cruisers differ widely in this. For a starter, estimate $50 per month.

Airline travel to U.S. or Canada. Almost everyone needs to make a trip back once yearly. Budget $165 per person per month for each trip.

Miscellaneous supplies and expenses

Try doing this exercise on a computer spreadsheet. It will make it easy to play with the numbers until you are satisfied with the results. Then, as things progress, the information can be fined tuned with reality.

Considering the cost of living in North America, the cost of cruising is not excessive. But, if your budget gets into a temporary pinch, hang out for a while at one of the low cost cruiser's haunts such as Belize, Guatemala, Honduras, Colombia or Venezuela.

Chapter 13
Fuel Management and Availability

13.1 FUEL AND EFFICIENCY MEASUREMENTS

With worldwide fuel consumption growing and relatively flat production rates the oil companies keep taking a bigger bite out of our budget. Unchecked, one shudders to think what the situation might be like in a few years. Perhaps in the distant future sailboats will be the only reasonable means of cruising. But for now, cruising liveaboards who depend upon *power* to maintain their first world standards, the best answer is fuel efficiency. Achieving efficient operation requires more than guesswork. The process has the following elements:

Determine the power setting for best economy. This may be done through the following steps:

calibrate the fuel system,
calibrate the engine tachometers,
make proper GPS adjustments,
make a speed v. rpm table or graph,
monitor and record fuel use carefully and
make a speed v. fuel consumption table or graph.

We will take these one at a time. Oh-oh, did someone say yeah-but? Understandably, non-technical or math challenged folks may desire to skip this section. Please stay with it or get some help; a little work here will pay large dividends.

Every boat is different and it is unrealistic to use "typical" performance data as a characterization of your boat's performance. Two identical vessels, with differently pitched propellers, can have very different characteristics. The efficiency peaks may be at different engine speeds and/or the overall efficiency may be different. For extended cruising, the range and operating costs are important issues needing careful consideration. The difficult part is ferreting out the data. After that, it is not much more difficult than checking your car's gas mileage.

13.1.1 Fuel system calibration

Unless the cruiser is fortunate enough to have differential flow meters (those that account for return flow also) or a calibrated day tank, making precise fuel consumption measurements can be difficult.

Factors that contribute to measurement error are:

fuel temperature change,
vessel attitude changes with fuel use,
poor dipstick or sight tube calibration,
poorly calibrated tachometer(s) and inconsistent measurement method.

The cruiser has to live with some of these factors, but not with others. Let's first eliminate the lesser contributors and then concentrate on those we can do something about.

You may have experienced the problem of filling a fuel tank with cool fuel, then, after running for some hours, heating the engine room and fuel tanks, fuel was found oozing out the overflow. However, for fuel use measurements, thermal expansion introduces only a small error. For example, with a 20° rise in fuel temperature the vertical height will increase by 0.01" for each inch of fuel height (¼" for 25" of fuel height).

Most boats with large fuel tanks have them centrally located such that fuel burn off does not greatly change the vessel's pitch attitude or cause significant error in fuel level measurement. However, the difference between full and empty water tanks may affect the boat's trim and be a factor in fuel measurement inaccuracy.

A large error-producing factor of fuel use measurement is poor dipstick or sight tube calibration. We can do something about this, although the measurement may, at best, have a frustrating 5 percent or so systematic error. However, a fuel management program with that amount of error can still provide useful data and lead to large savings.

Calibration of the dipstick(s) or sight tube(s) by making marks while fueling is not a satisfactory method. What is needed is a complete set of carefully made fuel tank physical measurements from which volume calculations can be made. It is rare for fuel tanks to be nicely rectangular; they frequently have odd vertical angles and are perhaps tapered fore and aft. Thus, the calculations may be a little difficult. Computer programs such as AutoCad® or other computer aided design programs can make fast work of the problem. Otherwise, if calculations aren't your thing, find any engineer boat owner who can help.

It will be good to have the data in a table that shows both the fuel remaining and fuel consumed (from full) in one-half inch or one-inch intervals. A graph may also be helpful. Establish full as that level having sufficient headspace to avoid vent tube overflow with fuel thermal expansion. For example:

Dipstick (inches from bottom)	Fuel remaining (gallons)	Fuel consummed (gallons)
26	325	0
24	295	30
22	265	60
20	236	89
18	208	117
16	181	144
14	155	170
12	130	195
10	106	219
8	83	242
6	61	264
4	40	285
2	22	303
0	0	325

Having a column for fuel-consumed makes it easier to answer the fuel dock attendant when asked how much fuel is needed.

After the calculations have been completed, carefully mark the dipstick. The spacing for the marked intervals should be such that after a half or full day of running a meaningful measurement can be made. Marks every inch should be sufficient. Don't bother to mark the dipstick too finely or make measurements too frequently. That may add to the errors.

The next step is to calibrate the fuel consumption at different engine speeds. But before proceeding, it is important that the vessel's tachometers have been accurately calibrated. Most often tachometers should be adjusted to be accurate around the middle of the operating range. They will, however, deviate from accuracy above and below that setting. Although that may be less than ideal, it will not affect the process of finding the settings for good fuel economy.

Within this context, fuel burn rate measurements are independent of sea state or currents. Long runs at a consistent engine rpm produce the most accurate data. It is reasonable to make the first cut at this data while motoring in the waterway, however, having to slow for *No Wake* areas, bridges, etc. will introduce error. The fuel use calibration can be improved later, at sea, with consistent long-term power settings. But until then, even a rough calibration can produce fuel savings. The table and associated graph below are examples of these measurements for a typical trawler.

Engine Speed (rpm)	Fuel usage (gph)
1200	2.8
1300	2.9
1400	3.1
1500	3.5
1600	4
1700	4.7
1800	5.4

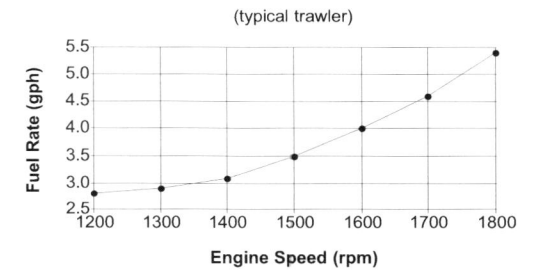

Vessel Fuel Consumption v. Engine rpm
(typical trawler)

13.1.2 Power settings vessel speed calibration

These measurements are relatively easy to make but take time and repetition to get good accuracy. Unlike fuel consumption measurement, wind, sea state and current will cause significant error.

GPS measurements are accurate for speed over the ground (SOG), but does your GPS speed readout bounce around a lot? If so, go to the GPS' setup menu, locate the speed setting that refers to slow, medium and fast. Change it to slow. This will average the displayed speed over a longer time and provide good accuracy. Unlike the ICW, offshore cruising is always done using nautical miles. For that reason, set the GPS' vessel speed to be displayed in knots.

Next, make a table of speed versus engine rpm settings. Clearly, the best measurements will be made with long straight stretches, no current and smooth sea conditions. Even small turns will reduce the accuracy of this measurement so it is a good idea to run with the autopilot. It is possible to make good measurements in bays or the ICW during slack tide conditions. After collecting the data, make a table and / or graph of speed versus engine rpm. The table and associated graph below illustrate this.

Engine Speed (rpm)	Vessel Speed (knots)
900	5.2
1000	5.7
1100	6.15
1200	6.55
1300	6.95
1400	7.28
1500	7.58
1600	7.85
1700	8.1
1800	8.3

Speed v. Engine rpm
(Typical trawler)

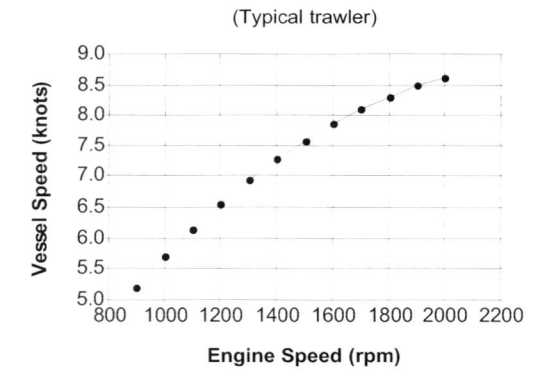

13.1.3 Finding the best compromise setting for fuel efficiency

Having created the tables or graphs of *Speed v. Engine rpm* and *Fuel consumption rate v. engine rpm* it is now a relatively easy task to produce a table or graph that expresses vessel *fuel efficiency v. engine rpm*. At last!

For all vessels, there is a best fuel efficiency power setting. For semi-draft and draft hulls lower engine power settings generally yield better fuel efficiency. But at very low engine speeds the engine, transmission and shaft frictional losses (overhead), become more significant. Efficiency drops off with further rpm reductions. At higher rpm settings, other non-linear factors such as bow wake, wetted surface area and propeller slip begin to dominate the equation, and fuel efficiency drops quickly with further rpm increases. This may be seen in the following table and graph.

Fuel Efficiency (naut. miles/gallon)	Fuel usage (gph)
2.32	2.8
2.37	2.9
2.34	3.1
2.17	3.5
1.98	4
1.77	4.7
1.55	5.4

Fuel Efficiency of a Typical Trawler
(from the data on previous pages)

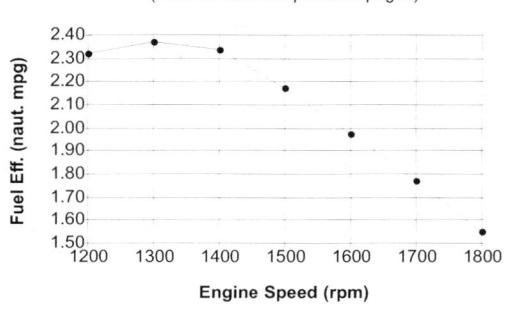

In the above examples, one can see that running at 1200, 1300 or 1400 rpm yields roughly the same efficiency, but at higher engine speeds efficiency falls off. Fuel efficiency as a function of engine rpm is independent of the sea state or current.

Skippers with a real zeal for data and whose boats are equipped with twin engines can repeat this process running on a single engine. It may be found that the vessel's range can be stretched by about 25 percent, but only with a similar loss in speed. Maintaining the normal twin-engine cruising speed with a single engine reduces the advantage significantly. But, as fuel prices rise, innovative means of reducing the undriven propeller drag and rudder angle drag may improve the single engine performance making it a more attractive option.

Those familiar with spreadsheet programs can produce a single spreadsheet having all of the data, calculations and graphs in a single file.

13.2 FUEL MANAGEMENT

The experiences of purchasing fuel around the Caribbean can range from horrific to euphoric. A horrific experience may be when the fuel delivery method is so bad that a large amount of fuel is spilled. Or, there may be no spill problem, but the fuel dock's pump delivery rate is only about 1 gallon per minute. More pleasantly, fuel may be delivered to the boat by dugout canoe and hand pumped from drums. But all captains will be in a state of euphoria when the price for good quality fuel is as low as 7 cents; -yes that's right-, seven cents per gallon (Venezuela, 2005).

Cruisers need to be able to plan fuel stops around their vessel's range. They also want to know where to buy good fuel at the best prices. Below is a chart listing many locations in and around the Caribbean at which to buy fuel. Each location has ratings for fuel price and quality. The rating scale for fuel price is 1 to 5 with 5 being the most favorable. Specific costs are not given because of the regularity of price changes. Rating fuel quality is not as quantitatively defined. Unless otherwise indicated the quality and delivery means is good.

Please note that the only locations given are those for which there has been first hand experience or in a few cases, where the information came from a trusted source. When a country or location is not represented, no inference should be made.

Fuel station comparisons chart

Location	Price	Quality	Delivery Rate
Most of south Florida	1,2	-	-
Fernandino Beach, Florida	3	-	-
Ft. Pierce, Florida	3	-	-
Boot Key Harbor, Florida	3*	-	-
Nassau, Bahamas	1	-	-
Luperon, Dom. Rep.	2	-	hand pump
Palmas del Mar, Puerto Rico	3*	-	-
Salinas, Puerto Rico	2	-	poor

(continued)

Location	Price	Quality	Delivery Rate
Chagaramus Bay, Trinidad	4	-	-
Isla de Margarita, Venezuela	5	-	-
Cumana, Venezuela	5	-	-
Puerto La Cruz, Venezuela	5	-	-
Cartagena, Colombia	4	-	-
Isla de San Andres, Colombia	4	-	-
Curacao	3	-	-
Colon, Panama	3	poor	-
Nargana, Panama	3	-	hand pump
Bocas del Toro, Panama	3	-	-
La Ceiba, Honduras	3	-	hand pump
Rio Dulce, Guatemala	3	-	-
Belize City, Belize	1	-	-
Isla Mujeres, Mexico	1	-	-
Cancun, Mexico	1	-	-

* known to give volume discounts. Elsewhere in the Caribbean discounts are seldom given.

13.2.1 Optimizing Range

From the Fuel Station table it is clear that fuel can be purchased to best advantage when the stops are planned and a vessel has the adequate range to skip the bad stops. But there are other things to consider also.

The ocean currents in the Gulf of Mexico and Caribbean Sea can be as high as 4 knots. Those extremes may be found in a few spots in the Straits of Yucatan, off NW Panama, the Mona Pass, etc. Such high current conditions are usually transient and localized. It is more usual to encounter currents in the 0.5 to 2 knot range. On a long haul, 1 to 2 knots of current acting on a 7-knot trawler significantly alters the fuel range.

If one chooses to circumnavigate the Caribbean Sea, the most usual and most practical approach is to go south from the Bahamas to the Leeward Islands, then the Windward Islands and to the north coast of South America. Then, with a favorable current go from Venezuela to the ABC islands, Colombia, Panama, and north along the coast of Central America. Continuing with a favorable current, leave Isla Mujeres, Mexico for the Dry Tortugas or Key West, Florida.

Alternatively, many cruisers choose only to go to the Western Caribbean. Very often working the coastal counter currents and cruising behind the reefs can minimize the exposure to adverse currents. Also, going south from Cabo Gracias Adios, Honduras, the large eddy current in the Southwestern Caribbean can be ridden to good advantage. However, cruising east along the Colombian North Coast toward the ABC islands is usually a very tough stretch with frequent high seas. For that reason it is seldom cruised west to east.

In the San Blas Islands of Panama, facilities are lacking. Fueling delivery is done with large dugout canoe (cayuca) and hand pumped to the boat.

Fueling on the Rio Caroni, a branch of the Rio Orinoco. Venezuela.

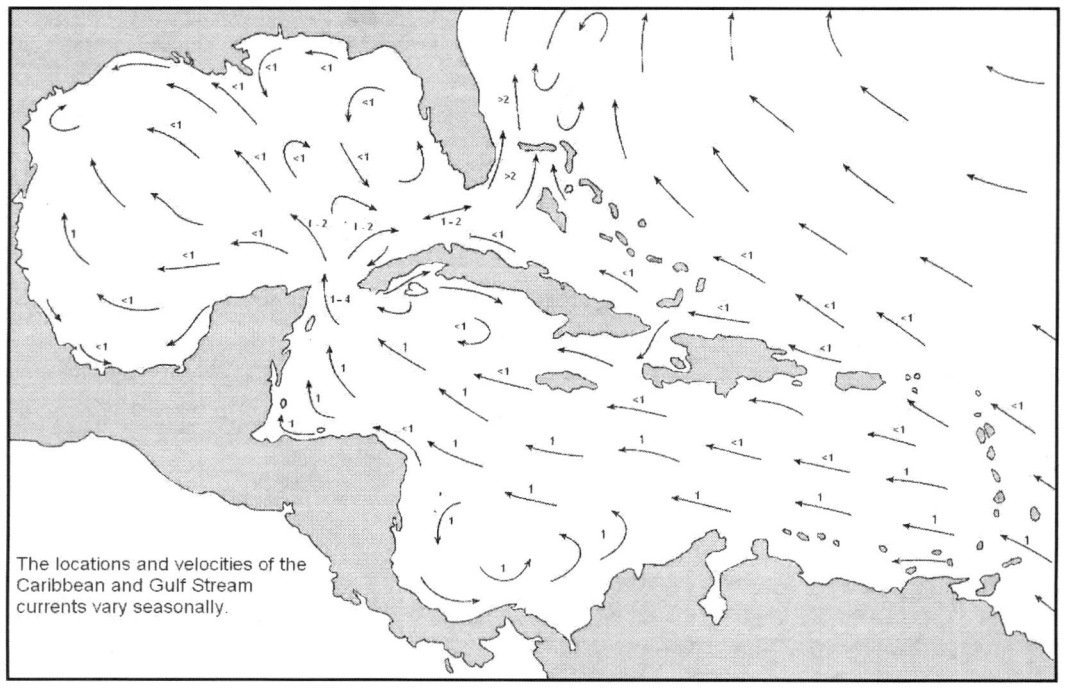

The locations and velocities of the Caribbean and Gulf Stream currents vary seasonally.

Ocean Currents

102 • EXTENDED POWER CRUISING

The most advantageous fuel stops might be as follows.

	Approx. Distance
Average 0.75 knots adverse current	
South Florida to Luperon, D.R.	624 nm
or	
South Florida to eastern Puerto Rico	1000 nm
(If the distance is too great, pick up a small amount of fuel at Luperon, D.R.)	
Puerto Rico to Trinidad	675 nm
or	
Puerto Rico to Puerto La Cruz, VE	725 nm
Average 0.75 knots favorable current	
Puerto La Cruz, VE to Aruba	400 nm
Aruba to Cartagena, Colombia	450 nm
Cartagena to Isla de San Andres (via Panama)	500 nm
San Andres to Rio Dulce, Guat.	600 nm
Rio Dulce to Key West, FL	725 nm

This all adds up to 4400 nm, but in reality, with side-trips it is more realistic to estimate the whole trip at 5000 nm. That is a good number for budgeting and for deciding on consumable stocks such as impellers, zincs, oil stock, filters, etc.

For a trawler with an efficient arrangement of batteries and energy use, the fuel consumption of an 8 kW genset (no air conditioning) can be approximated at 100 gallons per month. With solar panels, this figure can be cut significantly. The vessel's fuel budget and estimated fuel range may then be adjusted to account for this overhead consumption.

The next part of optimizing range is about improving the boat below the waterline. When diesel fuel was under a dollar a gallon and trips were short, a poorly fared hull was not of great concern, but we need to look at it more seriously now. On most trawlers, the back end of the keel is squared off. That geometry produces more drag than if it were tapered. Other unnecessary drag inducing elements include the squared off strut mounts and other protrusions such as the old style depth sounders. These can all be nicely fared in at reasonable cost. At this writing, we can't comment on the degree of improvement that might be expected, but it is obvious that all improvements will yield fuel savings for the remainder of the boat's life.

13.2.2 Fuel Tankage

Hopefully your cruiser/trawler will have adequate tankage for a range with reserve of at least 600 nm. But even if you have a range of 1500 nm or more, carrying additional fuel can provide savings. Fuel in Venezuela and Colombia can be purchased at bargain prices. Thus, a fuel bladder or plastic barrels secured on deck may help both the range and cruising budget.

13.2.3 Special Fuel Concerns

VENEZUELA. As mentioned above, in 2005, the price of diesel fuel in Venezuela was about $0.07 (USD) per gallon. There are some provisos, however. Foreign vessels are limited to purchasing a maximum of 1000 liters once every three months. Above that limit, any amount of fuel could (in 2005) be purchased at what is called the International Price of $0.48 (USD) per gallon.

Also, in Venezuela, fuel can at times be bought on the black market for about $0.25 per gallon. For many years, this has been an acceptable means of buying fuel. Usually it is brought to the boat by pickup truck or in a boat. We have not heard of any fuel problems, but depending upon the political climate, there could be a risk of being fined, along with the seller, for buying fuel in this manner. Check with fellow cruisers for current information at each location.

COLON, PANAMA. It has been reported for years (and we experienced it in 2004) that the fuel sold at the Panama Canal Yacht Club has very low viscosity and poor lubricating properties. It is very much like kerosene. This creates two problems for the cruiser. First, the low lubricity can and has ruined fuel injector pumps. The second problem is that the fuel produces less energy per gallon than good diesel fuel. Thus, a vessel's fuel range can be significantly reduced (perhaps as much as 25 percent. We also experienced this). In 2004, this fuel was NO bargain at $1.60. However, given no alternative, it has knowledgably been reported that adding one quart of 2-cycle engine oil to 100 gallons of PCYC fuel will make the fuel safe for injector pumps.

NARGANA, PANAMA (San Blas Islands). Fuel can be delivered to the boat by large dugout canoe and hand pumped from 55-gallon drums here. In 2004, the price was $1.60 per gallon. It appeared to be good fuel and no contamination problems were experienced. The pumping process does not take as long as one might expect.

CARTAGENA AND ISLA DE SAN ANDRES, COLOMBIA. The fuel sold at these locations has been found to be clean and of good quality. It has a slightly gray color and may be a little more viscous than U.S. fuel. It was a bargain at $1.00 per gallon in early 2004, but jumped to $1.90 by January of 2006.

GALAPAGOS ISLANDS. Fuel is available at the islands. However, current information is needed before venturing there.

BELIZE CITY, BELIZE. Fuel is available at the city dock at St. Georges. Be warned, however, that the onshore breeze along with frequent boat traffic creates a very choppy condition at the pier. The dock's construction makes it difficult to adequately fender boats and some amount of dock rash is almost a certainty. Together with one of the highest fuel prices anywhere, avoid buying fuel there if possible.

ISLA MUJERES, MEXICO. Fuel prices in Mexico are high. They can be made all the greater at Isla Mujeres, Mexico where there have been numerous reports of cruisers being charged for more fuel than their boats could hold. We experienced this and had to pay for 100 gallons more than we got. If you must buy fuel here, test the pump calibration with a 5 gallon bucket and make sure the pump meter is set to zero at the beginning. Alternatively, fuel can be purchased across the bay at a yacht club near Cancun.

One last bit of information.

To convert liters to gallons, multiply by 0.264

To convert gallons to liters, multiply by 3.79

Chapter 14
Maintenance

THE CHAPTER, *GAINING CONFIDENCE*, provided a long list of cruising boat subsystems. In that context, the process of familiarization with the onboard equipment was begun. Now, however, it is time to look at components in terms of their care and feeding.

A potential new cruiser, especially one without a technical background, may be feeling a bit queasy about now. After all, are you kidding yourself about being able to handle the quagmire of wires, pipes, machinery, etc.? Are you being realistic about this?

The answer is that there is a small percentage of people who should not try to sharpen a pencil or hang a picture. They already know that machines are their enemy and in any confrontation, that enemy will win. Without help, extended cruising is not for them and they know it. You, however, know that motivation born of need and desire is a strong ally. You will prevail.

This chapter is organized in terms of the various types of maintenance required to keep a vessel sea worthy. Those categories include:

Things that wear out
Things that need periodic adjustment
Routine maintenance
Safety equipment routine maintenance
Other maintenance tips
Repairs in foreign ports
New equipment installations

By taking each type of maintenance activity separately it will be easier to gain an understanding of all the needs. Cosmetic maintenance is not included.

14.1 THINGS THAT WEAR OUT OR OTHERWISE DETERIORATE (PROPULSION AND GENSET)

In the process of preparing a boat for extended cruising, the first consideration is to evaluate the status of your equipment and correct the deficiencies. This section will also be useful toward gaining a general understanding of the long-term maintenance requirements and spare parts needs.

For the purposes of this chapter, things that wear out are expendable items like hoses, belts, etc. Each component to be described will have an approximate lifetime described either in engine hours or calendar time. Please note that the lifetimes given may not be in agreement with the manufacturer recommendations or the experience of others. Use the replacement periods as a starting point for building your own preventive maintenance schedule.

14.1.1 Belts*

Replace every 3 to 5 years or around 3000 hours. Replace anytime if they are shiny, cracked or shedding. Keep in mind that too much belt tension can cause water pump bearing failure and too little tension will cause belt slippage resulting in excessive belt wear, loss of tachometer calibration and unsatisfactory alternator operation. Refer to the engine manual for the correct belt tension.

14.1.2 Hoses*

Replace every 5 years. If a hose has been softened by fuel or a solvent, chaffed, bulging, collapsed, cracked or hardened and has brittle edges, replace it.

14.1.3 Coolant reservoir cap*

Replace every 5 years or if leaking. During day-to-day operations and unless a loss of coolant is suspected, it is not recommended that the coolant level be checked more frequently than about once a month or after a period of inactivity. To do so more frequently causes excess wear on the cap retaining flange.

14.1.4 Engine and transmission oil coolers*

Several different types of coolers are on the market. One type requires replacement every 2500 to 3000 hours; other types have greater longevity. Check with the manufacturer or a knowledgeable service technician. These are not expensive items so, if in doubt, change it out. Then, cleanup the old serviceable units and retain them for spares.

If the engine oil cooler begins leaking internally, the engine oil level will drop more quickly than usual. In calm water, with the engine running an unusually large oil film may be seen coming from the exhaust. Over time, with the engine shut down, that same internal leak can also fill the engine with saltwater if it is below the water line. In a pinch, without a spare cooler, the bad unit can be bypassed and the engine operated at reduced power settings. Have bits and pieces of hose/clamps and the necessary oil line coupling in the spares kit.

14.1.5 Engine coolant heat exchanger

These assemblies are good for many thousands of hours. But, they require monitoring and occasional cleaning. At least once a year remove the end caps and clean out the bits of zinc salts and other material that has accumulated. At the same time, inspect the channels for salt and dirt build up. If the build up has narrowed the channels, the heat exchanger should be cleaned or boiled out at a radiator shop. The channels of the heat exchanger are made of thin wall copper tubing. With care, the channels can be cleaned using a wooden dowel, but it is safer and better to have them chemically cleaned.

If a leak should develop during a cruise and a competent repair shop is not available, do not attempt to re-solder the leak. It is most probable that the heat of the torch will open up more leaks. For both internal and external accessible leaks, a temporary repair can be made using JB weld or other good epoxy compound. Five-minute epoxies are not recommended for use anywhere unless the repair is only needed to last five minutes.

An internal leak in the heat exchanger will be evident from a loss of engine coolant. Tiny external leaks are easily spotted from a salt cake buildup around the leak.

14.1.6 Engine coolant fresh water pump

These pumps can last for many years or for just a few hundred hours. The useful lifetime of coolant pumps is dependent upon the age of the bearing seal, belt tension, and manufacturing quality. An early warning of impending failure will be a slight trail of dried or drying coolant just below the belt pulley. This inspection should be part of your regular engine room checks. At a minimum one spare pump and gasket should be in your kit.

14.1.7 Engine coolant raw water pump

Raw water pumps require a lot of care and feeding. The rubber impellers may need replacement as frequently as every 300 hours or once a year which ever comes first. Keep a good log of the hours accumulated on the impellers.

Initially, and after the first 300 hours, inspect the impellers every 100 hours to check for cracking. Impellers can be inspected by stressing each of the impeller blades to the maximum deflection in both rotational directions. If cracking has begun it will be evident at the base of the blades. After inspecting and replacing two or three, the proper impeller replacement interval can be added to your checklist.

If one waits for the water pump impeller to fail, it may deteriorate quickly creating bits that plug the oil cooler and engine heat exchanger. Thus, there will be a dramatic reduction in pumped coolant accompanied by impeded flow in the heat exchangers. The result can be a quickly overheating engine and potential engine damage. By far the best policy is to replace the impellers regularly and with adequate time margin to prevent impeller destruction.

Approximately every 1500–2000 hours raw water pumps need to be rebuilt with new wear plates in order to perform efficiently. It is wise to have a rebuild kit(s) in the spare parts inventory. It is also a good idea to have one complete raw water pump as a spare as seal or bearing failures usually require shop repair.

14.1.8 Engine exhaust elbow

Exhaust elbows are generally cast iron. They deteriorate both from use and age so it is difficult to predict when they will fail. For example, an elbow that is 10 years old, but has only 2000 engine hours, may crumble. Or, it may be 3 years old, but have 4000 hours and still have useful life left. Unless the elbow is already leaking, you may not be able to determine the condition by looking at the outside. To check the elbow, remove the exhaust hose, then tap at the edges with a hammer and probe inside with a blade screwdriver. If great chunks of rust fall out leaving little sound wall thickness, it is time for a change. Carry a spare(s) in any event.

If you have the misfortune of an exhaust elbow leak, either replace it immediately or make a temporary (epoxy) repair. Unchecked, in a short time the leaking hot salt water can cause a lot of damage to the starter, damper plate, housings, alternator, control linkages, etc. Few things are more corrosive than hot saltwater.

14.1.9 Engine heat exchanger zinc pencil

Have a good stock on board. Zinc pencils need to be replaced every 100 to 200 hours or when they are more than ½ eroded away. Without them, the heat exchangers will be eaten away. Don't forget the genset too.

14.1.10 Engine fuel injectors

Diagnosing the health of fuel injectors is best left to a diesel engine mechanic. Suffice it to say that if there is an unusual amount of fuel in the exhaust water, a skipping engine or excessive smoking after a cold start-up the problem may be fouled or mal-adjusted injectors. Injectors do require periodic refurbishing.

14.2 OTHER LIMITED LIFE COMPONENTS

14.2.1 Batteries

House batteries need special mention because they are normally connected in parallel or series-parallel. When a cell fails it will become a continuous drain on all of the other cells and can cause the premature demise of the other batteries. It can also be an explosion and fire hazard.

To determine which battery has a failed cell, charge the bank fully. For standard wet cell batteries, use a hygrometer to find the bad cell. (It may be the battery that has been drinking excess water lately.) For maintenance free batteries, gel- cells and AGM batteries, after charging, it will be necessary to disconnect one terminal on each battery and measure the individual batteries' voltages. The battery with a low voltage will be the bad guy. The latter technique works with standard wet cell batteries as well, but the hygrometer test method is usually easier to perform.

Replacement batteries must be of the same type as the rest of the bank. Minor variations in voltage and capacity of individual batteries can degrade the whole system. If the batteries of a bank are all old and tired, it is best to replace them.

14.2.2 Cutlass bearings

These are the propeller shaft bearings under the hull. Normally, these bearings last a very long time. If they were in good condition when you bought the boat, it is possible that you may never have to replace one.

However, premature cutlass bearing failure can be caused by bad engine alignment, fishing line, rope, a plastic bag, defective manufacture and marine growth impeding water flow. Fishing line wrapped on the shaft at the bearing is especially bad and can ruin a bearing in just a few hours.

It is always a good idea to check the condition of the props, shafts and regions around the cutlass bearings any time you dive the anchor or are just in for a swim.

If while running, a sudden vibration is detected, there's a good chance a propeller picked up a rope, plastic bag, Sargasso weed or other debris. It could also be a skipping engine. Try briefly reversing the drive; you might get lucky. Otherwise, if it is not a skipping engine, stop and dive the prop(s) before any damage is done.

Sudden catastrophic cutlass bearing failure occasionally happens, usually with very new bearings or very old ones. Sudden failure occurs when the rubber-bearing sleeve comes loose from the outer bronze or fiberglass cylinder. This is a serious condition. The vibration may be so bad that the engine must be shut down as soon as it is safe to do so. Continued running may risk damage to the shaft and transmission.

More commonly, a gradually increasing vibration level will signal cutlass-bearing deterioration. Bearing replacement is a job to be done in the yard.

14.2.3 Shaft packing gland(s) (stuffing box)

There are several types of "drip-less" shaft seals. For these, check with the manufacturer regarding maintenance and recommended spare parts. If, on the other hand, the boat is equipped with the old-fashioned packing gland shaft seal(s) they will require occasional attention. After a year or so, many miles of operation and repeated tightening, the old packing material becomes compressed and hard. When that occurs, too much water will be leaking past the packing, and further tightening risks damage to the flange. Over tightened, the flange assembly will run warm and the shaft can be scored. The normal temperature may be a few degrees above the seawater temperature; it should not be hot.

Normally replacement of the packing material is not difficult and can be done anytime. It is astonishing, however, that a few boat designs make this job nearly impossible. Hopefully, your boat is not one of them. Packing replacement can be done while the boat is in the water. The main difficulty may be to keep the incoming stream of seawater away from components that will rust. As a precaution, before going to work, spray adjacent components with a lubricant as a surface barrier.

Next, using a mandrel (pvc pipe or ?) the same size as the shaft, cut the new packing material in individual one-turn rings making diagonal end cuts to produce an overlapping joint.

Remove the packing nut or adjustment flange. Use a small screwdriver or pick to remove the old packing material. Avoid scratching the shaft. The water flow may be annoying, but it will not be serious.

Install the new packing material with the same number of rings as were removed. Be sure to stagger the alignment of the diagonal end cuts to insure a proper seal.

For the next few hours of operation, several adjustments will have to be made as the new material settles in.

Note: Teflon® impregnated packing material will last longer and run cooler with less frequent dripping (or no dripping) than material without Teflon®. Keep enough material in the spares kit for at least one full replacement for the rudder(s) and propeller shaft(s).

On *Francesca*, we have found that the propeller shaft packing material has needed replacement every 4000 to 6000 miles.

See Packing Gland Adjustments in the *Periodic Adjustments* section of this chapter.

14.2.4 GPS

GPS units are sealed with a dry nitrogen purge and may also have silica gel packages inside. They are made that way to minimize the level of humidity within the package. Even the slightest amount of moisture condensation will cause a GPS to become intermittent or at least temporarily fail.

Seals begin their road to failure the day they are assembled. In just a few years an expensive GPS can become unreliable. Early signs of this may be experienced when the activated GPS takes longer and longer to locate satellites and calculate a position. By then the unit will be of such an age that the manufacturer won't support it. What to do?

Even with bad seals, most GPS units will function reasonably well so long as the internal self-heated temperature is elevated to remove or prevent minor condensation. Therefore, even when the GPS is not in use, keep the power on. For the equipment's longevity and to avoid attracting bugs, it's probably best to adjust the screen intensity to a low level when it's not in use.

To get the longest life out of a GPS, keep it shielded from direct sunlight and covered up when not in use.

Also, think about your backup GPS. Brand spanking new, but left in a drawer for a year or two, it may not work without hours of cookout. That won't be helpful when it's really needed.

GPS external antennas can also fall victim to moisture condensation. Sometimes they can be brought back to life with a little careful surgery and a good drying out. Having a spare GPS antenna along may be useful for analyzing a problem as well as for replacement.

14.2.5 Watermaker

Watermaker manufacturers often recommend changing the membranes every three years. That is, if you are fortunate enough to get that much time out of them. Membranes are easily and frequently damaged by:

fuel contaminated water,
water with a heavy biological burden,
chlorinated water,
not operating the watermaker frequently enough,
poor pickling methods,
too high membrane pressure
salinity changes (approaching a river)
or a dozen other bad practices.

Take all of the precautions and maintenance tips given in the owner's manual seriously.

If the age of the component is unknown, replace it.

14.3 THINGS THAT NEED PERIODIC ADJUSTMENT

This class of maintenance, while periodic, is not routine.

14.3.1 Engine alignment(s)

Engine alignment is critical to the long-term health of the transmission(s) and the cutlass bearings. It may be necessary to do this procedure after haul-outs, once every two years, or perhaps even more frequently depending upon the boat's history. With the acquisition of any boat, these adjustments should be on the list of things to do before beginning any cruise. What's more, adjustment may require several iterations. That is, after a significant adjustment, the engine mountings will settle to a new stable position after several hours of operation. The new engine position may not yet be in good alignment with the shaft and require subsequent albeit lesser alignment adjustments.

Proper alignment is checked by taking the bolts out of the transmission / shaft mating flanges. Then, use a feeler gauge to see that the flanges are all around parallel to within 0.005 inches. Also check for flange vertical horizontal alignment. The shaft may sag significantly under its own weight. If so, the determination of vertical alignment can be a little subjective. Check to see that the shaft is centered in the packing gland flange.

Engine alignment must be done properly. If there is doubt about your abilities to perform this task, get competent help and be a good observer so that you can do it yourself the next time.

Also periodically check the security of the engine mounting bolts.

If there is excess vibration while underway it can be engine alignment, propeller damage, a bent shaft, a failed cutlass bearing, debris on a prop or a skipping engine. Diagnosing vibration problems may take a bit of work, but before hauling the boat, check the engine alignment.

14.3.2 Valve adjustments

If you lack confidence in doing this job, by all means get competent help here. Engine damage can result if this is not done properly. Valve adjustments are required only infrequently; check the engine service manual for the correct schedule.

14.3.3 Tachometer(s)

Most analog electric marine tachometers receive their drive signals from an output from the engine alternator(s). Analog tachometers aren't very accurate, especially when there are wide temperature variations and the alternator belt tension or belt condition is poor. Even after calibration, their accuracy is not constant over the operating range. Analog tachometers are, however, relatively easy to adjust if you have access to a hand held mechanical tachometer.

The tachometer adjustment potentiometer may be found on the backside of the instrument. It is generally a small screwdriver adjustment perhaps covered with a plug or label. With the engine running at a calibrated rpm (using a mechanical or digital tach. and at a mid range setting), adjust the analog tachometer. After adjustment, put the panel back in its normal position and check to make sure the reading has not changed. Most analog marine tachometers are position sensitive.

Properly adjusted tachometers can help save fuel and simplify engine synchronizing. Adjustment should be done anytime the calibration becomes suspect.

But, before making the adjustments, check to make sure the alternator belt(s) are in good condition and properly tensioned.

14.3.4 Packing gland adjustment (engine and rudder)

Adjustment of these devices is kind of touchy-feely. If Teflon™ impregnated packing material is installed on the propeller shaft(s), it may be possible to run with no water drip. Other materials may require a slight drip (one drip every one to three seconds) to run cool. The rudder glands, however, should be tight enough to preclude any dripping or leakage whatever.

14.4 ROUTINE MAINTENANCE

Maintenance that is scheduled purely around engine hours or calendar time and repeated with regularity is routine. For a cruising vessel, the list of routine maintenance items is surprisingly long. A sample checklist is included in the appendices.

14.4.1 Engine oil and filter changes

Refer to your engine manual for frequency, oil type and filter recommendations. For replacement full flow filters, it is important to fill them with fresh oil prior to installation; otherwise, the engine will run without oil until the filter is full.

It is astonishing in this day and age that the manufacturers of oil filters have yet to address the mess created when changing their filters. To help avoid oil spills, put a plastic shopping bag around the filter before the flow begins. It doesn't solve the problem by any stretch, but it does confine it some.

14.4.2 Transmission oil changes

Considerably less frequent than engine oil changes, but nonetheless important. Refer to your engine manual for frequency, oil type and filter recommendations. Have the transmission oil analyzed every year or so. Each analysis costs around $25 and it can provide early warning of failure.

14.4.3 Injector pump oil change.

This is a requirement only for vintage Ford Lehman engines. The manufacturers recommendation is to change the oil every 50 hours. The main concern is apparently for reduced lubricity due to oil dilution by diesel fuel Begin by changing the oil between 50 and 100 hours. If the dilution is minimal, and the oil is clean, extend the oil change time. On *Francesca*, the dilution has become less each year. We now change injector pump oil at the same time the engine oil is changed.

14.4.4 Fuel filters

It is best to have a vacuum gauge(s) across the main fuel filter(s) to detect when a filter is loading up. Prior to any long run, if the gauge(s) indicates loading, it or they should be changed before the engine begins to be starved for fuel. With reasonably clean fuel, the filters should not require replacement for hundreds of hours. With dirty fuel it may be required in just a few hours. When there is any question about the cleanliness of the fuel you plan to purchase, have a gallon pumped into a bucket for inspection.

Baja filters are portable devices for filtering fuel as it is fed into the boat. They are popular with sail boaters who require only a few gallons of fuel. However, they are impractically slow for the fuel quantity needed by trawlers.

It is unusual to get dirty fuel, but maintain a large stock of fuel filters just in case.

14.4.5 Heat exchanger zincs

Replace every 100–150 hours or whenever there is less than 50% of the pencil remaining.

14.4.6 Raw water pump impeller, main engines

Replacement can be required with as little as 300 hours of running time. Even less if the vessel has not been used regularly over a long period of time. After the first 300 hours, inspect the impeller(s) every 150 hours to check for cracking. It is far better to replace a still functional impeller than to wait for the telltale exhaust sounds, fouled heat exchangers, runaway engine temperature and risk an expensive engine overhaul.

Examine the impeller blades by stressing them at extreme angles and check for signs of cracking especially near the base.

14.4.7 Raw water pump impeller, generator set

For most generator sets, impeller replacement is not needed more often than every 800 to 1000 hours. However, the impeller should be inspected every 150 hours after the first 500 hours. Replace it and record the hours at the first hint of cracking.

14.4.8 Engine mounts

Check all of the mounting bolts and nuts for tightness. These fasteners can work loose after the punishment of vibration, jarring and rolling at sea. Not only is a loose mounting tough on transmissions and cutlass bearings, engines have been known to come loose at sea.

14.4.9 Batteries

Maintain batteries in "topped up" condition using only distilled water or double processed watermaker water. Water contaminants create an ever-present discharge path and reduce the life of a battery.

14.5 SAFETY EQUIPMENT ROUTINE MAINTENANCE

Next in line for routine maintenance and inspection are the safety items required to be kept aboard. A checklist such as the one found in the next chapter is necessary to be assured of maintaining a safe vessel. However, rather than fill the pages recounting Coast Guard requirements we have included only a few tips about safety equipment. The prudent skipper will be knowledgeable about the legally required safety equipment.

14.5.1 Fire extinguishers

Extinguishers hang quietly on the bulkheads and get little attention. These devices offer comfort in the knowledge that should a fire start, they are ready and capable of putting out a fire. Well, maybe. If your type B, C dry chemical fire extinguisher has been on the bulkhead more than a few months, without being shaken, there is a good chance it will be useless when needed. Every couple of months, and especially before beginning a cruise, it is necessary to vigorously shake these extinguishers. When the extinguisher is shaken, the cake of powder can be felt to break loose from the bottom. Thereafter, continue shaking the bottle for about 30 seconds to insure that the powder is well distributed in the propellant.

14.5.2 Life jacket strobe lights

For night passages, a clip on personal strobe light is a small investment for greatly improved safety at sea. Make sure the strobes are functional and have fresh batteries before making night passages.

14.5.3 Ditch bag

This is a bag in which survival gear is stored for use in the very unlikely event of a sinking. Periodically change the food, water and flashlight batteries. Also include copies of current passports, vessel documentation, credit cards and a little cash.

Further information may be found in the chapter, *Maintenance Checklist*.

14.6 OTHER MAINTENANCE TIPS

Here are a few ideas that we, and others, have tested over the years.

14.6.1 Bent propeller

In many regions propeller shops are non-existent. With a bent propeller, one has three choices. Run with the bent prop, replace the prop with a spare or attempt a repair. Clearly, and for the sake of the running gear, continued operation with a bent propeller is not a good choice particularly if there is significant vibration. If a spare prop is not available, then the following field repair method may get you out of a spot. This repair technique requires that there is at least one good blade on the damaged prop.

First, of course, for the big boat you need to have a prop puller aboard. These can be purchased or made at any machine shop for $100–$200. Also have a wrench aboard that fits the prop nuts.

Even in murky water, it is not too big a trick to remove a prop while snorkeling or on a hooka rig. Scuba is an option but less desirable because of the bulk and likelihood of getting fouled with the rudder or prop. Take care to have the prop tied off and don't drop the cotter pin, nut, key or tools.

Once the prop is aboard and cleaned up, use Bondo®, concrete, or fiberglass and resin to make a solid casting of a good blade. Bondo® is by far the easiest and quickest material to use and it's a good idea to have a couple of quarts or a gallon of this inexpensive material aboard for all kinds of temporary repairs.

To make a casting of Bondo®, form several layers of tape around the edge of a good propeller blade. This will serve as a dam to retain the slightly soupy Bondo® on the blade. Next, coat the blade with a thin film of grease or cellophane tape to prevent the Bondo® from adhering to the blade. Lay up a half dozen 1/8–1/4 inch layers of Bondo® to make a casting approximately 1 inch thick.

Bondo® generates heat while curing. So, to avoid warping or a potential fire, build up multiple layers with time for cooling in between each layer.

After the casting is thick enough and cooled, remove it from the good propeller blade. You now have form with which to help return the bent blade(s) back to a more normal condition.

The next step is very subjective. If the blade is too badly bent, attempts to cold form it back to the original shape may result in cracking. In any event, reforming must be done gently and with slow deliberation. Never try to bend any section of metal more than a slight amount and always work the damaged material in stages all along the blade. A portable vice with wood spacers may be helpful. In other cases a wood backing and a hammer striking wood or plastic on the blade will work. Clearly, a prop with only minor damage is the best candidate for this technique, but seriously damaged props have been repaired this way also. With a little time and care a prop can be returned to a condition where it is difficult to detect that any damage had occurred.

14.6.2 Marine growth in port

Visits to foreign ports have a way of stretching from a few days to months. Many places are called cruiser traps because they are so pleasant. Just as often the bay water supports accelerated marine growth that will flourish on unprotected propellers. Within a few weeks propellers can become indistinct blobs. The problem can be eliminated by placing a plastic bag(s) over the prop(s). Barnacles and worms are filter feeders; if there is no water flow (food supply), they cannot exist. Most of us don't savor diving in port waters, but local divers can be found that will do the job for you.

14.6.3 Alternator failure

Many cruising boats are outfitted with high output alternators of 100 amps or more. These seem to fail much more frequently than the lower output units. Most likely, the failures occur because high output alternators also create more heat. Without good ventilation, the rectifiers and semiconductors in the regulator can easily exceed their temperature limits and fail. If you experience this type of failure, it may take a little creativity to improve the alternator cooling.

14.6.4 Main engine or genset engine won't start

Oddly, in this case the primary problem is usually not so big a problem. Unless there is difficulty with cranking, the problem is usually fuel related. Fuel pumps, poorly bled fuel lines/filters or fuel system air leaks are highest on the list of potential offenders. But, for some engine installation, a bigger problem can be created with continued starting attempts. With no exhaust pressure, water can back up in the exhaust system and do serious damage to the engine. For installations where the exhaust manifold is above the muffler and waterline this shouldn't be a problem, but do take the time to understand your exhaust setup before cranking a stubborn engine too much.

14.6.5 Outboard motor fuel contamination

For cruisers, their dinghy is their car. Dinghies are used nearly every day and are needed for all facets of fun, foraging and shopping. When an outboard motor problem occurs it needs fixing quickly and reliably.

By far the greatest problem is one of fuel contamination. If water, trash or both are in the fuel, the result is the same-, unreliable operation. It is an even greater problem with 4 cycle engines because the carburetor apertures are significantly smaller than with 2 cycle engines.

To protect against this problem, either mount a spin on fuel filter on the dinghies transom or put a large inline filter such as a Fram 51 inside of the engine cowling.

Spark plugs, prop, fuel filter and water pump impellers nicely round out the needed spare parts inventory for the outboard. A spare prop might be handy too.

14.6.6 Dinghy repairs

Perhaps a leak or two are discovered in the dinghy's Hyperlon™ tubes or bits are beginning to delaminate and fall off. You then get out the trusty little repair kit, follow the directions to a tee and in a few days are disappointed with the results. What to do? Well take heart. 3M, 5200 adhesive works better than the stuff found in most repair kits by a country mile. Just make sure the surfaces are clean and have been lightly abraded with sandpaper. As long as there is little or no UV exposure, a patch attached with 5200 will be a permanent fix. Even for pinhole air or water leaks, a small bit of 5200 applied to a dry surface, without a patch, and allowed to cure (without pressure on the tubes) makes a good semi-permanent fix. Ancient dinghies can be kept in service almost indefinitely with this technique.

14.6.7 Sick watermaker

There you are 2000 miles from south Florida where the watermaker was purchased. The watermaker output is still all right for taking showers, but it tastes slightly salty. If you have a salinity tester, it might be found that the salinity exceeds 400 ppm but is less than 1000 ppm. This is a common range for the output of dying membranes. But, getting a new membrane will be difficult and may take weeks.

Here's a solution that may let you finish your cruise with only minor inconveniences.

Flushing the watermaker with fresh water is a task that you have done many times. During the fresh water flush the pressure is usually reduced to zero. However, by raising the membrane pressure to a level no greater than 200 psi it is possible to reprocess the slightly brackish tank water and capture very good drinking water in jugs. Here's how it works.

A healthy watermaker membrane, will remove the salt from the seawater with better than 99% salt removal. If that deteriorates to only 97% salt removal, that results in about 1000 parts per million of salt remaining and bad tasting, even dangerous drinking water. By reprocessing that water you wind up with 97% removal of the 1000 parts per million of salt – or excellent drinking water. Using this procedure, there would have to be a large decline in the membrane's health to preclude getting good potable water.

The authors' experience with a deteriorating membrane over a one-year period has yielded excellent drinking water at all times.

This technique works well when at the dock also. In many areas of the Caribbean, the dock water is of questionable purity. Bacteria and parasites may be present in the water. Yet, by filling the boat's tanks with dock water and then processing it through the watermaker into a separate tank or jugs assures good water.

Take care, however, chlorinated water will damage a watermaker membrane. Be sure that a proper carbon block filter, in good condition, is used to remove chlorine and chlorine compounds (bleach) before processing the water through the watermaker membrane.

14.6.8 Dock power cord deterioration

At every marina, dock power pedestal connectors show damage from overheating. The same problem often occurs at the vessel's shore power connections. Unless precautions are taken, expensive dock power connectors and cables can be fried within a year or two.

The problem occurs when minor corrosion raises the resistance of the connections and power is dissipated at the connection. The heat then accelerates corrosion and the problem gets worse. Eventually, the connection temperature is sufficiently high to melt the plastic or even start a fire.

The fix is simple and long lasting. Coat both ends of the power cord connections with a film of an anticorrosion product like Noalox®. Reapply this material every year or so. Products like this can be purchased at electrical supply houses. Your shore power connections need never fry again.

Dock cords left dangling in the water are unsightly. More importantly, if the insulation is old and even slightly cracked, there is a risk of accelerated rudder and shaft zinc deterioration. Left long enough, stray currents can go to work on all the metal components below the waterline including those of your neighbors' boats.

14.6.9 Other boat electrical problems

Corroded or loose connectors and terminals account for at least 80% of the problems with boat electrical systems. If one knows where to look, many, if not most, of those problems can be solved without technical assistance.

In the inspection process, first make sure the power is off then systematically tug on the wires to terminals to find bad crimp connections and loose terminals. Where necessary, clean contacts, tie up cables, provide stress relief loops and an occasional drip loop. Use an antioxidant compound where appropriate.

Having done these things systematically, many potential problems can be eliminated before they occur. This process doesn't require much technical expertise, just observation and good sense.

If the wiring behind a panel is a rat's nest, it may be worthwhile to take one wire at a time and clean it up. If you're not comfortable doing that, get some help, but try to do as much as possible. Rat's nest panels are difficult to troubleshoot. They are also prone to connection failures caused by the stress of frequent servicing.

For all new electronics installations, where possible, leave cable lengths long enough to enable testing the equipment in convenient positions without undue cable and connection stress.

14.7 MAINTENANCE AND REPAIRS IN FOREIGN PORTS

This brief section may contain surprises for new cruisers. Everyone expects that third world labor will be low cost and often the quality of work will be poor. However, with planning it is possible to get good quality work done very inexpensively.

In countries like Guatemala, Panama, Colombia and Venezuela, labor rates can be very low. In 2004, it was not unusual to be able to employ reasonably experienced craftsmen for $2.00 per hour or less. The trick is to get referrals and to see the quality of work that has been done. Teak refinishing, painting, fiberglass work, carpentry, and boat cleaning / airing are services that can usually be found at low hourly rates.

More serious work such as transmission and engine repairs, where shop rates are incurred, can also often be obtained at low cost. For example, in Panama, a transmission repair on *Francesca* cost $260. That included pickup, repairs with a few parts, a little machining, return, installation and testing of the transmission. In this case, the key to success was a referral from the transmission manufacturer's service organization. Conversely, a trawler captain at Isla de Margarita needed minor engine work. After the engine was striped down and many of the parts taken to the mechanics shop, the work was discontinued. The captain had to pay to get his parts back and find another mechanic to finish the job.

Replacement parts can be a problem, but many of the service people are very resourceful. It may be expeditious and less expensive to have a part fabricated rather than wait for it to be shipped in. In Trinidad, Venezuela, Panama and Colombia, there are many machine shops.

In Cartagena, Colombia and elsewhere in the southern Caribbean it is possible to have a boat's exterior completely refinished from the bottom of the keel to the top of the mast. This can be done with gel coat or various other paints. Often the work is not as good as a modern U.S. paint shop, but the cost can be a small fraction of that in the States. Complete blister jobs are done routinely. In Colombia, specialty paints and epoxies may not be available. If possible, bring what you need.

Imron and Awl Grip paints need to be brought in from the U.S., otherwise, locally available two-part polyurethane auto paint makes a nice job. Quality interior work is not as readily available, but with referrals good craftsmen are out there. There are ready supplies of teak, mahogany and other hardwoods at bargain prices.

Thus, with a single visit to the southern Caribbean your somewhat tired looking vessel can be transformed into much of its former self at rates you can't afford to pass up. One cruiser put it this way, "I saved so much money I had to go to the ATM nearly every day." For all services, it is usually best to negotiate a total price up front rather than pay by the hour.

14.8 NEW EQUIPMENT INSTALLATIONS AND UPGRADES

New equipment and equipment upgrades, as always, are only as good as the installations. Unfortunately, there are more tales of woe than tales of praise.

Yardwork at Cartagena, Colombia

Here are a few sad stories.

> A cruising sailboat had a long section of active HF-SSB antenna (not coaxial cable) installed inside the wooden mizzen mast alongside the radar and lighting power cables. The other wiring absorbed most of the antenna's radiated energy. Besides having very poor SSB performance, many of the boat's systems were badly affected by the rf energy.
>
> A cruising trawler had over 500 feet of wiring variously installed to accommodate new installations. The added wiring was haphazardly installed and contributed to general electrical unreliability and servicing difficulties. The wire additions had been unnecessary because the trawler had been manufactured with ample spare wires and breakers.
>
> A cruising sailboat had multiple new electrical installations and other modifications done over a period of years. These were poorly documented if at all. Subsequent problems and servicing costs were excessive. The complexity was beyond the depth of the owner who gave up and sold the boat.
>
> During outfitting, a new aluminum power catamaran had extensive additional stainless hardware installed on the weather deck. Within a year galvanic corrosion blistered the paint around the hardware. It had not been properly sealed and insulated from the aluminum deck.

Colombian yardworker friends take a brief cruise

You get the idea, huh!

At every marina, if one asks who does good work, someone will say that so-and-so is the best. That may or may not be the case. It may be that the one who makes the recommendation has no real knowledge of the technology. Get recommendations for service people from knowledgeable cruisers. Then, make sure that new installations or modifications are well documented and understood.

Chapter 15
Maintenance Checklist

Elsewhere in this book, the diverse maintenance requirements of a boat were likened to a small community where all of the various service infrastructures are provided. The small community advantageously has individual departments to maintain each primary element and contractors that handle the downstream functions. But, on a cruising boat, the captain and mate have these as well as other responsibilities including navigation, piloting, cooking, foreign liaison, cleaning, research, etc.

Unless there is a programmed system of regular review, too many maintenance items tend to fall through the cracks. In time, sloppy maintenance will lead to failures, inconvenience, delays and unnecessary expense. We have talked with many captains about the problem. Often they describe some canned computer program that guides them along. But it is surprising how suddenly enlightened some captains are when they first see the checklist method presented in this chapter. The simple system is a common sense approach to timely maintenance, yet for some reason it has not been an obvious approach. Patented inventions are often like that. They are simple, but not obvious solutions to a problem or need.

The checklist that follows has evolved and grown over the years. It is still growing. Yet, even today and although there are over 100 items on the list, it seems odd that it could not have been written completely in a single setting. That alone puts a sharp point on the fact that we cannot possibly keep all of the functional needs and the associated periodicities in our heads. Properly done, performance of the checklist will require several days to a week to complete.

As a whole the checklist also provides a maintenance and travel history for the vessel. Whenever the vessel is sold, it will be important to any potential buyer. It may also have some nostalgic value to seller.

We used a computer spreadsheet simply because it was a convenient means of making an open ended array. There seemed no need to add the complications of an automated flagging or dating system. While the reader may have his or her own preferences about how to set it up, the most important features of the checklist are the listing, scheduling and tracking of the needed items.

The pre-cruise checklist, provisioning and spare parts spreadsheets can be downloaded from our website at: www.cruisingfrancesca.org

After downloading, they can be tailored for your needs.

Francesca									
Date	Nov. 30, 2003	Dec. 28, 2003	Aug. 10, 2004	Dec. 15, 2004	Jan. 25, 2005	Mar. 15, 2005	April 27, 2005	June 17, 2005	Sept. 10, 2005
	Isla San Andres	Rio Dulce, Guat	NMB, SC	Luperon, DR	Salinas, PR	Trinidad	Pto. La Cruz, VE	Trinidad	Pto. La Cruz, VE
Port Engine									
Engine Hours	5159	5258	5481	5685	5738	5863	5917	5985	6090
Engine Oil	OK	Changed	Changed	OK	Changed	Changed	OK	OK	Changed
Inj. Pump Oil	OK	Changed	Changed	Changed	OK	Changed	OK	Changed	Changed
Transmission Oil	OK	OK	OK	OK	OK	OK	OK	OK	Changed
Engine Oil Filter	OK	Changed	Changed	OK	Changed	Changed	OK	OK	Changed
Racor Fuel Filter	OK	OK	Changed	Changed	Changed	Changed	OK	OK	Changed
Eng. Heat Exch. Zinc	Changed	OK	1/3 gone	Changed	OK	Changed	OK	OK	Changed
Coolant Level	OK	OK	OK	OK	OK	OK	OK	OK	Refreshed
Raw Water Strainer	OK	OK	OK	OK	OK	OK	OK	OK	OK
Water Pump Impeller	OK	266 hrs	Rebuilt, new	OK	OK	Changed	OK	OK	OK
Eng. Heat Exchanger	OK	OK	Cleaned	OK	OK	OK	OK	OK	OK
Eng. Oil Heat Exch	Repaired	OK	New	OK	OK	OK	OK	OK	OK
Xmiss. Oil Heat Exch	OK	OK	OK	OK	OK	OK	OK	OK	OK
Battery Levels	OK	Topped Up	Topped Up	Topped Up	Topped Up	Topped Up	Ok	Topped Up	New 8D
Inspect Exhaust Elbow	OK	OK	OK	OK	OK	OK	OK	OK	OK
Inspect Hoses	OK	OK	OK	OK	OK	OK	OK	OK	New
Check Belt Condition	OK	OK	OK	OK	OK	OK	OK	OK	OK
Clean Oil Catch Pan	Cleaned	Cleaned	Cleaned	Cleaned	Cleaned	Cleaned	Clean	Clean	Cleaned
Adjust Shaft Packing Gland	Adjusted	OK	Adjusted	Adjusted	Adjusted	Repacked	OK	Adjusted	New Packing
Check Engine Alignment	Adjusted	–	–	–	–	–	–	–	–
Adjust Valves	–	–	Adjusted	–	–	–	–	–	–
Engine Maint.	–	–	Nw Inj. Oil seals	–	–	–	–	–	–
			New Damper Plt						
Gen'l Op. Performance	Satisfactory	Satisfactory	Satisfactory	Satisfactory	Satisfactory	Satisfactory	Satisfactory	Satisfactory	Satisfactory
Spare Parts Inventory	Satisfactory	Satisfactory	Satisfactory	Satisfactory	Satisfactory	Satisfactory	Satisfactory	Satisfactory	Satisfactory

Francesca

Date	Nov. 30, 2003	Dec. 28, 2003	Aug. 10, 2004	Dec. 15, 2004	Jan. 25, 2005	Mar. 15, 2005	Apr. 27, 2005	June 17, 2005	Sept. 10, 2005
	Isla San Andres	Rio Dulce, Guat	NMB, SC	Luperon, DR	Salinas, PR	Trinidad	Pto. La Cruz	Trinidad	Pto. La Cruz, VE
Starboard Engine									
Engine Hours	5145	5258	5472	5676	5729	5854	5907	5975	5998
Engine Oil	OK	Changed	Changed	OK	Changed	Changed	OK	OK	Changed
Inj. Pump Oil	OK	Changed	Changed	Changed	OK	Changed	OK	Changed	Changed
Transmission Oil	OK	OK	OK	OK	OK	OK	OK	OK	Changed
Engine Oil Filter	OK	Changed	Changed	OK	Changed	Changed	OK	OK	Changed
Racor Fuel Filter	OK	OK	Changed	Changed	Changed	Changed	OK	OK	Changed
Eng. Heat Exch. Zinc	Changed	OK	1/3 gone	Changed	OK	Changed	OK	OK	Changed
Coolant Level	OK	OK	OK	OK	OK	OK	OK	OK	OK
Raw Water Strainer	OK	OK	OK	OK	OK	OK	OK	OK	OK
Water Pump Impeller	OK	266 hrs	Rebuilt, new	OK	OK	Changed	OK	OK	OK
Eng. Heat Exchanger	OK	OK	Cleaned	OK	OK	OK	OK	OK	OK
Eng. Oil Heat Exch	Repaired	OK	New	OK	OK	OK	OK	OK	OK
Xmiss. Oil Heat Exch	OK	OK	OK	OK	OK	OK	OK	OK	OK
Battery Levels	OK	Topped Up	Topped Up	Topped Up	Topped Up	Topped Up	Ok	Topped Up	Topped Up
Inspect Exhaust Elbow	OK	OK	OK	OK	OK	OK	OK	OK	OK
Inspect Hoses	OK	OK	OK	OK	OK	OK	OK	OK	OK
Check Belt Condition	OK	OK	OK	OK	OK	OK	OK	OK	OK
Clean Oil Catch Pan	Cleaned	Cleaned	Cleaned	Cleaned	Cleaned	Cleaned	Clean	Clean	Cleaned
Adjust Shaft Packing Gland	Adjusted	OK	Adjusted	Adjusted	Adjusted	Repacked	OK	Adjusted	New Packing
Check Engine Alignment	Adjusted	–	–	–	–	–	–	–	–
Adjust Valves			Adjusted						
Engine Maint.	–	–	Nw Inj. Oil seals	–	–	–	–	–	–
			Nw Damper Plt						
Gen'l Op. Performance	Satisfactory	Satisfactory	Satisfactory	Satisfactory	Satisfactory	Satisfactory	Satisfactory	Satisfactory	Satisfactory
Spare Parts Inventory	Satisfactory	Satisfactory	Satisfactory	Satisfactory	Satisfactory	Satisfactory	Satisfactory	Satisfactory	Satisfactory

Francesca

Date	Nov. 30, 2003	Dec. 28, 2003	Aug. 10, 2004	Dec. 15, 2004	Jan. 25, 2005	Mar. 15, 2005	Apr. 2", 2005	June 17, 2005	Sept. 10, 2005
	Isla San Andres	Rio Dulce, Guat	NMB, SC	Luperon, DR	Salinas, PR	Trinidad	Pto. La Cruz	Trinidad	Pto. La Cruz, VE
Generator									
Generator Hours	1251	1297	1407	1481	1612	1722	1808	1875	1970
Engine Oil	OK	Changed	OK	Changed	OK	Changed	OK	Changed	OK
Engine Oil Filter	OK	Changed	OK	Changed	OK	Changed	OK	Changed	OK
Fuel Filters	OK	OK	Changed Racor	OK	OK	Changed both	OK	OK	OK
Heat Exch. Zinc	Changed	OK	Changed	OK	Changed	Changed	OK	OK	Changed
Coolant Level	OK	OK	OK	OK	OK	OK	OK	OK	OK
Raw Water Strainer	OK	OK	OK	OK	OK	OK	OK	OK	OK
Water Pump Impeller	OK	OK	OK	OK	OK	Changed 800hrs	OK	OK	OK
Exhaust Elbow	OK	OK	Leak repaired	vy slight weap	vy slight weap	vy slight weap	slight weap	Replaced New	OK
Battery Levels	OK	Topped Up	OK	OK	OK	OK	OK	OK	OK
Inspect Hoses	OK	OK	OK	OK	OK	OK	OK	OK	OK
Check Belt Condition	OK	OK	OK	OK	OK	OK	OK	OK	OK
Clean Oil Catch Pan	Clean	Clean	Clean	Clean	Clean	Clean	Clean	Clean	Clean
Spare Parts Inventory	Same	Less 3 oil filters	Purchased	Less 1 oil filter	Unsatisfactory	Same	Same	Same	Same
House Equipment									
Port Inverter Batteries	OK	OK	6 new Trojans	Topped Up	Topped Up	Topped Up	OK	Topped Up	Topped Up
Stbd Inverter Batteries	OK	OK	4 -Topped Up	Topped Up	Topped Up	Topped Up	OK	Topped Up	Topped Up
Salon A/C Filter	OK	OK	Cleaned	OK	OK	OK	OK	OK	Cleaned
Aft Cabin A/C Filter	OK	OK	Cleaned	OK	OK	OK	OK	OK	OK
Aft Shower Sump	OK	OK	Cleaned	Cleaned	OK	Cleaned	OK	Cleaned	Cleaned
Aft Shower Sump Pump	OK	OK	New Switch	OK	OK	OK	OK	OK	OK
Fwd Shower Sump	OK	OK	Cleaned	Cleaned	OK	Cleaned	OK	Cleaned	
Fwd Shower Sump Pump	OK	OK	New Pump	OK	OK	OK	OK	OK	OK
Macerator Pump	OK	OK	Rebuilt	OK	OK	OK	OK	OK	Rebuilt

Francesca

Date	Nov. 30, 2003	Dec. 28, 2003	Aug. 10, 2004	Dec. 15, 2004	Jan. 25, 2005	Mar. 15, 2005	Apr. 27, 05	June 17, 2005	Sept. 10, 2005
	Isla San Andres	Rio Dulce, Guat	NMB, SC	Luperon, DR	Salinas, PR	Trinidad	Pto. La Cruz	Trinidad	Pto. La Cruz, VE
Boat Hull & Fittings									
Bottom Paint	OK	OK	OK	Vy Poor	Vy Poor	New w/epoxy	OK	OK	OK
Rudder Zincs	OK	OK	OK	OK	OK	OK	OK	OK	OK
Shaft Zincs	OK	OK	OK	OK	OK	New	OK	OK	Poor
Hull Screens	OK	OK	OK	OK	OK	OK	OK	OK	OK
Thru Hull Fittings	OK	OK	OK	OK	OK	OK	OK	OK	OK
Sea Cocks	OK	OK	OK	OK	OK	OK	OK	OK	OK
Haws Pipes & Cleats	OK	OK	OK	OK	OK	OK	OK	OK	OK
Bilge Pumps	OK	OK	OK	OK	OK	OK	OK	OK	OK
Bilge Condition	Clean/dry	Clean/dry	Clean/dry	Clean/dry	Clean/dry	Clean/dry	Clean	Clean	Clean
P & S Rudder Packing Glands	OK	OK	OK	OK	OK	Tighten/greased	OK	Weaping	OK
Ground Tackle									
Danforth Shakle/Rode	Rode Poor	Rode Poor	New 300' 5/8"	OK	OK	OK	OK	OK	OK
Delta Shakle/Swivel/Chain	OK	OK	OK	OK	OK	OK	OK	OK	OK
Lunch Hook Shakle/Rode	OK	OK	New Swivel	OK	OK	OK	OK	OK	OK
Snubbers	OK	OK	OK	OK	OK	OK	Fair	Poor	New
Dock Lines	Fair Cond.	Fair Cond.	Fair Cond.	Fair Cond.	Fair Cond.	Fair Cond.	Fair Cond.	Fair Cond.	Fair Cond.
Dock Fenders	Good Cond.	Good Cond.	Fair Cond.	Fair Cond.	Fair Cond.	Fair Cond.	Poor Cond.	Poor cond.	Poor Cond.
Tow line / Spare Rode	short	short	200' used 5/8"	OK	OK	OK	OK	OK	OK
Safety Items									
Flare Gun (Qty & Date)	OK	OK	3 exp. 11/07	OK	OK	OK	OK	OK	OK
Flares (Qty & Date)	OK	OK	3 exp. 11/07	OK	OK	OK	OK	OK	OK
Air Horn & Emerg. Horn	OK	OK	OK	OK	OK	OK	OK	OK	OK
Hand Held Radio	OK	OK	OK	OK	OK	OK	OK	OK	OK
Life Jackets	OK	OK	OK	OK	OK	OK	OK	OK	OK
Personal Strobe Lights	OK	OK	New Batts, OK	OK	OK	OK	OK	OK	OK
Fire Extinguishers	OK	OK	4 shaken	OK	OK	4 shaken	OK	OK	4 shaken
Ditch Bag	OK	OK	Restocked	OK	OK	OK	OK	OK	OK
Lighting									
Navigation lights	OK	OK	OK	OK	OK	OK	OK	OK	OK
Anchor Light	OK	OK	OK	OK	OK	OK	OK	OK	OK
Gen'l lighting	OK	OK	OK	OK	OK	OK	OK	OK	OK

Francesca

Date	Nov. 30, 2003	Dec. 28, 2003	Aug. 10, 2004	Dec. 15, 2004	Jan. 25, 2005	Mar. 15, 2005	Apr. 2, 2005	June 17, 2005	Sept. 10, 2005
	Isla San Andres	Rio Dulce, Guat	NMB, SC	Luperon, DR	Salinas, PR	Trinidad	Pto. La Cruz	Trinidad	Pto. La Cruz, VE
WaterMaker									
Operation	Fair Water	Fair Water	New Plumbing	New Membrane	6 gpm	6 gpm	5 gpm	6 gpm	6 gpm
Pump Oil	OK	OK	OK	OK	OK	OK	OK	OK	OK
Carbon Filter	OK	Changed	Changed	OK	OK	Changed	Changed	Changed	Changed
10 micron Prefilter	Changed	Changed	Changed	OK	Changed	Changed	Changed	Changed	Changed
Spare Parts Inventory	OK	OK	Deficient	OK	OK	OK	Deficient	Deficient	OK
Dinghy and Outboard									
Engine Oil	OK	OK	OK	OK	OK	OK	OK	OK	
Oil Filter	OK	OK	OK	OK	OK	OK	OK	OK	
Lower End Lub	OK	OK	Changed	OK	OK	OK	OK	OK	
Dinghy Exterior	OK	OK	Fair	Fair	Fair	Fair	Fair	New cover	OK
Propeller	OK	OK	OK	OK	OK	OK	OK	OK	OK
OB water pump impeller	OK	OK	New	OK	OK	OK	OK	OK	OK
Security Cable	OK	OK	OK	OK	OK	OK	OK	OK	OK
Anchor & rode	OK	OK	OK	OK	OK	OK	OK	OK	OK
Davit Cables	OK	OK	OK	OK	OK	OK	OK	OK	OK
Spare Parts Inventory	OK	OK	OK	OK	OK	OK	OK	OK	OK

Francesca

Date	Nov. 30, 2003	Dec. 28, 2003	Aug. 10, 2004	Dec. 15, 2004	Jan. 25, 2005	Mar. 15, 2005	Apr. 27, 2005	June 17, 2005	Sept. 10, 2005
	Isla San Andres	Rio Dulce, Guat	NMB, SC	Luperon, DR	Salinas, PR	Trinidad	Pto. La Cruz	Trinidad	Pto. La Cruz, VE
Fly Bridge Electronics									
VHF Radio	OK	OK	OK	OK	OK	OK	OK	OK	OK
VHF Handheld Radio	OK	OK	OK	OK	OK	OK	OK	OK	OK
Radar	—	—	Installed used	OK	OK	OK	OK	OK	OK
GPS	OK	OK	OK	OK	OK	OK	OK	OK	OK
Autopilot	Poor	Poor	Replaced	OK	OK	OK	OK	OK	OK
Depth sounder	OK	OK	New	OK	OK	OK	OK	OK	OK
Compass	OK	OK	OK	OK	OK	OK	OK	OK	OK
Lower Helm Electronics									
VHF Radio	OK	OK	OK	OK	OK	OK	OK	OK	Failed
Radar	OK	OK	OK	OK	OK	OK	OK	OK	OK
GPS	OK	OK	OK	OK	OK	OK	OK	OK	OK
Autopilot	—	—	Replaced	OK	OK	OK	OK	OK	OK
Depth sounder	Poor	Poor	New	OK	OK	OK	OK	OK	OK
SSB Radio	OK	OK	OK	OK	OK	OK	OK	OK	OK
Email TNC	OK	OK	OK	OK	OK	OK	OK	OK	OK
Computer	OK	OK	OK	OK	OK	OK	OK	OK	OK
Compass	OK	OK	OK	OK	OK	OK	OK	OK	OK

Chapter 16
Weather

16.1 WEATHER (GENERAL)

It is important for the new cruiser to understand that with reasonable attention, the weather extremes of large storms should never be part of a powerboat cruisers offshore experience. Thus, a general understanding of the weather is needed for the cruiser to plan comfortable, safe passages and to select safe havens when storms are forecast. To that end, the information provided herein is meant as an introduction with particular emphasis on the Caribbean Sea and the Gulf of Mexico.

Most cruising guides attempt to describe the weather conditions for the specific region covered by the guide. They discuss rainy seasons, hurricane seasons, seasons with northers or tropical waves and so on. That is useful, but a more general understanding of the major tropical weather features is needed for extended cruise planning. This short chapter describes the weather patterns for the Gulf of Mexico and Caribbean Sea in a broad introductory sense.

Starting with the basics of weather, moving air masses such as highs, lows, ridges and troughs and their interactions are responsible for our changing weather. In the northern hemisphere, highs rotate with a clockwise motion and lows counterclockwise. In the broadest of terms, weather systems north of about 15°-north latitude move from west to east. Below 15°-north weather systems move east to west. However, major frontal systems and hurricanes often move contrary to these generalizations.

16.2 WINTER WEATHER CONDITIONS

During the winter months in the Gulf of Mexico and northern Caribbean, weather systems sweep down from the western U.S. in a general southeasterly direction. As they move toward Cuba, the movement tends to be a bit more easterly.

With low-pressure systems in the southern Gulf of Mexico and northern Caribbean, the wind clocks around from the west to north to northeast as the low passes. For small systems the wind can clock around to a much greater extent.

Each system has an associated front that is the interface between air masses of different temperatures. For any system the peak winds generally occur during frontal passages. For lows, the worst wind conditions most often come from the northwest to northeast and vessels should be appropriately sheltered. The typical conditions associated with frontal passages are winds anywhere from 20 to 35 knots, but they can be much worse. Wind velocities in excess of 50 knots are not all that rare.

Winter high-pressure systems also move through the Gulf of Mexico and northern Caribbean with the same northwest to southeasterly direction. As the high approaches, the wind will clock from the north to east and then southeast. Peak winds of those frontal passages generally come out of the north or northeast (occasionally the northwest). Fronts associated with moving high-pressure systems are not often as energetic as the low-pressure fronts, but they are to be respected just the same.

Both types of weather systems move and extend as far south as a line from Nicaragua to the Dominican Republic with lesser effects yet further south. During strong frontal passages cruising vessels should be secure at a dock, anchorage or mooring.

South of about 13° north latitude the wintertime wind conditions are much more benign and the trade winds are the dominant feature. However, coastal conditions may vary significantly because of land effect winds. Land effect breezes are significant along coastal Belize, Honduras, Panama, Colombia, the Dominican Republic and Puerto Rico. With the exception of a part of the Colombian coast, the winter conditions along the north coast of South America are much like the summertime conditions, albeit the trades are a bit stronger. The special Colombian features are discussed later.

16.3 SUMMER WEATHER CONDITIONS

Above about 20°-north and aside from the occasional squall, the summertime conditions settle down to gentle breezes and calm seas. Below 20°-north latitude, as the northers die out in April, tropical waves begin their marches from Africa across the Atlantic. Typically spaced they pass every 4 to 7 days. Most tropical waves are relatively benign having only rain and less than 25 knots of wind. Occasionally, however, they will move through with greater energy.

During the summer, areas like the Bahamas and the eastern Caribbean are at their cruising best. But with tropical depressions, storms and hurricanes, just being there is like rolling the dice. Aside from the personal risk, cruising vessels are rarely insured against named storm damage within the boundaries of the region of probable hurricanes. Most insurance carriers put the lower boundary of the hurricane belt at 12.5° to 13°-north latitude. But, in the years 2004 and 2005 the island of Grenada, just at and above 12° N, was hit hard. Insurance carriers may begin reducing the lower latitude limit to include Grenada.

The South American coast, as near as 75 nm south of Grenada, has had only one hurricane hit in the past 100 years. Thus, coastal Trinidad, Venezuela, Colombia and Panama are popular havens for cruisers. With one regional exception, near Colombia, the coast provides excellent cruising conditions year round.

The region along the northeastern coast of Colombia is well known for having frequent severe sea conditions. Low-pressure systems, seemingly trapped by Panama to the west, often become stationary north of Colombia. That factor combined with an eddy current that bucks the trades tends to produce punishing seas in this area. Cruisers, therefore, seldom make the passage west to east, bucking those seas. But the passage, in either direction, can be smooth and a patient wait for good weather will be rewarded. The months of December through March are not generally favorable for this passage. From Aruba to Cartagena, Colombia is about 400 nm. There are a couple of ways to make the trip. One school of thought is to stay well offshore (some say 200 miles), and tough it out while the other school says that cruising boats should go in groups and take the easier inshore route. Considering the sea conditions, inshore cruising is favored as safer; making mostly day trips with stops at good anchorages. However, the inshore route is less favored when considering the potential for banditry.

16.4 OTHER FEATURES THAT AFFECT SEA CONDITIONS AND SAFETY

The affects of weather combined with ocean currents create very diverse sea conditions. In the Gulf Stream and other ocean rivers, a modest wind against the current can create short interval chop that punishes boats and crewpersons

A visually threatening, yet benign squall at Bocas del Drago, Panama

alike. Around points and capes (puntas and cabos), the current together with even a light wind can generate confused seas. Large ocean swells originating many days before and a thousand miles away are impressive and affect progress. Fast moving tight squalls with high winds, although seldom the source of large seas, are fleetingly intimidating. While the squally wind may whip up the seas, conversely a heavy rain can settle it. These are a few of the day-to-day factors of weather and sea state. Without understanding, they are all threatening. Given time, your understanding and tolerance for the sea conditions will mature. However, to put it all in perspective, there are times to be timid and times to be a little less so. Was there any mention of being bold?

Frequently mentioned in tropical weather reports is the Inter-Tropical-Convergence-Zone or ITCZ. This region is usually located between 5° north latitude and 5° south latitude. The ITCZ is a band that stretches from Africa to South America. In the zone, the northeast and southeast trade winds converge and create rising air or convection. The convection can later spawn tropical storms. The ITCZ is sometimes called *The Doldrums* because there is often little surface wind in the zone.

Lightning is discussed in Security at Sea, Anchor and Ashore.

16.5 FORECASTS

In port, the means of obtaining weather forecasts are countless and include the Internet (dozens of websites), AM/FM radio, TV (local and national news), The Weather Channel, NOAA weather radio, weatherfax, VHF radio, satellite TV and so on. At sea there are fewer options, but they are no less informative.

Weather information can be acquired through several common means using HF-SSB radio. The first and simplest method is to listen to the various marine or Ham nets. Every day, each net has a volunteer who provides current and forecast weather information. That information will often satisfy cruisers' day-to-day needs.

16.5.1 Automated voice weather on HF-SSB

The U.S. Coast Guard broadcasts automated voice weather information to the Caribbean on the following schedule.

	TIME (UTC)	FREQUENCIES (MHZ)
	0400	4.426, 6.501, 8764
	0530	same
All	1000	same
NMN	1130	6.501, 8.764, 13.089
(Portsmouth, VA)	1600	same
	1730	8.764, 13.089, 17.314
	2200	6.501, 8.764, 13.089
	2330	same

For the purpose of planning passages, more complete weather information can be acquired using the weatherfax system.

16.5.2 Weatherfax broadcasts

Weatherfax transmissions are a free service of U.S. Coast Guard and the U.S. National Weather Service. The equipment needed for WeFax reception can be of two types. The first is a dedicated WeFax receiver/plotter system. These units are effectively SSB receivers/printers with limited capabilities and which require a dedicated antenna. With a big equipment budget, it would be nice to have such a system. Just punch a couple of buttons and, bingo-, weatherfax.

For those not having a big budget, a satisfactory alternative is to use the SSB communications transceiver to receive weatherfax transmissions. When operated in conjunction with a computer, this system offers the same capability as a dedicated WeFax receiver. At least one WeFax software system requires only software and uses the microphone input on the computer. Other systems require a small demodulator that plugs into a communications port on the computer. Compared to the dedicated WeFax receiver, these alternatives are quite inexpensive. Although it may sound a little complicated, once the few wires are connected and software is installed, it is not difficult to use.

At sea and while at anchor the weatherfax broadcasts are good sources for gaining weather and sea state information. WeFAX transmissions emanate from the U.S. Coast Guard Station (NMG) at New Orleans, LA. The transmissions are made using upper sideband (USB) on the following frequencies: 4.3179 MHz, 8.5039 MHz, 12.7899 MHz and, between the hours of 1200Z to 2045Z, on 17146.4 MHz. Broadcast times for the weather products are listed below.

	TIME (UTC)	PRODUCT
	0005	Tropical surface analysis (west half)
	0020	Tropical surface analysis (east half)
All NMG (New Orleans, LA)	0035	24-hour wind/wave forecast
	0045	48-hour wind/wave forecast
	0055	72-hour wind/wave forecast
	0105	24 hr surface forecast
	0115	48 hr surface forecast
	0125	72 hr surface forecast
	0150	72 hr wave period/swell direction
	0200	GOES tropical satellite image
	0215	00 hr sea state analysis
	0225	High seas forecast (text)

Add six, twelve and eighteen hours for the other broadcast times.

Additional information regarding weatherfax products, broadcast times and frequencies may be found at the website: http:// weather.noaa.gov/pub/fax

The FAX weather products display the various weather features overlaid on a surface map. Monitored daily, the sea states and movement of weather systems can be tracked and evaluated in terms of affects on cruise planning.

Beginning on each of the six hour scheduled broadcasts, the Tropical Surface Analysis chart of current conditions is transmitted. On this presentation, the lines of equal surface pressure (isobars), the positions and pressures of the low and high-pressure regions, frontal boundaries and more are displayed. The spacing of the isobars is indicative of wind speed and direction. Regions with closely spaced lines (higher pressure gradients) have higher winds. The wind direction can be deduced from the clockwise or counterclockwise wind rotation about highs and lows respectively.

An example of The Western Tropical Surface Analysis may be seen below.

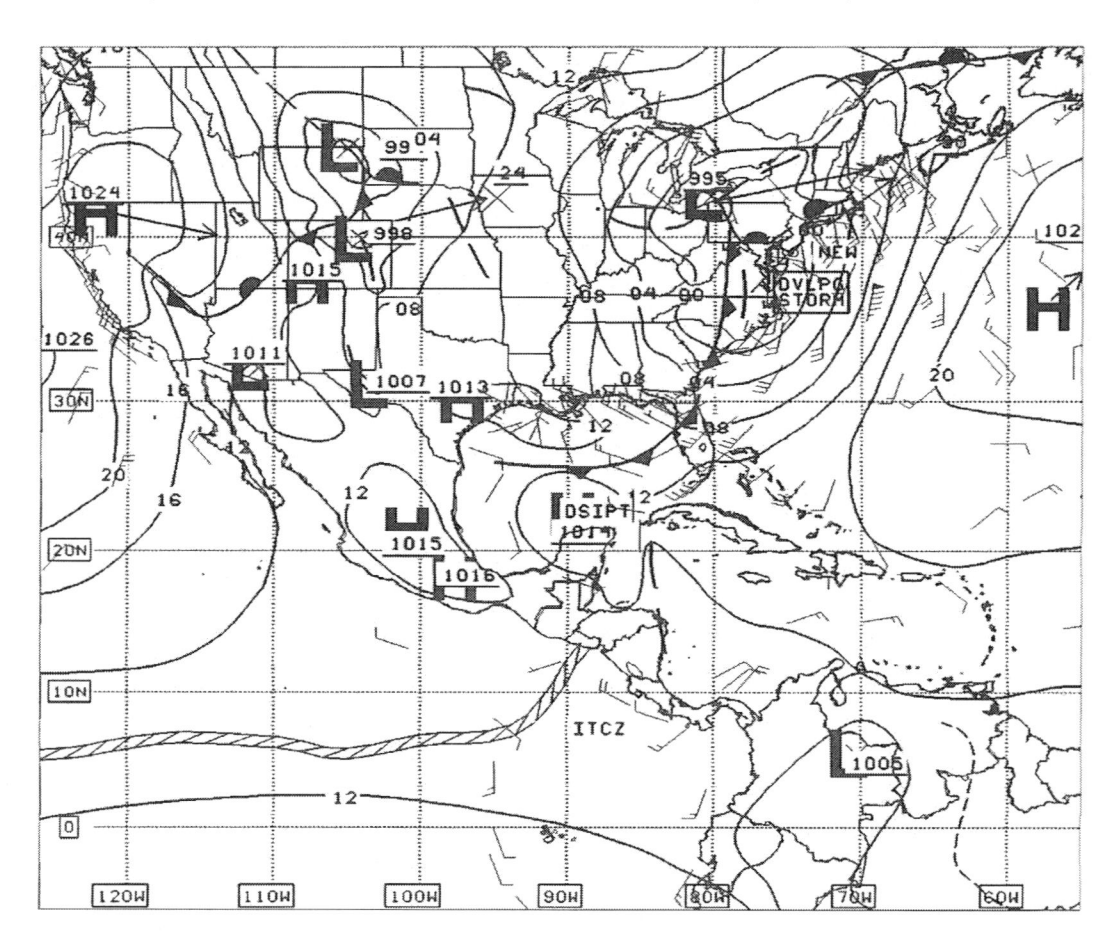

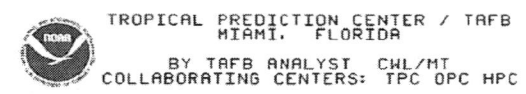

134 • EXTENDED POWER CRUISING

Fortunately, we don't have to make assumptions about the wind speed and direction from the chart above. That data, as well as the sea conditions, are provided by the 24, 48 and 72 hour Wind / Wave and Surface Forecasts.

Below is an example of a typical Wind/Wave Forecast. In this weatherfax product, the wind speed and direction can be determined from the "wind arrows" and "arrow's feathers." The arrows point in the direction of the wind and the feathers are coded for wind speed. A short (half) feather denotes 5 knots; a long feather equals 10 knots. Thus, for example, an arrow having two and one half feathers indicates the wind speed is 25 knots. Lines of equal wave height are shown and the numbers indicate the wave height.

Although the weatherfax broadcasts (for the Caribbean area) emanate from a U.S. mainland Coast Guard facility, the system can't always be relied upon. If the radio signal propagation is poor, the chart clarity may be degraded badly. At times, there may be no broadcast and occasionally the broadcast simply states, "the chart is not available." Also, in 2005, hurricane Katrina damaged the USCG Communications Station (NMG) at New Orleans, LA and it was off the air for about a month. The Bush Administration is also proposing to discontinue the free general distribution of weather products.

16.5.3 Email access to weather

The weather charts above and other weather products can be obtained by way of the Internet, or as GRIB files via the SSB SailMail service, SSB Ham Winlink service or satellite email services. This alternative can be more convenient than working with the weatherfax schedules or dealing with the other problems associated with those broadcasts. The email

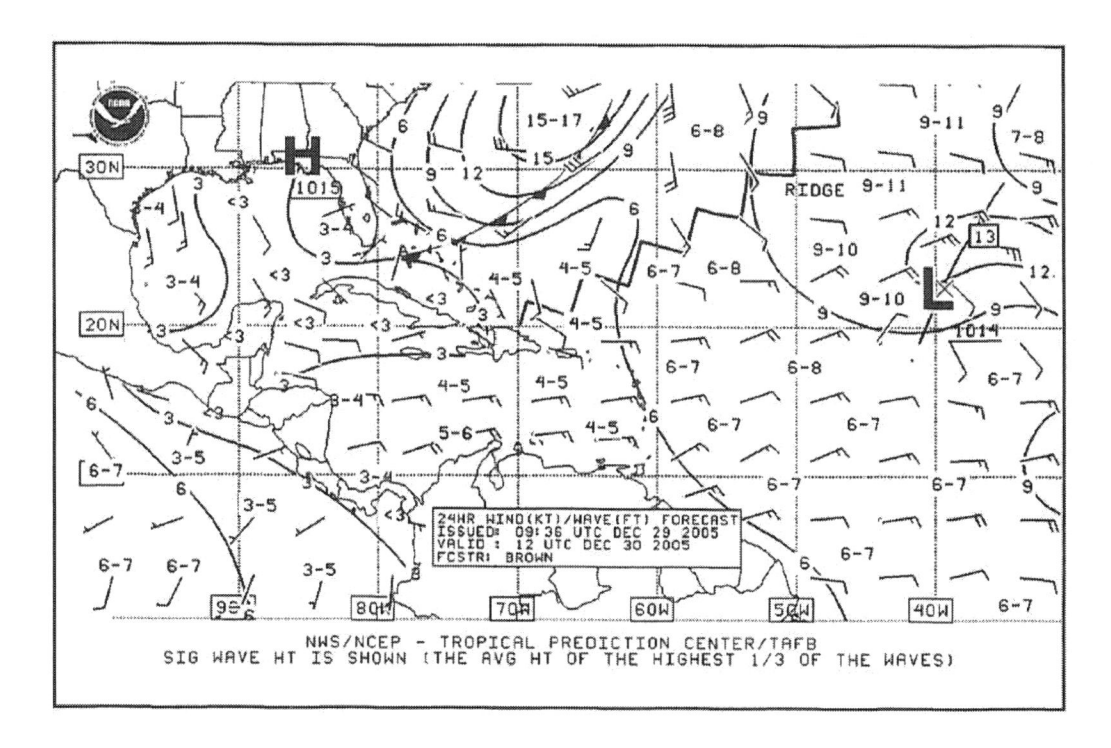

WEATHER • 135

download airtime on Sailmail or Winlink can be excessive.

Buoyweather.com is another excellent source of information. For a very small fee, cruisers can receive, by email, a variety of weather forecast and archival products. For example, a seven-day plain text wind and sea state forecasts can be obtained for any chosen position at sea. The arbitrary positions are called virtual buoy locations and the weather and sea state information is calculated from National Weather Service base data. The following is an example of a seven-day virtual buoy forecast.

BUOYWEATHER.COM Virtual Buoy Forecast
Location : 11.0N 63.5W
Cycle : 20050717 t00z
UTC–4 Hours

		Wind		Seas	
DATE	HR	dir/deg	range(kt)	dir/per	range(ft)
7/16	20	ENE 70	11—15	ENE 4sec	3—5
7/17	02	E 90	11—15	ENE 3sec	2—4
7/17	08	ESE 102	10—14	ENE 3sec	2—4
7/17	14	E 82	10—13	ENE 3sec	2—3
7/17	20	ESE 109	13—18	E 3sec	2—4
7/18	02	ESE 124	11—14	E 3sec	2—4
7/18	08	ESE 120	8—11	E 4sec	2—4
7/18	14	ESE 103	10—14	NE 8sec	2—4
7/18	20	E 90	12—16	E 3sec	2—4
7/19	02	ESE 108	12—16	E 3sec	2—4
7/19	08	ESE 116	11—15	E 3sec	2—4
7/19	14	E 95	11—15	E 3sec	2—4
7/19	20	ESE 101	14—20	E 4sec	3—5
7/20	02	ESE 113	12—17	E 4sec	3—5
7/20	08	ESE 111	12—16	E 4sec	3—5
7/20	14	E 88	16—22	E 4sec	3—5
7/20	20	E 97	15—21	E 4sec	4—6
7/21	02	ESE 117	11—16	ENE 5sec	3—6
7/21	08	ESE 110	11—15	ENE 5sec	3—5
7/21	14	E 98	13—18	E 4sec	3—5
7/21	20	ESE 101	12—16	E 4sec	3—5
7/22	02	ESE 104	10—14	NE 7sec	3—5
7/22	08	ESE 120	9—12	NE 7sec	2—4
7/22	14	ENE 79	11—15	NE 7sec	2—4
7/22	20	E 83	11—15	E 3sec	2—4

(continued)

DATE	HR	Wind dir/deg	range(kt)	Seas dir/per	range(ft)
7/23	02	ESE 102	10—14	NE 7sec	2—4
7/23	08	ESE 106	9—13	ENE 7sec	2—4
7/23	14	ENE 78	12—16	ENE 7sec	2—4
7/23	20	ESE 103	12—16	ENE 3sec	2—4

Yet, other sources for weather information are the various SSB nets that cover the Caribbean. Volunteers selflessly spend many hours collecting, reviewing and disseminating information to fellow cruisers. These nets are discussed more fully in the chapter on *Communications*.

Satellite email services such as *Skymate*™ also offer a variety of weather products.

16.5.4 OTHER VOICE WEATHER SERVICES

Some cruisers find it helpful to get personalized interactive voice weather briefings on marine HF-SSB radio from sources such as Chris Parker, Herb Hilgenberg, and others. These individuals are highly competent weather analysts. Their services are by subscription. To evaluate these services they may be heard by listening at the following times and frequencies.

Chris Parker	beginning at 1200Z	8.137 MHz
Chris Parker	beginning at 1230Z	8.104 MHz
Chris Parker	beginning at 1300Z	12.359 MHz
Herb Hilgenberg	beginning at 2000Z	12.359 MHz

Voice weather information is also provided as a free service on the Ham

San Blas Sunset

frequencies by George.

beginning at 1115Z	7.241 MHz
beginning at 1130Z	7.086 MHz

With all of those sources of weather data and a little homework, bad weather should not be an adversary except when at anchor or at the dock. Choose adequately long weather windows for crossings and find protected anchorages with good holding for approaching storms.

The weather needs of *power cruisers* are different from our sailboat friends. In that regard, may you have light winds and following seas.

Chapter 17
Overnighters

FOR SAILBOATS, OVERNIGHT PASSAGES ARE A READILY ACCEPTABLE NORM. However, often there are looks of astonishment by non-cruisers at the suggestion of making overnighters with a powerboat. Why do you suppose that should be? Most likely it is because we tend to think of powerboats as having limited range and questionable sea worthiness for conditions that the imagination suggests might be encountered.

It's doubtful anyone would argue that sailboats aren't more seaworthy than most cruising powerboats. By necessity sailboats were bred to withstand greater extremes in sea conditions because their forward progress is less predictable. But, in general, seaworthy powerboats that have good range are capable of making passages more predictably and quickly than a sailboat. With predictable passage time the powerboat can take advantage of weather windows that offer light winds and calm seas.

Over the years we have made many single and double overnighters. Every round trip to Central and South America requires at least a half dozen such passages. During our first year of offshore cruising, access to weather was equipment limited and a few slam-bang nights were experienced. However, with weather-fax, virtual buoy information and weather from the various SSB nets there's no reason to have those kinds of experiences.

Here are a few ideas that will help make overnighters less stressful.

The most pleasant overnighters are done when the phase of the moon is near full. The moonlight doesn't provide any navigation safety advantage, but it does allow a horizon reference and makes it easier to move about the boat.

Plan overnighters such that the destination arrival time does not crowd sunrise or sunset. Sea conditions and ocean currents can shift arrival times either way by several hours.

With two people aboard a good shift schedule to try is two on, two off. For most people, drinking coffee during the night inhibits their ability to sleep while off shift.

Heavy ship traffic may require both the captain and mate to be up and alert. Near shipping lanes there may be times when a dozen ships are in sight. Remember, if a ship's bearing does not change but the range is closing, you are on a collision course. Binoculars (with a lighted compass), radar and/or a lighted hand-bearing compass will help sort it out.

With some trawlers, a trip from the fly bridge to the head below requires exposure to the weather decks. Even in calm conditions, there is a risk of slipping or tripping and few things are more dangerous than a nighttime man-over-board situation. Thus, during exposure to weather decks, the least precaution is for the person going below to wear a life jacket with a strobe light (not active) attached. The person remaining on the fly bridge should observe that the one making the trip below does so successfully. A better solution is to have a porta-pot, hospital type plastic urinal or a simple equivalent on the fly bridge to minimize the number of trips below.

Engine room inspections with the noise, heat and boat's movement make a very dangerous combination. A piece of clothing caught up by rotating machinery will be disastrous. Everyone has to work through the tradeoffs regarding the frequency of inspections. For example, there should be enough experience with the engine(s) to know how often oil must be added. In between those times, an engine room visual inspection for unusual conditions should be sufficient. A high water alarm will reduce the frequency of bilge inspections, but a check once or twice a night is a good idea.

With the unfortunate exception of a load of bad fuel, having known fuel filter conditions (e.g. vacuum gauges) will minimize the need for filter changes while underway. Think through the possibility of having to do such work in the engine room under adverse conditions ahead of time.

Improper instrument lighting and other lights aboard can be unreasonably fatiguing and limit the watch standers ability to see dimly lit vessels. In that regard we have found that a single red light dimmed and focused on the instrument panel from above is far better than the individually lit instruments (even when those lights are red and dimmed).

During crossings, record the time and your position every hour. If there were to be an electronics failure, you can begin dead reckoning without too much initial error. It is also wise to maintain a daily communications schedule on SSB or make timely position reports by email with a friend. When possible, make daily SSB check-ins and position reports with the morning nets.

If the sea conditions deteriorate, manage the situation by slowing down and/or tacking.

Upon leaving any anchorage, enter a sufficient number of waypoints such that, if necessary, it will be possible to return to that location at any time without assistance.

No discussion about nighttime cruising should be left without considering things that go bump in the night. There are hazards out there, but the likelihood of hitting them is small. Having said that, in our travels at night, we have hit two logs, two unyielding clumps of Sargasso weed and snagged lobster pot lines three times. One of the log collisions caused moderate propeller damage, but only once was it necessary to dive and clear a lobster pot line. In the other incidents it was possible to clear the propellers of weed and line with careful, short duration propeller reversals. The logs and Sargasso weed events took place off Panama in a known, but unavoidable, region of frequent debris. Those are the total nighttime collision events of *Francesca* over eight years and at least 80 overnight passages while cruising the Caribbean.

More seriously, there is no doubt that container ships lose many containers. Reports by the insurers have confirmed that. Intuition tells us that containers are most likely lost during heavy sea conditions and most go to the bottom in a relatively short time. We powerboat cruisers, on the other hand, are not at sea during or shortly after heavy sea conditions. Thus, we postulate (hopefully), that it is unlikely containers will be in our paths. Yet, every so often there is a report of an encounter.

Nighttime cruising under the Southern Cross can provide many pleasant and memorable experiences. The bright full moon playing on gentle seas is serenely picturesque. And when the moon has waned, the spectacle of the Milky Way and occasional meteorites are stunning. These are times for reflection, thoughtful conversation with your partner and inner peace.

Chapter 18
Anchorages and Anchoring

MOST BOATING PERIODICALS CARRY ARTICLES ABOUT ANCHORING. They give the ABCs of anchoring which all sound fairly simple. After a few dozen times anchoring in the Intracoastal Waterway, that impression is further reinforced. But for those who then believe that the art of anchoring is not particularly challenging, this chapter should be a good dose of reality. The fact is that many very experienced cruisers consider anchoring a critical and difficult skill to master. Why are there such divergent views here?

The answer is a little complicated. First, weekend boaters don't encounter a wide variety of conditions and are seldom out in bad weather. They tend to drop the anchor, put out an unknown amount of scope, let the current or wind have its way, call it good, and go off to play with water toys. No problem.

At the next level, the majority of domestic cruisers are sailboats of 36 to 44 feet in length. Almost universally, these sailboats' original equipment included a 44 lb CQR anchor. Very often, sailboat captains with a few years of experience endorse their CQRs and say that they rarely *drag*. Again, what's the big deal! Anchoring is just a simple routine. Drop and set the hook, get a cocktail and dreamily watch the puffy little white clouds drift by as the western horizon rises to meet the sun. But, maybe it's not that simple.

The best cruising boats are equipped with two anchors. Often they differ in type. The first and most frequently used is a general-purpose plow type anchor such as a CQR or Delta. These are good in sand, grass and hard mud. The second anchor will often be a fluke type such as a Danforth or Fortress. They are good in sand, mud and soft mud. Both types of anchors fill a need. Just as important, however, are the anchor's size, how it is connected to the vessel, how it is set and then how it is monitored. But, before going any further with this let's start thinking about anchoring in terms of serious cruising.

There is a kind of universal law that states, the worst storms occur between the hours of midnight and 2 AM. If you have never dragged anchor, the following little story may help to give an idea of how much fun it is.

After a difficult overnight crossing and a long day the trawler *Low Orbit* found refuge in the lee of a small-uninhabited palm covered island. Bill and Louise dropped and set the hook in sand and grass. It was an ideal setting with a lovely beach and an inviting coral reef nearby. Just before arriving, they had caught a black fin tuna. Bill grilled the fillets while Louise made the trimmings. It was a great meal after which they enjoyed a couple of cocktails and a picture perfect sunset. Aaaah and sigh.

After such a tiring trip, the couple retired about 8:00 PM and they were soon fast asleep. But sometime later, the GPS anchor drag alarm awakens Bill from a deep sleep. A glance at the clock-, it's 1:30 AM. Oh, oh, got to wake up fast, Bill thought. He calls out, "Honey, wake up, we're dragging." Quickly out of bed, he looks out a window. It is pouring down rain and the wind is blowing about 30 knots with higher gusts buffeting *Low Orbit*. There they are in the middle of nowhere and, with the exception of occasional lightning strikes, total darkness surrounds the boat. A quick look at the GPS confirms they are dragging. There had been a sudden wind reversal and the anchor, having pulled free, was skating along the bottom. Even after having dragged a couple of hundred feet it would not reset itself. Note: The chain, a conch, grass or mud may have fouled the anchor or they may be dragging too fast for a reset.

Low Orbit is dragging parallel to the island and there is at least one patch reef out there to worry about. With no time to dawdle, Bill starts the engines and gets ready to retrieve the anchor. The boat is laying side to the wind, rolling in the chop and moving quickly through the small safe area of the anchorage. Louise turns on the RADAR, nuts-; it takes two minutes to warm up.

Bill says, "Louise, I'll go out and retrieve the anchor. As soon as it is up, get us pointed into the wind and back to the anchoring waypoint." Of course, Louise is upset, but she knows that it is critically important to keep her head.

Out on the bow, the blowing rain stings Bill's face and renders his eyeglasses useless. The waves are up and combined with the wind it is difficult for him to stand in the bow. A quick look with a flashlight reveals that the anchor chain is lying back under the boat and chafing on the hull. "Crap, there goes the new paint job," Bill mutters to himself. Then, the boat turns a bit and the chain jumps out of the bow roller and begins gnashing the toe rail. Bill yells into the wind, "Port engine reverse and starboard ahead 800 rpm." Louise does not respond; she cannot possibly hear the command. Realizing his mistake, he hurries back to the helm station, repeats the message and scurries back to the bow. While doing this, Bill badly bangs a shin on something or other. It hurts doubly because there is no time to swear about it and it slows him down.

Louise has done well at the throttles and the boat comes around so that Bill can muscle the anchor chain back onto the bow roller. During this process, he pinches a finger and knows that it is bleeding. The extent of the injury is difficult to tell because the pitching deck, roaring sea, pummeling wind and stinging rain overload his senses. Louise yells that she can see white water close astern. Bill has the windlass engaged and the chain is being retrieved. Finally the anchor is on the chute, but not before it had swung on a large arc and banged into the bow; more paint damage. Bill then finds that the anchor is fouled with about 50 lbs of grass and sticky coral mud. He grabs the boat hook and after a little struggling manages to clear the anchor.

Returning to the helm station Bill finds Louise working to get the boat back to their anchor waypoint. The RADAR, now functional, is a confusion of rain and sea state clutter. It takes a precious few seconds for Bill to punch the right buttons and get a good view of their position. Hmmm-, there's blood on the RADAR. Where did that come from? Oh nuts, there is blood streaked all over the place.

Thankfully, Louise is doing a creditable job of closing on the waypoint. The situation is getting under control, but by now Bill's mouth is so dry he finds it hard to talk.

After a minute or two they close on the anchor waypoint and Bill goes back out on the bow. At the waypoint Louise brings the boat to a stop and Bill deploys the anchor. But the wind quickly turns *Low Orbit* sideways and again the chain threatens to jump out of the roller. Louise sees the developing problem and engages the starboard engine at idle to keep the boat into the wind. It is working, but she can't tell if the boat is running over the chain. Bill gives her hand signals to engage and disengage the drive while letting out chain. Alas the boat turns sideways again. The drifting boat drags the anchor too quickly for it to settle and grab.

After repeating the effort of anchor retrieval and maneuvering to the waypoint three more times the anchor finally grabs.

Soaking wet and tired Bill gets back to the helm station, sheds clothes, towels off and expectantly hovers over the GPS and RADAR. Louise gets a couple of band-aids for Bill's finger and then works to sop up water. The wind and rain continue, but the anchor holds. After 3 more hours and with daylight looming, the storm began to abate.

Well, that's how it goes sometimes. The cruisers were prepared with good reliable equipment and this dragging event ended more or less happily.

If, on the other hand,
- the windlass had been too slow or tended to jam,
- the anchor was too small and would not reset,
- the captain or mate made a serious error,
- the dinghy painter wrapped in a propeller,
- the boat had drag into another boat,
- the captain lost a finger working with the chain,
- or any number of other unhappy details,

then in all likelihood, the boat or boats might have spent the night on a reef, shoal, lee shore, or worse.

That story isn't a fairy tale. Because of unknowable conditions, such as bad bottom, fouled anchor, wind reversals, etc., dragging occasionally happens to everyone and, for a few, a little too frequently. On *Francesca*, we had a number of such experiences before realizing our boat had too much windage for the size anchors being used. But, even with improved gear and having anchored over a thousand times, we know there is no such thing as immunity from dragging.

Many cruisers are at anchor the better part of each year and change anchorages every few days or weeks. With weatherfax and participation in local SSB networks, there can be reasonable forewarning of upcoming windstorms. Once in a while, however, predictions fail and cruisers are caught by surprise. Even then, unless there is a wind reversal, a well-anchored vessel should not drag. But whenever a storm threatens, a well-prepared crewman should be standing anchor watch just in case.

Cruising is in one respect similar to all other lifestyles; it has good and bad times. The rest of this chapter describes practices, equipment, and a few more stories that will help to take much of the bad out of those bad days and nights.

18.1 ANCHORING BASICS

Many books and articles discuss the art/science of anchoring, yet only a few successfully describe it from a cruisers point of view. Anchoring is one of the most technical issues of cruising and because the conditions are so diverse and subject to individual judgment, it is far more art than science.

Let's start with the basics just to be sure they aren't overlooked.

18.1.1 Rode or Chain

For anchoring in the tropics, all chain is recommended for the primary anchor. Occasionally, the bottom will be decorated with coral or rock that can quickly ruin rode. If all chain is not an option, then use as much chain with the rode as possible. A good case for all chain is that if you drag, chain will not foul the prop(s), rudder(s) or stabilizers as rode might.

18.1.2 Scope

For normal conditions, when deploying an anchor, the amount of chain to be let out should be at least 5 and preferably

7 times the sum of the depth of the water and the height of the bow off the water. The amount of chain thus deployed is referred to as scope. For rode, the scope must be at least 7 times the sum of the depth and the height of the bow. With rode there must be at least 15 feet of chain attached to the anchor even when there is no coral or rock to chafe upon. The chain helps to keep the anchor shank low to the bottom for good holding. One rule of thumb is that there should be enough chain to equal the weight of the anchor. Others state it differently saying that 15 to 25 feet of chain is adequate for the anchor to have the maximum holding power.

For heavy storm conditions or with bad bottom, the scope should be increased. Remember, chain or rode in the locker isn't helping to do anything but weigh down the bow. Use it when you can. The only disadvantage of using more scope is that there will be greater retrieval time if you drag. However, with more scope, dragging becomes less likely.

There are lots of tricks to improve the holding of an anchor and chain combination such as sentinels, a second anchor on the same chain, etc. These are not necessary for normal conditions given that your vessel is equipped with a satisfactory anchor(s). Sentinels and secondary anchors and anchoring for hurricane winds are not discussed in this book. The intent of this chapter is simply to make you aware of the safest and simplest means of anchoring for normal conditions. That includes all conditions short of a named storm.

> A little side note: Be sure the bitter end of the chain attached to the boat with line that can be cut quickly if necessary. In that regard, always have a float and line available on the bow to tie on as a marker for later anchor retrieval.

18.1.3 Anchors

The next principal player is the anchor. Everyone seems to think that they have the best anchor for their boat. To be sure, if any type of anchor is really bad, it won't be very popular. Still, there are classes of anchors that are better suited for particular bottom conditions than others.

A Danforth type anchor works well in mud and sand, but is not well suited to grassy bottoms or very hard mud. With grass over soft mud, if the Danforth drags, chances are that it will be fouled and require precious time to clear before any attempt to reset it can be tried. Keep in mind that the clearing process is likely to be needed during bad conditions with whatever broomstick or boat hook that is available. A conch shell, can or plastic container may jam in the flukes causing further delays. Still, the Danforth is a necessary part of the anchoring arsenal. There are times when it is clearly the anchor of choice. In the same conditions, but to a lesser degree, the Bruce anchor can also have a tendency to foul.

Plow type anchor (CQR, Delta and others) are very popular among cruisers. They are better suited to most bottoms with the exception of soft mud. In soft mud, they often require settling time before they can be set. If they become fouled with grass and muck, they are more easily cleared. They also have a better chance of resetting themselves after a sudden wind reversal than does the Danforth.

Whatever your needs or preference, make sure your anchor is plenty large. It is a good idea to buy anchors that are one or even two sizes larger than the manufacturer recommends. Scrimping cannot compensate for lost sleep, anxiety and potential damage to your boat.

18.1.4 Snubbers and bridles

Most experienced cruisers use snubbers or bridles to transfer the load on the chain to hard points on the boat. If you have a bow pulpit they are especially necessary to avoid having the bow pulpit ripped off the boat during heavy conditions. The snubber line(s) should be 10 to 20 feet long and made up of stranded Nylon® line. Because Nylon® stretches significantly under load, the longer the snubber or bridle, the less shock the cleats, boat, chain, shackles, swivel and anchor will experience.

For trawlers and many sailboats, a bridle snubber satisfies several needs. First, of course, is the load-shock thing, but it also distributes the load to two different hard points. Another benefit is that a bridle greatly reduces the boat's wind driven "sailing" arc.

To reduce chafing on Nylon® line it's a good idea to use a protective sleeving at strategic points. Flexible plastic tubing and fire hose material are popular for this purpose.

18.1.5 Setting the anchor

This is a difficult issue to deal with. You often hear about people setting their anchors with full reverse power while others use much less. The problem is that full reverse for a 32-ft sailboat with 18 horsepower is not much force when compared to a trawler with large props and several hundred available horses. For the trawler, full reverse might well exceed the yield of the chain or other ground tackle components including the bow cleats.

To properly set an anchor enough force is needed to at least partially bury the anchor in hard sand. For trawlers, the throttle(s) setting(s) may be less than 1000 RPM, yet still applying roughly 1000 lbs of setting force. But just because an anchor appears to have been set, there are many bottom conditions to deceive a captain. On a scoured out bottom an anchor may be hooked on the edge of a shallow depression or a small coral formation. On grassy bottoms, notorious for poor holding, it may be useful to test the set with a higher throttle setting. On the other hand, with a very soft mud bottom, it may not be possible to set an anchor successfully without allowing it to settle for an hour or more. But even on good bottom, an anchor may be lying on its side or otherwise poorly set. When possible, it is a good practice to check the anchor's set either by diving it or by observation from a dinghy using a glass bottomed bucket.

18.1.6 Multiple anchors

Most cruisers agree, "If one anchor will do, don't use two."

If an anchorage is crowded and the other boats have out two anchors, then two anchors may be necessary to avoid swinging into other boats. But think ahead, if you drag, two anchors will have to be retrieved and the chances are good that they will foul one another.

It is time for another little story.

> *Francesca* was in the Bahamas during the winter of 1997–8. It was an especially bad year for frequent and violent northers. *Francesca* was equipped with a 44 lb. Danforth on rode and a 44 lb. CQR on all chain. Having already experience dragging twice the previous month and with the expectation of the next norther, both anchors were deployed. *Francesca* was in the company of another trawler, *Heide*, which also had two anchors out. The anchorage was small, the island had a rocky shore and the bottom was grassy sand.
>
> Around midnight the storm blew in with winds around 30 to 35 knots. After a sudden wind reversal, *Francesca* had one anchor let go and within a few seconds, the second also let go. There was no time to recover the anchors before the boat would have foundered on the rocks, so the boat was negotiated seaward with the engines in reverse and the two anchors dragging. Then in open water, the anchors were retrieved. Fortunately, the chain on one anchor and rode on the other had not wrapped around one another.
>
> With the wind reversal, *Heide's* two anchors also let go. But before the vessel had drifted far the all chain anchor hooked up. The second anchor's rode, however, had found its way to both props and also fouled one of the stabilizers. If *Heide* had needed to get underway it would have been impossible.

In congested anchorages, it may be necessary to use the "Bahama" anchoring technique. But, rather than run the risk of dragging with two anchors deployed or being dragged into by others, it may be better to find a spot with more room and drop just one hook. Sometimes the safer anchorage will be a 1/2 mile or more from an island. Keep in mind that protection from the wind is often highly over-rated. It may be better to experience a little wind and wave action than lose sleep worrying about tight quarters, your neighbors, lobster pots, the reef or rocks.

18.1.7 Lighting and radio

There are many places that are so remote and traffic so light that there is little need to display an anchor light. Indeed, many energy-limited sailboats frequently opt not to use their precious watts. However, when there is more than one boat in an anchorage the anchor lights may be the only indicators that will let you or a neighbor know one of you is dragging. Similarly, if the VHF radio isn't on, no one can let you know either.

Here's another story.

> Several sailboats were anchored in a lovely little half moon shaped lagoon in the Bimini Islands. During the night, a squall moved through with a large wind shift and heavy gusting conditions. An upwind sailboat began dragging. Their radio was not on nor was the crew awakened by the storm. A downwind sailboat, with

> a crew standing anchor watch, tried to call the dragger. No response, of course. The next action was to shine a spotlight on the dragger. No response. Finally, as the collision became imminent, the alert crew was outside yelling at the dragger. After the collision there was, of course, a response by the crew on the dragger.
>
> Fortunately, in this incident there was little damage, but it could have been much worse. The dragger could have dislodged the second sailboats anchor and then they would have both been in trouble.

For your and others safety, it is just plain smart to *always show an anchor light* even if you are all alone. In most areas, small fishing boats run at speed at all hours of the night. Other cruising boats may also enter the anchorage after dark.

If you are with other boats, agree on a channel to guard and have the radio on. If the weatherman says it's going to blow, set an anchor watch. And if you think it is likely that you are going to drag, start the engine(s), watch the RADAR and GPS and have recovery plans made in advance.

Here's another good tip. When in an anchorage with other boats and one or more of them is dragging, turn on deck lights, but not spreader lights. Spreaders and spotlights are too bright and can cause more confusion than help. Several deck lights, on the other hand, can help a dragger to judge his distance from you while regaining control.

18.1.8 Drag alarms

Now that GPS *Selective Availability* is a thing of the past, the GPS anchor alarm is a reliable drag indicator. Most GPS units have a remote output for a really loud awakening alarm. When set properly the GPS can give a very early indication of dragging. The setup is simple. First set the alarm threshold. That setting will likely be in nautical miles. If the plan is to deploy 100 feet of chain or rode, then a reasonable threshold might be 0.03 nm. Experience has shown that 0.02 nm yields too many false alarms. However, 0.03 nm will only be useful if the alarm is set when the anchor first touches bottom. Then, the threshold is set for the anchor swing radius. If the alarm is set after the chain has been deployed, then the threshold must be set to a greater amount to account for the full diameter. In that case 0.04 nm should work with only a few false alarms for chain lengths up to about 125 feet.

In small anchorages when there is a prevailing trade wind and no wind or current reversal is expected, the anchor alarm threshold can be tightened up to advantage.

If the vessel is equipped with modern radar having a positional alarm *and* the power to run it during long hours at anchor, this can also be an effective drag alarm.

Shore lights may be excellent positional references, but unless they are from a public facility, they may be turned off when you need them. Also, if there is an intense squall, visibility may be cut such that shore lights are not visible. Often in the Bahamas and Caribbean there are no shore lights to use as references.

18.1.9 Dinghies

A dinghy, trailed behind an anchored boat during a blow, is asking for trouble. If an anchored vessel trailing a dinghy drags, there is a strong possibility the painter will foul the prop(s) and rudder(s). Even independent of that problem the dinghy may (as we have witnessed) run up under the swim platform damaging both. But, pulling a dinghy up on a davit(s) during bad weather is difficult and dangerous. If caught with a dinghy astern, tie it alongside for the storm's duration. Then, add a second securing line. Dinghies tied alongside tend to chafe lines quickly.

18.2 ANCHORAGES

The variety of anchorages is unlimited and there are several factors to consider at each.

18.2.1 Bottom type

Clearly the best bottom is clean deep sand. Throughout the Bahamas and Caribbean, one may expect to have this kind of bottom only about 20 percent of the time. The worst condition will be jell-o like mud with heavy grass. Depending upon the perception of holding and weather conditions, it may be prudent to stay far away from other boats or even seek out another spot. Even with good holding, clustering is not a good idea. In a bad blow, there will often be a dragger.

18.2.2 Plan your escape

Lagoons, lee shore, island groupings and bays all require different strategies for protection during bad weather. The best advice is to have an escape plan in advance of situations that might occur. Rarely, will it be necessary or advisable to put out to sea to ride out the weather. However, that would be the case for a lee shore coastal anchorage. At other times, the GPS cookie crumb trail will help, but unless the GPS is set properly and the captain has practiced tracking the trail, it can easily be strayed from. The GPS position filter needs to be set on fast and the map orientation set to *track up* for this technique. A more straightforward solution is to set an adequate number of waypoints on the way into the anchorage and have the initial escape heading planned. Also, the RADAR layout of the anchorage should be understood. It is easy to get confused during adverse conditions. Then, even if it is necessary to turn donuts all night, you are prepared.

As a backup, take bearings and have a compass course determined for an escape route. A GPS, RADAR or other electrical failure would be just the thing to ruin your night.

18.2.3 Failure points

The last thing anyone wants to happen during a storm is to have a part of the ground tackle fail.

A little story.

A sailboat was happily anchored at Puerto Cortez, Honduras when a surprise storm occurred. The sailboat was not using a Nylon® snubber and was relying only on a deck fastened chain stop to take the load. The wind picked up to greater than 50 knots during the evening and the chain stop broke under the

> heavy load. All of the chain paid out and the captain watched helplessly as the end slipped over the side. Not having a second anchor aboard, the vessel had to put to sea and ride out the storm all night.

A proper chain snubber would have prevented this mishap. Also, the bitter end of the chain should have been tied off with a section of Nylon® line. A few days later the sailboat had divers recover his chain and anchor. If the boat had been in more confined water such as a lagoon, it is probable that the boat would have been hard aground and perhaps seriously damaged before morning.

Another little story.

> During that same storm, *Francesca* was anchored in a small lagoon also on the north shore of Honduras. The lagoon deceivingly appeared to be very secure. It was in fact a trap. When the storm hit, *Francesca's* anchor was well dug in and a 20-foot bridle insured that the strain and peak loads were damped and distributed.
>
> However, when the seas built to 8 feet and the wind was at its highest, the chain hook deformed sufficiently to come loose. The entire chain load was then transferred to the bow pulpit that was never intended to take such heavy loading. The bow pulpit, windlass, second anchor, bow rail and bow toe rail were all ripped free and pulled into the water. Fortunately, Ben was out on the bow when this happened and was able to put a rolling hitch on the deploying chain and snub it off to a cleat before it had paid out entirely. Two other load-distributing snubbers were then put on the chain. The boat was saved and suffered no further damage, but it was later found that only 10 feet of chain was left in the locker. The line tying off the chain's bitter end would have certainly failed under the load.
>
> The bow pulpit, and all of the other bits were recovered the next day. After emergency repairs were made, the chain hook was tested under a heavy engine load and it again popped free of the chain.
>
> Reflecting on the incident, too much trust was put in the weakest point of the ground tackle system. After the bow pulpit, windlass and second anchor were lost over the side, few options remained. Had the chain been lost it might have been possible to maintain the vessel's position with power. But the second anchor's rode was still connected as were the windlass power cables. It would have taken 5 minutes or more to clear these problems and in that time *Francesca* would have been on the rocks. As it was, she rode out the night in only 4 to 5 feet of water with heavy seas and rocky bottom only a few feet aft of the rudders.

Chain hooks are convenient and easy to use, but they may not be reliable. They also tend to fall off during slack wind/current. If they are used during storm conditions, it may be wise to have a backup snubber attached to the chain with a rolling hitch (followed by a half hitch for security). A better solution for a bridle is to use a slotted chain plate similar to those sold at marine stores. There is a concern that the commercially available plates may be too thin for the loads expected during heavy storm conditions. However, any machine shop can quickly fabricate a rugged plate suitable for your chain.

18.3 SAFETY

Always keep in mind that the bow is one of the most dangerous places to be on a boat. It becomes even more dangerous during heavy weather conditions and that fact is further exacerbated by machinery, taught lines, loose lines, pitching bow, slippery deck, bad visibility and so on. Good communication with your partner is imperative. Hand signals and a minimum dependence upon voice communications are always best. The processes of anchoring and anchor retrieval require careful coordination between crewmembers. A lack of planning causes the process to deteriorate to yelling, confusion, mistakes, injury and boat damage. After dropping the hook at a new anchorage and before settling down for cocktails, discuss your contingency plans in detail. Then, when awakened at 2:00 AM by the anchor alarm, there will be no delays, indecision or fuzzyheaded logic.

18.4 LEGAL ISSUES REGARDING ANCHORED VESSELS

This is a confusing set of issues that we regret to say is not answered here. To provide an idea of the problem's complexities here are a few incidents to ponder. Consider also that there is no obvious negligence and the vessels described below have good equipment.

A little story.

> A first vessel anchored away from others in a secluded spot. Later another boat dropped the hook nearby. Still later, the wind rose significantly. The second boat was astern of the first. During the night the first vessel dragged into the second and caused the second boat to drag. The entanglement then caused both vessels to wind up hard aground with damage. Who is the injured party here?
>
> Or, a vessel entered an anchorage with other boats. The captain found a spot, seemingly having lots of room, and dropped the hook with an appropriate amount of scope. Later, in the wee hours of the morning, the wind shifted and another boat, having out much more scope, swung into the vessel causing cosmetic damage to both vessels. The captain of the vessel with more scope claimed that it was needed for expected weather conditions. Who is at fault?
>
> Or, a boat in the anchorage was unattended. It dragged and several other concerned cruisers got it under control and re-anchored. Had it not been for

> their efforts, other boats in the anchorage may have been damaged. Later, the unattended vessel dragged again and was damaged. Did it pay to be a Good Samaritan?
>
> Or, a vessel was on a mooring provided by a marina or municipality. Rent was paid for the use of the mooring. During the stay, the mooring parts and the boat drifted aground with damage. Recourse?
>
> Or, during the night a vessel's anchor light burned out and a local launch rammed into it with damage and injuries. Oh, oh!

Reading published case studies, we tried to look into a few of these matters. But the water is very muddy. Often the fault is spread about with, for instance, one vessel being charged with 20 percent of fault and another 50 percent and yet another at 30 percent.

In relatively minor accidents where insurance isn't involved, most of us will be inclined to sort out what is fair and settle it straight away. But, the causes of accidents in anchorages are often clouded with shifting winds, bad weather, unknowable holding, etc. Yet, there must be some relatively simple criteria by which we can be guided. Won't some knowledgeable sea lawyer please write a book for the layman on this subject? We're all flying blind here.

Chapter 19
Medical Concerns, Issues and Opportunities

19.1 ROUTINE HEALTHCARE AND MEDICINES ABROAD

Traveling outside of the U.S. and Canada can present some health challenges. Language differences, the distance to proper medical care or a medical emergency of any kind can be daunting problems. However, there are ways to reduce the risks and manage most situations.

Clearly, people everywhere need hospitals, pharmacies, doctors, dentists, and other therapists. Even at small ports, these services will be represented. When in port, local information regarding medical services can be obtained through marinas, other cruisers, the local VHF net, or any of various area communications nets. Perhaps the facilities won't be up to North American standards, but reasonable healthcare can be found almost anywhere.

Specialists of all kinds can be found In population centers such as Port of Spain (Trinidad), Puerto La Cruz (VE), Caracas (VE), Cartagena (Col), Panama City (Panama), San Jose (CR), Guatemala City (Guatemala.), etc. and modern diagnostic equipment such as CAT and MRI are available. Doctor referrals are not needed to visit specialists. Appointments are usually not necessary and the cost of visiting a doctor is most often a fraction of that in the U.S.

In Latin America, we have found medical doctors to be generally competent and caring. Their offices are usually small having one to three rooms and they typically counsel one patient at a time. Many doctors are English-speaking; frequently having received training in North America or Europe, otherwise, the language problem can be solved using an interpreter.

With regard to medicines, arguments have been made to discourage U.S. citizens buying inexpensive foreign products. One such argument suggests that the medicines may be substandard. However, the pharmaceutical companies that make products sold in the United States and Canada also make most of the medicines sold abroad. That would suggest pharmaceutical companies such as Merck, Pfizer, generic producers and others make good quality products for North American distribution, but make cheap, less efficacious products to sell elsewhere. That view seems cynical in the extreme. Everyone needs good medicines.

Another argument we hear is that counterfeit medicine manufacturers produce and sell poor quality products under the labels of reputable companies. There is perhaps a chance of that, but medicines are sold at licensed farmacias (pharmacies), not on the streets. We have never heard of any such complaints. One wonders what is the greater sin, condemning all foreign drugs on the basis of unproven misconduct or withholding less expensive alternatives for those who need it.

In the Caribbean, medicines are often much less expensive and most non-narcotic drugs can be purchased over the counter without a doctor's prescription. In some areas, drugs containing codeine may also be purchased over the counter. Unlike the United States, where it is often difficult to get more than one or two months supply of medication, quantity purchases can be made in most foreign ports. For regularly needed drugs such as high blood pressure medications, the savings can be significant. There is more on this later.

19.2 MEDICAL EMERGENCIES

The special medical problems of the cruiser are not the lack of competent doctors or efficacious medication while in port. But, emergencies at sea are another matter. These are most problematic during a long crossing or when anchored and weathered in at a remote location.

In a medical emergency while isolated, the cruiser has several options. Advice may be sought through various area cruisers' radio nets that are held daily on both marine and amateur radio (Ham) single sideband frequencies. For example, the marine radio nets include: the *Northwest Caribbean Net*, the *Panama Connection Net*, the *Eastern Caribbean (Safety and Security) Net* and the *Bahamas Net*. There are also many Ham radio nets such as the *Caribbean Net*, and the *Breakfast Club Cruiser's Net*. These and others are active during the morning hours. See the chapter on *Communications* for a listing of the most popular nets.

The amateur radio *Maritime Mobile Service Net* on 14.300 MHz is active during the hours of 1600Z to 0300Z. On this net, a doctor is on call to aid in emergencies. It does not matter that you are not a HAM. *In an emergency, medical or other, it is permissible to use any frequency necessary to resolve the problem.*

High frequency radio has limitations however. At night, radio wave propagation (skip) lengthens greatly and on higher frequencies, communications may not be possible at all. Thus, in a time critical situation, it may be difficult to make contact using this medium. Satellite telephone is a more reliable means of communications, but only a small percentage of cruisers have this equipment aboard. During the past 5 years, there has been only a small reduction in the costs of satellite services. But the situation may be improving. If so, more cruisers will be using satellite telephone, Internet and email services.

During times of isolation at sea or at anchor, cruisers frequently maintain scheduled communications with other vessels, nets or shore stations. Position/condition reports are often sent periodically to a friend. Regular communications is seldom more than a few hours away.

For scuba divers, Divers Alert Network (DAN) provides emergency evacuation and other services for a very small annual fee. For more information, visit their website at: www.diversalertnetwork.org

19.3 BITES, STINGS, MARINE ENVENOMATIONS AND ALLERGIC REACTIONS

This section may read like a great set of reasons not to visit the tropics. But don't get paranoid. While aboard your vessel it is possible to avoid most insect bites. The best practice is to anchor as far from land as practical. However, there's not much point in cruising to foreign lands if you can't also enjoy inland travel. This section deals with how to avoid bites and stings where possible and what to do when bitten. Whenever a bite or sting produces unexpected or severe effects, seek qualified medical assistance.

19.3.1 Mosquitoes

Window screens are a necessity in much of the Caribbean. Mosquitoes can be a problem in the late afternoon, early morning and occasionally at night. It's a good practice to close up unscreened openings by 5 PM. Also, maintain an ample supply of insect repellents. These can be bought locally almost everywhere, but may be more expensive outside of the U.S. For bites, we have found that a watery paste of *Adolph's Meat Tenderizer*™, or similar product having the active ingredient papain, applied to the bite quickly reduces the itching and irritation.

Mostly, mosquitoes are the same nuisance as in North America, but becoming infected with malaria is a possibility. Preventive medication is an option, yet there may be side affects. The arguments for or against taking a prophylaxis go something like this:

> Mefloquine (Lariam), Chloroquine (Aralen), and other prophylactic medications have potential side effects and the decision to take these agents should be weighed against the risk of contracting malaria. People visiting the tropics, but not the malaria hot spots or those who stay for extended periods may be better off not taking them. Also, taking a prophylaxis does not guarantee that one cannot contract malaria. (Note that in the U.S. these drugs are expensive. In Central and South America they are generally available and very inexpensive.)

In the Caribbean, the strains of malaria are usually very treatable and the cure is inexpensive, quickly effective and readily available. The most common types are those that are chloroquine sensitive (NW Carib.) and those that are chloroquine resistant (Panama and Northern South America). The malarial strains, the prophylaxis and treatment differ from region to region. Check with a local farmacia (pharmacy) for the proper medicines to have aboard. Another good source of information is the Center for Disease Control (CDC) website at: www.cdc.gov/travel.

Whether you use prophylaxis or not, it is a good idea to have the medicines aboard to effect a cure. In most countries they are sold over the counter. One medicine that is used to avoid future relapses is primaquine. But, for people with G6PD (glucose-6-phosphate dehydrogenase) deficiency, this medication can be dangerous to take. Ask your North American doctor about a test for G6PD deficiency before beginning the first cruise.

Also keep in mind that malaria-like symptoms can be confused with the symptoms of other serious infectious agents and the right diagnosis needs to be made as soon as possible. Malarial infection may require hospitalization.

Dengue fever is another very unpleasant, often painful, disease spread by mosquitoes. The symptoms are non-specific with general body aches, fever, malaise and/or weakness lasting around 10 days, but there can be an extended period for full recovery. Dengue can have hemorrhagic complications. For that reason, do not take aspirin if dengue is suspected. Fortunately, cruisers are only rarely infected with dengue fever.

19.3.2 No-see-ums, chitris (pronounced cheetrees), sand gnats and sand flies

These are names for mostly the same kind of little beast, but there are variations. When they can be seen, the coloration may be anything from light brown to black. In a few locations, their bite can cause swelling, sores and possible infection. Some people react worse than others to the bites, but only rarely are there complications. We know of only one case where a cruiser was bitten and infected with the parasites causing leishmaniasis.

19.3.3 Tabano and conga flies

These critters look a lot like deer flies, but there is a big difference. Tabanos are found irregularly in western Caribbean coastal lowland areas. Congas are localized to a few inland river regions. During the daylight hours, just one or two in the boat can be a real nuisance. For most people, the reaction to a bite clears up in a day or two, but there can be a bad reaction with swelling, itching and pain that lasts several weeks.

The tabano fly is a very stealthy fellow and has a way of biting without drawing attention to itself. They favor elbows, fingers, the backs of the knees and ankles. After being bitten, apply a watery paste of meat tenderizer as soon as possible. We have found that relief is usually immediate. This treatment is somewhat less effective when applied to older bites. More conventionally, topical steroids such as Cortaid are helpful in reducing the discomfort.

19.3.4 Coral and jellyfish stings

In the Caribbean, swimming, snorkeling and diving are a big attraction. Stings from various common jellyfish, the Portuguese Man of War and stinging coral are all nicely treated with meat tenderizer too. Skin damage, pain and itching can be minimized with immediate treatment.

Coral stings or scratches can be the beginning of a bacterial infection some of which can rapidly involve surrounding tissue. An hour after the treatment with meat tenderizer, wash the area with soap and water and apply a good topical antibiotic. Fungal infections are also a possibility. They can be serious and aggressive. If the area becomes infected, see a doctor as soon as possible.

19.3.5 Sea urchins

Divers routinely regard some types of sea urchins as the most dangerous animals in the sea. A misstep, knee, or hand in the wrong place and you have a painful, perhaps long lasting injury. Long spine black sea urchins are the worst to tangle with. The spines are very sharp and easily bury deeply into flesh. For all but surface material, removal is next to impossible and attempts to do so generally make matters worse. The best means of dealing with it is to clean the area, soak it in hot water (up to 114° F) for 10 minutes or until the pain eases. Then, apply topical antibiotics and a loose bandage to protect the area from contamination and further injury.

19.3.6 Stonefish and scorpionfish envenomation

A bad encounter with one of these fish is very rare. Hot water immersion therapy (up to 114° F) will provide pain relief, as the venom is heat sensitive. Stonefish envenomation is reported to be more painful than the scorpionfish. Untreated, the worst pain should subside in about 12 hours. Analgesics may be helpful.

19.3.7 Stingray wounds

This too is rare, but occasionally a person wading near the beach has an unfortunate encounter with a stingray. The wound can be deep and very painful. Hot water treatment is also recommended for this venom. Thereafter treat the wound with topical antibiotics and a loose bandage.

19.3.8 Ciguatera fish poisoning

Eating fish that have toxins in the meat from microorganisms called dynoflagellates causes this illness. Fish such as barracuda, jacks, snapper, grouper, mackerel and triggerfish can carry the toxin. Barracuda is one of the most likely offenders. Larger fish tend to concentrate the toxin by eating smaller reef fish that routinely ingest dynoflagellates.

The symptoms of ciguatera poisoning are numbness of lips and extremities, intestinal distress and cardiovascular disorders. These often occur within 6 hours of the time of ingestion. Generally the disease is non-fatal and of short duration. If poisoning is suspected discontinue eating all fish and see a doctor as soon as possible. Treatment is supportive and symptom driven.

In each region visited, check with the locals regarding the incidence of ciguatera poisoning and which, if any, fish types are involved.

19.4 PARASITES AND OTHER TROPICAL DISEASES

Parasites and other diseases in the tropics can be a problem. It's a good idea to visit the websites of the Center for Disease Control (CDC) and World Health Organization (WHO) for information about each area you intend to visit.

The best policy is not to swim, wade or otherwise expose one's self to river, creek or lake water, unless informed cruisers or local medical professionals say it is not a problem. The exceptions to this are hot springs and high mountain resort areas where the water is generally free of parasites. Cruisers are most often barefoot aboard their boats, but no one should go barefoot ashore. Several serious diseases including schistosomiasis are caused by parasites that enter the body directly through small cuts in the skin.

19.4.1 Chagas disease

This condition is caused by a parasitic infection as the result of being bitten by a bug known variously as the reduviid, vinchucas, harbeiros, assassin or kissing bug. The bug is endemic to Central and South America and it is estimated that tens of millions of people in the region are infected. The infection can be acute and life threatening, but most often it is a chronic disease that later causes heart problems. The chronic infection reduces lifespan by an average of 9 years. Bites mainly occur at night when a person is sleeping under the thatched roofs or in the forest where the bugs live. The bites most often are on the face, thus the name *kissing bug* darkly fits. However, the infection is not passed to the victim directly from the bite. While the reduviid feeds on blood (as much as 1 ml) it deposits infested excrement near the wound, thus causing the infection. Cruisers need never be exposed to this infection.

19.4.2 Contaminated water and produce

Finding good drinking water is usually not a problem. Check with the other cruisers about their long-term experience with the water supply in every location. Giardia, amebiasis, bacterial diarrhea and viral gastroenteritis are not uncommon and most cruisers will experience some kind of intestinal problem during any six-month period. Intestinal infections can come from a number of other sources including: uncooked foods, iced drinks (with contaminated water) and improperly washed fruits and vegetables. Your own watermaker water or bottled water are the safest sources of drinking water.

Washing fruits and vegetables with a solution of chlorine bleach (two tablespoons for 1 gallon of water) kills most bacteria and parasites, but does not kill the cystic form of amoeba and other protozoa that can cause intestinal infections. However, a solution of 10 drops of povidone-iodine 10% per gallon of water is said to be an effective overall disinfectant. Soak all produce for 10 minutes to minimize the chances of infection.

In most countries, medication that effectively covers the range of common intestinal bacterial and parasitic infections can be inexpensively purchased at a local farmacia (pharmacy) without a doctor's prescription. Go with the pharmacist's recommendation. Depending upon the type of medication, it may be a single dose or may require several days to complete a course of medication. The medicines we have used seem to have little or no side affects. The symptoms of bacterial and parasitic intestinal infection usually include more than one of the following: flatulence, larger than normal fecal volume, visible mucous along with the fecal mass, abdominal churning sensations, cramping and diarrhea. With the signs of intestinal infections, most cruisers do not go to the trouble of having a stool culture done to identify the culprit; they just take the cure. Usually, within one to three days the infection and symptoms clear up. However, if you have other health problems, it would be good to check with a doctor about these medications before leaving on an extended cruise.

19.5 OTHER HEALTH CONCERNS

Travel to many areas of the Caribbean should not be done without immunization for diseases such as yellow fever, hepatitis (A & B), meningitis, influenza, typhoid fever, tetanus and perhaps cholera. Check with the local county health department for current recommendations regarding the regions that are to be visited. The immunization process can be expensive and take a number of weeks so it is necessary to begin early. One possible exception might be the yellow fever shot. In the U.S., they are very expensive, but in Venezuela and elsewhere they cost only a few dollars.

Eating out in the various countries is one of the delights of cruising. If precautions are taken, the experiences will be generally good. But it should be understood that because a restaurant has a nice presentation there is no guarantee that the fresh salad or iced drink won't make you ill. Also, street food, while of questionable origin and character, is usually well cooked, tasty and seldom a bother.

The water supplies in many municipal areas have been greatly improved since the bad old days. Most municipalities now have chlorinated water. Yet, there can be cracked underground pipes, or other compromises to the water system's integrity. Thus, at restaurants, tap water, iced drinks, fresh salads and other uncooked, unpeeled produce should be ingested with understanding that there may be a price to pay. Some say that an iced drink with alcohol is safe. Don't believe it. At restaurants, the best bet is to consume beverages as canned or bottled sans-ice. Make sure that all the food is well cooked and only eat fruit that has been pealed. Restaurants and certain foods get a reputation for being good or bad. But take the advice of others guardedly. Their experience may have just been lucky or unlucky. After being in an area for a while, it will become clear where the salads and slaw can be eaten.

This last bit has nothing to do with the tropics, but everything to do with spending hours folded up working in the engine room. Leg cramps at night are a very unwelcome wake up call. We have found that BENGAY® provides quick relief and even reduces the likelihood of getting cramps. A tube by the bedside may save a lot of discomfort. Dehydration and mineral deficiencies are also believed to be causes of cramps.

19.6 MEDICINES TO CONSIDER HAVING ONBOARD

The list of pharmaceutical products to have in the medical kit need cover only the most likely problems that might occur. Of course, there should be the patent medicines for headache pain, antiseptics, band-aids, sunburn preparations, sunscreen, etc. But most cruisers believe that there should also be a supply of what we have come to know in North America as prescription drugs.

In addition to a cruiser's prescribed medications that may be taken regularly, the following table lists medicines to consider as stock items for the medical kit. The list includes a few patent medicines.

Allergic reactions (severe)
    epinephrine (Epi-pen) — Allergic reactions, e.g. bee stings
    albuterol inhaler (with spacer) — Asthma
Antibiotics — Used for
    amoxicillin
    amoxicillin-clavulanate
        (Augmentin) — Respiratory, ear, sinus infections
    cephalexin (Keflex) — Skin infections
    ciprofloxin (Cipro) — Systemic infections, traveler's diarrhea
    doxycycline — Prostate and urinary infections
    penicillin V — Respiratory infections
    TMP-SMZ (Septra, Bactrim) — Traveler's diarrhea, urinary infections
    azithromycin (Zithromax, Z-pack) — Respiratory infections
Antibiotic eye drops for conjunctivitis
    Polysporin drops
Anti-constipation
    Mineral oil or various patent medicines
Anti-emetics (vomiting)
    Phenergan (oral or rectal) — For the prevention of dehydration
Anti-diarrhea
    Imodium or equivalent
Antihistamines
    Benadryl, loratadine (Claritin) or equivalent
Anti-inflammatory, pain medicines
    Ibuprofen (Motrin, Advil), naproxen (Aleve), aspirin, etc.
Other pain medicines such as:
    Acetominophen (Tylenol)
    Narcotics, e.g. acetominophen w/codeine or hydrocondone (Vicodin)
Herpes simplex viral infection topical treatment
    Acyclovir
Intestinal Infections
    TMP-SMZ (Septra, Bactrim)
    Ciprofloxin — Bacterial infections
        Parasitic infections
Malaria therapy medication (oral)
    Chloroquine resistant strain
        quinine,
        along with Fansidar to prevent recurrence
    Chloroquine sensitive strain
        chloroquine
        along with primaquine to prevent recurrence
Nasal decongestant
    Afrin or equivalent

Seasick pills/patches
> Dramamine
> Cennazine, Bonine, Meclizine (Antivert)

Swimmer's ear, prevention (after swimming)
> Drops of dilute alcohol solution
> or
> Drops of 1:1 alcohol and white vinegar

Toothache pain relief
> Orajel or equivalent

Topical antibiotic creams
> Neosporin, Equate triple antibiotic

Topical antifungal creams
> Monistat, Mycelex or Lotrimin — Ringworm, tinea infections of the scalp and skin. Not effective for candidiasis.
> Nystatin, Mycostatin, Nilstat — Candidiasis, thrush

In many regions of the Caribbean (mostly south and west), these and other drugs can be purchased at a fraction of the cost in the States. Exceptions to this are medicines that are under patent restrictions. Otherwise, be prepared for a pleasant surprise. For example, in Colombia, an entire year's supply of a common blood pressure medication was recently available for a little over $4.00. Other items may not be as inexpensive, but a course of antibiotics will often cost just a few dollars.

However, be aware that most drugs have a shelf life. Some become less potent with age, but others, such as antibiotics with names ending in –cycline, can become significantly more potent with age, perhaps even toxic.

For the medications and various illnesses listed, we make the disclaimer that this text is not intended for self-diagnosis and/or self-medication. Use the information discriminately and at your own peril.

In addition to a supply of medicines, it is also recommended that you have a book or two on emergency medical treatment aboard. Those reference books, intended for doctors involved in emergency medical treatment, are not easily read by the layman, but can be helpful just the same. Books on emergency treatment have also been written for the layman. But, lets face it, for the layman, self-diagnosis and treatment is a little chancy and sometimes the stakes are high. We don't have the many years of training needed to make proper differential diagnosis or the knowledge to understand medicinal affects and interactions. Yet, it doesn't hurt to be prepared. In some situations, the alternatives may be worse.

Chapter 20
Security at Sea, Anchor and Ashore

I (BEN) GREW UP IN A SMALL TOWN IN IOWA. At that time nobody locked their doors and the biggest neighborhood security concern was that my pet raccoon might visit a neighbors house and do mischief. More seriously, there would be an occasional car wreck, farm accident or drowning, but those involved were seldom ever acquaintances. We all know that life isn't that simple anymore. These days there are too many incidents of theft, mugging, murder and carjacking. Security is an issue everywhere. It is important to keep this in mind when reading this chapter.

Another issue needs to be prefaced. That is, secondhand stories of security problems in the Caribbean should not be given much credence or perpetuated with additional telling. Indeed there are security problems, but they seldom live up to the ugliness of the many times told and embellished tales. The important thing is that almost all the security problems are avoidable with common sense precautions. It's kind of like making a decision whether or not to stroll through a bad part of a city at night. The degree to which you present yourself as an opportunity to the bad guys is a matter of choice and practice.

The issues are broken down into three main categories: security at sea, security at anchor and security ashore.

20.1 SECURITY AT SEA

Everyone has heard or read about piracy and boardings at sea. For cruisers venturing to far off places there may be concern and trepidation. But how real is the problem? To begin with, think about the problem from a pirate's viewpoint. Far away from land, the pirate must wait for his victim. It's a big ocean and the wait could be a long one. The pirate's fuel and food may run out before a proper victim candidate crosses his path. After all, the vessel(s) may not be to his liking, e.g. too big, too fast, too many crewmen or the crew may be armed and meaner than the pirate. That's too much uncertainty for any businessman. Still, there is always a small chance of a nefarious fish-boat crossing one's path purely by chance. Reasonable or not, and especially in areas with a history of problems, there should be measured concern when another vessel follows or closes on your position. When that does occur, a course or speed change may be warranted to check out their intentions. Far away from land, there is a much greater likelihood of being boarded by the Coast Guard or a foreign Navy than a criminal adversary.

Coastal cruising in a few regions, is yet another matter. Parts of Honduras, Nicaragua, Columbia and Venezuela have gained a deserved reputation. Until the situations improve, they should be given a good measure of leeway. The main concern is one of being spotted from land or by near-shore fishermen-bandits. With a fast boat, they can approach quickly. Confronted with that situation the three options of flight, fight or give up have been reduced to the less desirable two. Once a vessel has been boarded, the consensus is that yielding to the bandits is less risky than attempting to fight them off. Thus, by far the best defense is the conscious choice to avoid the near shore trouble spots. Networking with other cruisers will be helpful in staying informed of regional problems.

20.2 SECURITY AT ANCHOR

It is a sad for us to say that during the last eight years we have had several friends and acquaintances robbed while they were at anchor. There were also a number of other incidents reported on the nets. The thefts most often involved dinghies with outboard motors, but a few boardings have occurred. Only rarely, however, were the robbers bold enough to board vessels while the crew was there.

Thankfully, we have not had a first hand experience, but here are a few stories where the information came directly from those involved. After reading them, you will see that all of the incidents could have been avoided. That's not to say that the cruisers involved were careless or cavalier about security. Circumstances were such that let their guards down a bit and the opportunistic thieves were ready to take advantage of the situation.

An experienced cruiser motored up the Rio Dulce of Guatemala to the familiar cruiser's community near Fronteras. In this area, most often, anchoring out is a bad idea. There are half a dozen marinas near Fronteras to accommodate several hundred boats. But, when our friends arrived there was a delay getting a slip. In such a case, it is usual to drop the hook just off the marina. While waiting for a slip, they launched the dinghy and went to town and to the bank to get cash for their upcoming trip flight and visit to Canada.

Returning to the anchored boat, they hid the cash and then dinghied to the marina for lunch. While they were away, the cash was stolen.

Lesson: There are competent thieves watching the banks, ATMs and boats. In this example, if it is necessary to anchor in an area having questionable security, even briefly, a crewmember should remain aboard, alert and occasionally visible.

Another experienced Caribbean cruiser motoring up the Rio Dulce of Guatemala anchored (alone) in a known problem area. During the night two men boarded the boat. The mate used pepper spray on one man. In this case, it was sufficient to drive them off.

Lesson: The crew was alert to the possibility of a boarding. Anchoring out was a considered risk. In this case, they were lucky that the borders were not armed or more persistent. Anchoring in known trouble spots, especially alone, may be looking for trouble.

A single-hand cruiser, seeking safe haven from a close pass by hurricane Emily, anchored (alone) in a small lagoon on the north coast of Gulfo de Cariaco, Venezuela. Over the years there had been only a few incidents of robberies reported in the area.

During the night four men boarded his boat and robbed him of food, clothes, radio, etc. The skipper was physically abused, but not seriously. Afterward, the cruiser pulled out of the lagoon and spent the night orbiting in the Gulfo waiting for daylight to go to the marina at Cumana.

Lesson: There is safety in numbers. One mile away, at another lagoon, 30 to 40 cruisers were at anchor. None were molested during the night.

Margarita Island, Venezuela is a popular cruiser's haunt. It also has a well-deserved reputation for dinghy theft. All visiting cruisers are warned that dinghies left in the water at night are fair game. But, with a little wind, the bay at Porlamar becomes choppy and dinghy retrieval can be a problem. In this story the cruiser's dinghy stowage required that the outboard motor be removed. Obviously to do this daily is a chore and a little risky, especially in choppy conditions. The cruiser decided to pull the dinghy close alongside the swim platform and secure it and the motor with a cable and padlock. During the night, the dinghy's outboard motor was stolen.

> That same night another cruiser's dinghy motor was stolen. The dinghy had been left afloat on its painter. It was a profitable night for the thieves.
>
> Lesson: There are places, known to everyone, where dinghy theft is as common as dirt. In those places, unless you plan to stay on watch all night, the only secure dinghy is one that is safely stowed out of the water. You will get little, if any, sympathy from other cruisers if your dinghy is in the water at night and subsequently stolen.

> Near the end of 2004, at Porlamar, Isla de Margarita, VE (again), cruisers were fed up with the thefts. About 80 boats were at anchor and they organized a security watch. Each morning on the VHF net, volunteers would be sought for the evening watches. The two-hour watch shifts began at 10 PM and ended at 4 AM. During each watch, a spotlight was intermittently shown about the anchorage. The thefts abruptly ended and none occurred for four months.
>
> As might be expected, with the lack of thefts and changing cruising boats, interest was lost and the security watch petered out. Sure as the sun rises, the thieves were back in business and within a few weeks, several dinghies were lost.
>
> In much of the Caribbean, the average income is very low. An outboard motor can be worth several months' wages to a thief. Thus, when an outboard can be stolen, even only once a month, the thief is doing well.

There are many such stories. Thankfully, most of them have been simple thefts not involving physical abuse. Thieves aren't too analytical, but they are conscious of the risk-reward relationship even if they can't spell it. The fact that few thieves are caught, or even seen, suggests that they are cautious and only act when the risks are low.

20.3 SECURITY ASHORE

Mexico, Central and South America abound with wonderful places to visit and traveling can be done inexpensively and safely. Inexpensive, comfortable, air-conditioned express buses travel almost everywhere. But the chicken buses should also be considered. They are cheap and certainly less comfortable, but they can be a most rewarding means of traveling inland.

Everywhere in the Caribbean tall razor wire fences, barbed wire, broken glass on the top of walls and armed guards are commonplace, seemingly these paint a picture of runaway crime. That, however, would be a distorted conclusion. Police are not as visibly evident around the Caribbean as in the U.S. and they are less apt to investigate minor crimes. Therefore, security is more a matter of establishing defenses and employing private security guards than depending upon the police.

Large segments of the population are economically deprived. And, as we have seen in the U.S., during times of a faltering economy, the crime rate soars. Thus, a high incidence of theft and other crime is a problem for many Caribbean areas.

Does that mean they are unsafe? Not if you take a few precautions. Where possible don't:

> travel alone,
> wear jewelry or carry an exposed expensive camera,
> dress flashy,
> walk the streets at night without knowing it is a safe area (duh!),
> carry anything you can't afford to loose,
> carry credit cards any more than necessary,
> display wallet, credit cards, etc. at a counter or telephone.

And do:

> carry a copy of your passport,
> carry strapped bags slung around the neck, held with one hand,
> spread your cash about in several places,
> carry small amounts of cash in your pocket to pay for bus or taxis rides,
> keep your wallet discretely secure in crowded conditions,
> examine your wallet only in relative privacy,
> be wary of unusually friendly passers-by.

Acting thusly, it is unlikely that you will be robbed while traveling. Thieves can tell the difference between a savvy traveler and an easy mark. The last bit of advice for which everyone agrees is: don't offer any resistance. If the other advice has been followed, there will be little for you to loose. Why take any risk of injury?

There are other issues besides robbery to think about. In every country it is necessary to get money exchanged. A few years back changing money on the street was more the norm than the exception. These days, money is most often changed at the bank or at a money exchange. But in Venezuela and a couple of other countries, black market money on the street is still a going business and it is true that there is always a better exchange rate on the black market than at the bank. But *don't buy it on the street*. On the street, it is likely the buyer will get phony money or any number of switch-a-roo scams. Those guys have had years to work out effective ways of separating you from your cash. At marinas there are people, known to the cruising community, who offer good rates and provide real, properly counted money.

Another problem to be aware of is that of counterfeit U.S. dollars. In particular, phony $100.00 bills may be encountered. Don't get them and don't accidentally pass them. Look for the watermarks and little inlaid vertical lines that indicate they are good bills. We have seen the bills folded in thirds such that the fold line appears like the line expected on a good bill. If there's a doubt, go to a bank for clarification. However, if you do get stuck with one or more counterfeit hundreds, keep one in your wallet along with the minimum traveling cash. If robbed, it may be helpful in satisfying a bandit and providing yourself with a little ironic satisfaction.

20.4 LIGHTNING

At sea, at anchor or at the dock, lightning is a threat. In places like the San Blas Islands of Panama and elsewhere in Panama, during the rainy season, lightning is a serious threat and each year several sailboats receive lightning damage. The types of damage include sailboat dismasting and the complete destruction of electronics. What can one do to minimize the risk?

A number of books are available that cover the subject of lightning protection aboard vessels. With a little paranoia, a boat owner can spend inordinate amounts of money and time working on the problem. But, before you run out and buy all kinds of paraphernalia and systematically pull your boat apart to improve the grounding, etc., there are caveats to consider. First, there is no sure fire protection from lightning. General systems that claim to offer protection have only anecdotal evidence of that protection and their laboratory tests carry little if any weight. Commercial products may be based upon ethical and scientific reasoning, but since lightning protection systems are untestable, you can't know if the effort and money were spent wisely.

Of course, it is reasonable to have very good grounding of all metallic elements on a boat. But that does not mean loading the boat down with heavy cables or copper strapping. Here's the problem. A lightning discharge doesn't simply follow a DC path to ground. The discharge will often leave a heavy ground conductor (such as a mast) and take a seemingly higher

While anchored in the San Blas Islands of Panama, boats are frequently visited by the Kuna Indians who sell and trade their wares.

resistant, longer path to ground. This is because the discharge locally creates high frequencies that opportunistically find other resonance related pathways. These can be curiously circuitous.

We always joke about finding the tallest sailboat in the harbor and anchoring near it. There may be truth in the assumption that it is a protective umbrella, but because the tall mast is also one of the more likely targets, a nearby strike can damage your vessel's electronics because of the electromagnetic pulse (EMP). EMPs are generated whenever a fast, high current discharge occurs. They damage semiconductor components by creating destructive voltages across tiny circuit elements. Thankfully, the damaging affects of EMPs diminish rapidly with the distance from the strike. So, while it may be nice to be near the tall mast, you don't want to be too near it. Sensitive electronics can be protected from EMPs by placing them in a tightly shielded metal enclosure known as a Faraday Cage. The oven and microwave oven are reasonable facsimiles of a Faraday Cage.

Another anecdotal cautionary note is, don't push your luck anchoring too long near a specific island where there are many palm trees without tops (e.g. variously in the San Blas Islands).

All this adds up to the following suggestions.

Prior to cruising, inspect-repair the vessel's bonding/grounding system.
Add surge suppressors where appropriate.
Check your insurance policy for lightning damage coverage.

Then, before a severe thunderstorm approaches the following may help.

Lower all of the vessel's antennas.
When reasonable, disconnect and if possible ground the antennas.
Unplug the computer, TV and other electronics.
Place the laptop computer and backup GPS in the oven or microwave oven for EMP protection.

Disconnecting appliances does not provide any protection from EMPs, but can save them from other destructive discharges.

20.5 SELF DEFENSE AT SEA AND AT ANCHOR

Nearly every country has a prohibition against visiting vessels carrying firearms aboard, yet only a few countries' officials will ask about weapons. If a cruiser has one and admits it, the weapon will have to be turned over to the Port Captain until the cruiser is ready to return to international waters. Most of the time the officials don't ask. To do so just means more paper work and responsibility for them. It's a sort of don't ask, don't tell situation. However, if later during an onboard inspection, a weapon is found the consequences can be serious. Having said that, many cruisers carry weapons and I can't recall anyone having been arrested. That is offered anecdotally and not as advice or a recommendation.

The arguments against carrying a firearm are that if there should be a need for one, it is very likely that the adversary or adversaries will be better armed. Or, if you thwart a robbery, but in the process maim or kill a person, how would that set with you? That could be very troubling, especially if the thief wasn't a personal threat, perhaps very young or the theft very petty. Also, using a weapon within a country's territorial boundaries may become a bigger legal issue than the inconvenience of a theft.

Many cruisers content themselves with flare pistols and a goodly supply of shells. These have been used effectively against boarders, but they are not likely to thwart multiple boarders who are better armed.

Pepper spray, bear spray and mace have all been used effectively against intruders. In a situation where the spray has not been used effectively, it is not likely to elicit a life threatening response from the bad guy. To my knowledge, these personal defense items are fully allowable on private vessels.

We all know the arguments for carrying a weapon and some are clearly valid. The use of a weapon really comes down to knowing when you are in danger and have a chance to mediate that danger. For the boardings of which we are aware, only one or two fit the criteria justifying the possession of a firearm.

At sea it may be a different story. When approached by a high-speed vessel with only a few bad guys aboard, a shotgun blast striking the water ahead of their bow might be a deterrent. It might also cause them to bring out automatic weapons.

The easiest answer to the weapons issue is to avoid the problem areas. At any point in time, thousands of vessels, local and foreign, are plying the waters of the Caribbean without incident. When trouble does occur, it usually falls into one of the OOPS categories described previously.

Without firearms, there are effective passive defenses against unwanted intruders. One such method is to purchase and install a farm type electric fence unit. Worked against the seawater as ground, the vessel's metal handrails, stanchions, ladders, etc. can be effectively and safely electrified. Wooden handrails can be electrified through the application of ¼ inch wide thin copper foil tape. 3M Corporation makes one such product. When applied to the underside of a handrail, the tape is secure, unseen, yet difficult to avoid. The output of many electric fencer units is approximately 10,000 volts (at low, non-injurious

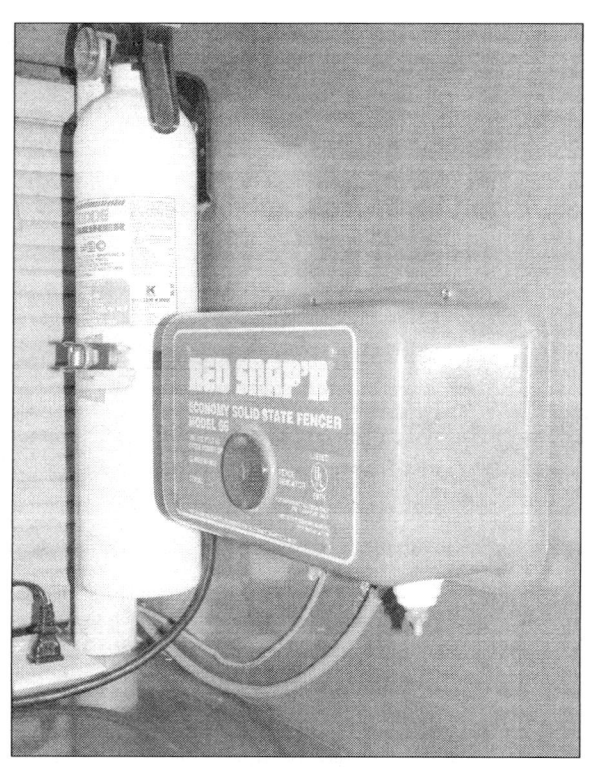

Livestock electric fencers are available with either 12 VDC or 110 VAC input power. Independently of that, two types of output are available. One type has a pulsed output of 8 to 10 thousand volts. The second type has a continuous output of about 800 volts. The higher voltage pulsed output should be used with wooden handrails where varnish may be applied over the conductive strip.

current). At this high voltage, the tape may be varnished over with many coats without interfering with the system's effectiveness. Clearly the high voltage can be easily defeated by a ground wire, but that is true only if the intruder is aware of its existence and is informed enough to understand how to defeat it.

Other passive systems include trip wire alarms, infrared motion sensors, and a series of treble hooks strung in the most likely regions of intrusion. All of these techniques work to some degree, but systems that prevent anyone from coming aboard in the first place are obviously preferred.

Most of the successful boarding/robberies have occurred when there has been no attempt to lock up the boat. Thus, the crew is awakened with a bandit standing over them. In troubled waters, lock the hatches and doors before going to bed.

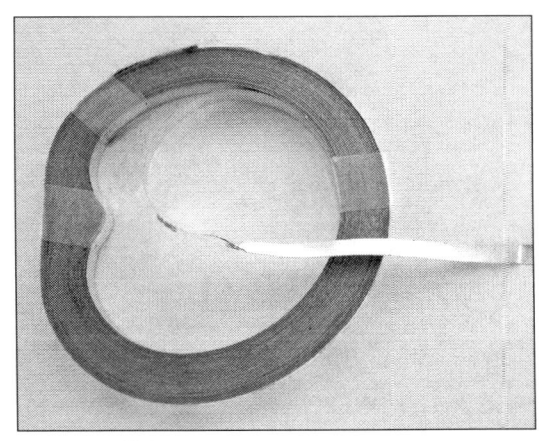

Copper Foil Tape

The Caribbean, like everywhere, has a few special problems. If you were traveling in Yellowstone Park it might be a bear problem, in Los Angeles a traffic problem, in the north in winter an ice and snow problem. So, there's no reason to get paranoid, just be aware and take reasonable precautions.

Chapter 21
Safety at Sea

WE SHOULD ALL KNOW WHAT SAFETY ITEMS ARE REQUIRED BY THE U.S. or Canadian Coast Guard. But extended cruising requires yet more safety equipment and an additional helping of awareness.

Illness and accidents at sea happen. Mostly they are only minor inconveniences like a cold, a stubbed toe or cut finger, but what if it is more serious. What if your mate falls down a ladder and injures his/her back or is unconscious. What if the electrical bonding of a seacock broke off years ago and the seacock finally broke. Or, how about getting caught in bad seas, the engine(s) stop due to fuel contamination and the boat is rolling to extremes in the trough. Most of these problems, taken individually, can be managed, but problems have a tendency to proliferate. Serious accidents are difficult to think about, but it is necessary to have them mentally categorized and know what to do. Here are the main types of problems that can and do occur at sea.

21.1 SERIOUS PERSONAL INJURIES / ILLNESS

Every year or two a cruiser on passage has a nightmare type problem. Here are a couple examples.

> In the southeastern Caribbean in 2003, a sailboat captain had a stroke during a crossing. He was mostly conscious, but had little comprehension of the situation. The problem was compounded by the fact that the autopilot had failed and the sea was up. His wife had difficulty keeping the vessel stable, making the

> needed radio calls and tending to her husband. She was able to get in touch with the Venezuelan Navy and the U.S. Coast Guard. Thankfully, the end result was a good one.

> In 2001, a man and his wife on a sailboat were crossing the Gulf of Mexico toward a port in south Florida. The winds weren't favoring their destination and progress was very slow. The captain had a heart attack. His wife changed course toward the Texas coast to favor the wind. She made the appropriate radio calls and got medical advice and other assistance. It was another good ending.

Difficulties such as this are often further complicated by weather and equipment problems. The two paragraphs above do not begin to do justice to the courage of those involved. One can only imagine their concerns and personal stress.

Lesser accidents occur more frequently. Scalds, falls, sprains, pulled muscles, strained backs, are all problems waiting for the careless seafarer.

For all serious accidents or sudden illness, what are the key issues to deal with? First, make sure that the boat is on a course that will not put it at risk. If the problem happens near the coast, change course to put it safely out to sea. If the vessel is in clear, but rough waters, it may be best to change course to improve stability and reduce the workload. Just be sure that, when attempting to manage a personal emergency, a vessel safety emergency doesn't compound the problem.

Next, tend to your distressed shipmate. Most of us aren't trained in emergency medicine, but it is primarily important to make certain an incapacitated person is positioned to minimize the potential for additional injury. After that, take whatever additional medical steps you're equipped and capable of administering.

Outside help is then needed. First, try VHF, channel 16. If another vessel is in hailing distance, they may be able to offer physical assistance as well as help with the radio work.

For further information regarding emergency assistance, review the procedures outlined in Chapter 8, *Communications* and in other texts.

21.2 MAN-OVERBOARD

This section does not include the basic seamanship of negotiating a vessel for the retrieval of a person in the water. That is left to other texts and should already be part of the cruiser's boating background. The reason for including this section is that new cruisers are likely to have little if any nighttime experience. On overnighters the challenges can include: ship traffic, watch keeping, perhaps hand steering in difficult conditions, equipment failure, squall conditions, and so on. If a crew has not thought it through, a man overboard accident after dark can have terrible consequences. Even prepared and in good weather conditions, a nighttime man overboard problem with only one crewman aboard can be extremely difficult to manage.

There are lots of reasons why people fall overboard. We will review a few of them, suggest ways to avoid the problem and finally discuss the emergency measures that need to be taken.

The most frequent reason for falling overboard is exclusively a male problem. The best advice therefore is to go below and use the head.

Sailboats, with lots of rigging and deck fixtures, have an especially hazardous deck upon which to maneuver. Fortunately safety harnesses are part of a sailor's everyday life and falling overboard can be avoided almost completely if safety procedures are rigorously practiced. But, on powerboats, safety harnesses are rarely used because there are no rigging accommodations.

There seems to be about a 50-50 mix of captains who like to run their vessels from the lower helm station and those who prefer the fly bridge. Certainly, those who operate from the fly bridge are at greater risk of an accident because of the frequent need to go below for bathroom breaks, food, coffee, engine checks, etc. In large seas at night, when no one wants to be on a weather deck, that's when there will be a need. The risk of all kinds of accidents goes way up in those conditions.

Given the realities, what should one do. Well, it is mostly just common sense. At night, when on a weather deck, always wear a personal floatation device (PFD) that is equipped with a waterproof strobe light (tested frequently and having fresh batteries) and a whistle. A handheld waterproof VHF radio can also be very helpful in coordinating a man-overboard situation.

Additionally, you and your mate need to keep track of each other at all times. Have prearranged signals for announcing movements when going below or returning to the fly bridge. Then, if there is an accident, the man overboard GPS waypoint can be set at the earliest possible moment. But, finding and assisting someone in the water at night, in anything but calm conditions will be difficult to say the least. Also, if the person in the water is unconscious, it is very unlikely that a one person aboard will be able to recover the MOB. Attempting to do so will also put them at great risk.

So, we shall limit the problem to a conscious person in the water. Having located the person, the boat should be brought upwind, but alongside (with plenty of clearance) and the transmission(s) put in neutral. Realize that without power, the boat will quickly round out and roll in the trough.

The person onboard then has several duties to perform. These must be done carefully, quickly and without risking either a fall or fouling of the rudder(s) or prop(s).

A tethered life ring must be thrown toward the person in the water. The tether should be a floating line. Next, the swim ladder must be lowered, but use a boathook and try to avoid getting on the swim platform.

Before the first overnighter, think about the problems and go over the procedures with your shipmate(s). Also, review the man overboard boat-handling procedures found in other texts.

21.3 FOUNDERED AND SINKING

Every year at least one cruising boat is damaged or lost while underway in the Caribbean. The good news is that only very rarely are those aboard lost with their boat. Also, because weather forecasting and forecast availability has greatly improved in recent years, heavy weather is seldom the primary problem for vessels lost or damaged while underway. However, weather can be a prominent secondary reason for serious problems at sea. For instance, the loss of power in 3 to 5 foot choppy seas can make efforts in a hot engine room quickly physically exhausting.

Let's take a look at a few other reasons cruisers have had sad experiences.

Chart errors. In many areas of the western Caribbean and elsewhere, the charts can be off by a mile or more. The extreme case is with a coastal chart M28130S0 (not 28130 which is OK), off Nicaragua and Honduras near Cabo Gracias Adios. On that chart, the latitude position is in error by 15 nautical miles. It was because of this that in 2003, a sailboat grounded heavily on the Media Luna reef in broad daylight. After a couple days, the Honduran Navy pulled the boat to safety with little damage.

A few other examples of charting discrepancies at popular locations include:

Mexico
    Isla Mujeres
    Chinchorro Banks
Belize
    Glover's Reef
    Lighthouse Reef
    Turneffe Reef

The above locations are off by up to a mile. Many other charting discrepancies exist, but usually to a lesser degree. Avoid close proximity to any land or reef structures during nighttime passages, especially if the wind and/or current will tend to drive a disabled vessel in that direction.

Running inshore (2 to 5 miles out). There are coastal regions, where because of offshore debris fields or current, running inshore at night is frequently practiced. But to do this safely requires the right weather, a good knowledge of the area, a functioning backup GPS and reliable tested waypoints. Engine failure with an onshore breeze could be big trouble.

Rogue Waves. Here is a problem for sailboats for which there are few answers. In 2001, a sailboat off Panama was hit by a rogue wave. The vessel rolled over and was dismasted. In that instance, thankfully the boat was saved and no one was seriously injured. Sailboats like to operate with favorable winds in the 15 to 20 knot range. If those conditions have prevailed for several days, moderately large seas are generated. Rogue waves are not freak waves; they can be up to twice as large as the average sea condition and there is a small probability that a rogue wave will be encountered at any time.

Serious wind generated rogue waves do not occur during reasonably settled conditions or even during transient squall conditions. Therefore, powerboats need not be exposed to this type of problem.

Inlet woes. In the Caribbean, few of the coastal inlets and reef entrances are buoyed or marked. Mostly, cruisers have to navigate these openings using waypoints and eyeballs. Cruising guides for each region often publish the approach and entry waypoints, but in all cases, they aren't to be trusted until tested. Even if the published waypoint is correct, a GPS entry error may have been made. A few years ago, a skipper tried to negotiate an unfamiliar reef entry on the Yucatan coast of Mexico at night. Although he and his wife were rescued, their sailboat was lost.

These are examples of problems that, for the most part, could have been avoided. There is no need to be paranoid about potential problems, but it sure makes sense to have thought through the various scenarios and to maintain a state of preparedness.

21.4 TAKING ON WATER

Your vessel was inspected from stem to stern and everything was in apple pie order. All of the engine, genset and air conditioner hoses and clamps were in good condition and there was no reason for it to take on water. But, once in a while, things just break. Maybe there was a manufacturing defect an electrical bonding that was not secure, or the engine raw water cooling failed and the exhaust hose has burned through or, or, or. In any event, with early warning from a high water alarm, these problems should not threaten a vessel. Even better, an indicator showing bilge pump operation should be viewable at the helm station(s). With time to react and only little water aboard, problems such as this can be corrected before they become serious.

Undetected, however, an open flow through a seacock or engine hose can be disastrous. In 2003, a thoroughly, newly refurbished sailboat was rounding Cabo Gracias Adios off the Honduran coast. It was daytime and the vessel was under sail. With all hands on deck and in the cockpit, hull flooding from an unknown source progressed beyond recovery before it was discovered. After a mayday call, the lifeboat was put over the side and the vessel abandoned. The U.S. Coast Guard picked them up within about 12 hours.

21.5 FIRE ABOARD

This can be one of the most serious accidents imaginable and one that can happen even with the best-maintained vessel. For diesel-powered vessels, cooking accidents or electrical shorts are the most frequent cause of fires. Make certain that chemical fire extinguishers are shaken periodically so that they can be effectively used. In fire situations, proceed approximately as follows:

> Engine room fire, when possible:
> > Shut down the genset (if operating),
> > Shut down the engine(s) (if operating),
> > Shut off all fuel supplies,
> > Switch off all batteries not needed for communications,
> > Operate fire extinguisher(s),
> > Make appropriate radio calls.
> Galley fire
> > Shut down the genset or propane gas supply,
> > Extinguish the fire,
> > Make appropriate radio calls.
> Other fires (electrical origin)
> > Shut down the genset (if operating),
> > Switch off all batteries not needed for communications,
> > Extinguish the fire.

If there is any concern about being able to manage the fire, get out a mayday call as soon as possible.

Chapter 22
Assisting Other Vessels

WITH THE VARIOUS TOWING SERVICES and insurance coverage in North America, few powerboat captains are called upon to provide assistance to other vessels. Indeed, only few emergencies would require it. Thus, powerboat captains seldom gain experience in the processes.

The bulk of the cruising fleet is of course sailboats. They have several attributes that make them vulnerable to difficult groundings. First, sailboats don't have a high vantage point from which to observe and avoid obstructions. Single hulled sailing vessels also have deeper drafts and don't often have much reserve power to help back off from a grounding.

Trawlers and some other types of powerboats have quite different features making them useful in assisting other vessels. These features include:

good visibility from the fly bridge for avoiding obstacles,
good maneuverability (twin engine or bow thrusters),
relatively shallow draft (for most),
plenty of power to tow other vessels
plenty of power to pull other vessels, off reefs and other groundings.

Thus, the few powerboats in the Caribbean often provide a safety net for the rest of the cruising, sailing, community. We have just about lost count of the number of sailboats *Francesca* has either pulled from various groundings, towed or given other assistance.

The first considerations in giving assistance is to take care that a bad situation is not made worse, that no one is injured and that no damage is done to any vessel. Admittedly, there can be situations and sea states when these conditions are not so easily met. At such times, both captains must be clear and communicate their decisions to take acceptable risks. The Good Samaritan rule generally applies, but if either vessel or crew is tested beyond their limits that will be of little comfort.

Here's a little story.

A sailboat was approaching La Ceiba, Honduras. The seas were running five to six feet with steep (3 to 4 second) chop and the weather was squally and deteriorating. The little harbor at La Ceiba is entered through a rock jetty. A few miles out, the sailboat discovered that their diesel engine would not run. Sailing in through the narrow jetty would not be a good idea even in good conditions.

Without assistance, the sailboat captain's only option would have been to stay at sea for a day or two and ride out the area wide storm. However, there were yet other problems with the boat and staying at sea would have been risky. The captain called on VHF for towing assistance.

At the time, *Francesca* was the only trawler available to help. We worked out a plan to meet the sailboat a short distance outside of the jetty. When we arrived at the jetty a potent squall move through and visibility diminished to less than 1/8 mile. During the half hour it took for visibility to improve, the sailboat was forced eastward past the jetty. Anchoring was not an option. By the time *Francesca* met up with the sailboat, it was about two miles down the coast and getting close to shore.

After the sailboat picked up our towline, we began a long, very slow (1 to 1.5 knot) tow back to the jetty. Sea conditions were such that the sailboat's bow was frequently buried. A faster tow would have put unreasonable stress on the towline and hard points. All went well during the tow and neither vessel nor crew suffered any injury.

Upon arriving back at the harbor, Francesca was gradually slowed to a stop. But, because of poor communications on my part, there was confusion about when the sailboat was to drop the towline. Since sailboats have much less drag than trawlers, the sailboat continued past *Francesca*, but the sailboat crewman did not drop the towline. *Francesca* was in tight quarters and unable to maneuver. When the towline went taught, *Francesca* was pulled around by the stern and narrowly missed a collision with a docked steel ferry. With the exception of my pride, we were fortunate that no damage occurred and the sailboat and crew were saved from a difficult situation. However, the rescue could have gone very wrong at several critical points.

Analysis: Passing a line between vessels in adverse sea conditions is risky business. Good seamanship is required by both captains to avoid a collision. Good line handling is also required to avoid fouling the towboat's rudders or props. If that were to happen, the towboat would be at greater risk than the sailboat. Finally, poor communications nearly caused an accident after both vessels were safely in the harbor.

22.1 TOWING A VESSEL FROM A GROUNDING

Wind, current and sea states will dictate how the towboat approaches an ailing vessel. It is assumed that the captain has sufficient experience to negotiate his vessel.

For the best maneuverability, the towline should be attached to the towboat about a third of the way up from the stern. That's not usually possible so we take the next best thing and use the stern cleats as towing hard-points. The use of a bridle is a further compromise, but distributing the load between two cleats is justified. A bridle can be made up quickly by tying a second line to the main towline using a rolling hitch. It is a good practice to slide a float or jug onto the bridle to keep the tie point visibly on the surface. The towline should be of a length to minimize the risk of towboat grounding, danger of collision and offer reasonable maneuverability for both vessels.

Use a dinghy to pass the towline if there is a risk of grounding the towboat. After the towline is secured at both ends and it has been determined that the line will not damage deck gear on either vessel, put the towboat in gear and take up the slack as slowly as possible. Then, gradually in small increments add power and pause to observe the effects. Use only as much power as is necessary to pull the vessel free. As the grounded vessel begins to move, reduce power and disengage the drive as soon as possible to avoid the sailboat gaining momentum.

Both crews must be kept clear of the towline except when it is not under load. They must also be prepared to release the tow at any time should the towing captain find it necessary to do so. Finally, as the little story above suggested, communicate with the other captain regarding a coordinated towline release.

22.2 TOWING A VESSEL AT SEA

To pass a towline to another vessel, a $3/8$" casting line with a monkey fist or otherwise nondestructive weighted end should be used to aid in the toss. In a pinch, a plastic jug (e.g. half gallon or gallon milk jug) partially filled with water works very well. Try casting the line for practice to determine how near a vessel must be approached to assure a successful throw. In all but light wind conditions, approach the vessel to be towed on the upwind side. This will aid in casting the line further as well as help to avoid a collision.

The towline should be 3 to 4 boat lengths long and made of Nylon™ or polypropylene for needed stretch to avoid high shock loads on the hard points. A spare, perhaps retired yet sound, anchor line works well for this. As in the previous example, a bridle on both ends of the towline helps distribute the hard-point loads and reduces chafing.

Towing should be done using enough power to achieve needed steerage, but not so fast as to put heavy strain on either vessel. Judicious throttle play may be needed to dampen out an alternating slack and taught towline.

Tack or otherwise make the course line such that sea conditions are the least punishing for the general direction of travel. Make only very gradual turns.

When approaching the towline drop point gradually slow to minimum speed. Sailboats can easily run up on the towline during this time. If, after the towed vessel drops the towline, the towboat cannot continue forward, the line handler(s) must be ready to bring in the towline quickly to avoid fouling the rudder(s) and propeller(s).

22.3 PASSING FUEL AT SEA

Now and then, a cruising vessel will come up short on fuel. For sailboats, five gallons will often be enough to satisfy the need. Passing fuel is easy and relatively risk free.

Toss a casting line to the other vessel. Have the jerry jug tied to the end. After the line has been caught, ease the jerry jug into the water. The other vessel can easily recover the welcome fuel and return the line and jug later.

Powerboat captains should be prepared for these eventualities by having the necessary lines and paraphernalia available.

22.4 CONCLUDING REMARKS

Cruisers, especially in remote regions, need to be ready to pitch in whenever needed. As powerboat cruisers, we have the equipment necessary to provide assistance relatively quickly and with sufficient power to save other vessels from damage and possible loss. Assistance can usually be affected with low risk if we are prepared mentally and appropriately equipped.

Chapter 23

Money

THERE WAS A LITTLE DISCUSSION REGARDING MONEY AND SECURITY in Chapter 20, Security at Sea, Anchor and Ashore, but a few more details need to be presented.

Before beginning a cruise, a common question is: how much money should we have aboard? Clearly, the route and duration of cruises all differ and the answer will be different for each case. Among other things, this chapter offers at least a partial answer.

23.1 CREDIT CARDS

The cruiser must decide about the degree to which using a credit card is acceptable. Very often fuel and other major items can be purchased using credit cards. But, credit card scams are a problem everywhere. It is a good idea to advise the credit card company of one's travel plans. Also, in Venezuela for instance, the official exchange rate used for credit card transactions may be as much as 15 percent below the black market exchange rate.

23.2 ATM MACHINES

ATM machines are nearly everywhere, but - There have been times when the ATMs receipts have indicated no transaction, but the banks have deducted money from cruiser's accounts. In all of the cases we're aware of (and they are few), the error was corrected, but not without worry, aggravation and many telephone calls. Be sure to save all transaction slips, even those that say no money was withdrawn.

ATM transactions are usually limited to a few hundred dollars, but there are places where the limit is less than $100. The transaction charge, while most often a dollar or two, can be as high as 5 dollars. These charges add up quickly.

23.3 BANK EXCHANGES

With a few exceptions such as Venezuela, the bank exchange rates are the only rates. The plural is used, because there are often minor (pennies) variations between banks. As with most things, however, there are other small complications and caveats.

At the banks in most Caribbean countries, one cannot exchange dollars for local currency without showing a passport (not a copy). Exchanging money at banks can be time consuming.

Most often, U.S. dollars that have any kind of pencil, pen, stain mark or tear are unacceptable for exchange. Before leaving North America, go through all your cash and exchange the imperfect bills at a bank.

Banks around the Caribbean are not often pleased to exchange money for small bills, e.g. less than $10. Yet, in a few countries, small U.S. bills are preferred spendable cash (without exchanging for local currency). Therefore, one not only needs to be concerned about how much cash to have aboard, but also the denomination distribution. Refer to specific regional cruising guides for help on this.

23.4 EXCESS FOREIGN MONEY

This is the least worrisome problem regarding money. Changing foreign cash back to U.S. dollars can be done at the bank, but there will be yet another transaction fee. It is best to ask friends or make a call on VHF radio offering it to other cruisers. Don't try to take the money from one country to another and expect to exchange it. In many cases, it will not be exchanged or the rate will be very unfavorable. U.S., Canadian, Pounds and Euros are the common cash of exchange with U.S. dollars favored the most.

23.5 CASH ON HAND — WHERE TO PUT IT?

Boats have a zillion hiding places for cash. Yet, cash is frequently stolen from boats. Robbers seem to have a sixth sense for locating it. The best policy is to spread the cash around in four, five or six locations; maybe they will miss one or two of them. But, be sure to keep a list of how much and where the cash is located. Designate one or two of the lesser (and less well-hidden) stashes, as expendable in case of a boarding. Don't forget to put any counterfeit bills you may have received in these places as well.

Chapter 24
Pets Aboard

24.1 PET SELECTION

A large percentage of cruisers have pets aboard. The pets range from parrots to large dogs. Frequently the pet will be a carryover from the previous land based lifestyle. But, the selection of a new pet to be company on long voyages should consider the various liveaboard restrictions. The list of concerns in selecting a pet includes the:

- ease of handling a pet into a dinghy for shore visits,
- amount of food needed to be stocked,
- amount of exercise the animal needs,
- amount of fresh water required for baths or rinses,
- need to relieve bodily functions at sea,
- sleeping space and other confinement,
- hair and dander problem,
- alertness for security,
- grooming needs,
- adaptation to conditions at sea.

Some pet owners are happy to deal with a lot of inconvenience and others less so. Choose a pet according to realistic expectations and personal commitment. Well selected, a pet will pay the owner back many times over with its affection and companionship. Poorly selected, both the owner(s) and animal may suffer.

Additionally, countries such as Trinidad and most of the eastern Caribbean Islands will not allow pets ashore. Thus, there may be extended periods when a dog cannot have more freedom of movement. In the western Caribbean, dogs can be taken ashore almost anywhere, but if there are local dogs about, they may be sick, parasite ridden, have skin diseases and can be a health risk for your dog. Yet, on the other hand, runs and swims on secluded, uninhabited beaches are a delight for both the dog and owner.

24.2 PREPARING FOR A CRUISE

Along with the normal shots for rabies, parvo and distemper, an *international health certificate* will be required. Only a few countries make a big deal about having a pet's current health certificate. Even then, officials realize that cruisers may have been underway for a long time and as long as the shots are current, they aren't often concerned about the age of a health certificate.

Pet foodstuff of the desired quality may not be available in many of the

Francesca's Maggie

countries of the Caribbean. But for a cruise in the tropics, dry pet food purchased in the States may not last more than a few months before going bad. Set aside a bit of room in the refrigerator or freezer to extend the supply.

Your pet will need a supply of medicines and hygiene products including that for:

heartworm and flea prophylaxis,
ear mites and other ear infections,
eye infections,
skin infections and itch control,
shampoos.

If one stocks heartworm and flea/tick preventive medication sufficient for the cruise it may be prudent to keep them refrigerated. Otherwise, these medicines are available at reasonable prices at every population center. Also, at or near most population centers, veterinarians will come to the marinas and administer rabies and other vaccinations to the pets on the boats. In general, they do this service for much less than the cost of an office visit in the States. Other pet health problems can be similarly resolved.

Chapter 25
Pest Infestations

THIS SECTION PROVIDES INFORMATION ON SOME POTENTIAL PROBLEMS in the tropics. It should neither scare nor be of unreasonable concern. The topic regards potential problems that can be avoided altogether or made to be of minor concern. Awareness and preparation are the best defense against unwanted guests.

Location has the most to do with pests and other "bug" problems. Surprisingly, most of the tropical rivers, jungles and rain forests we visited have very few bugs. The worst areas are usually the coastal plains and mangroves. Pests such as mice, rats and snakes can be a problem at the marinas.

25.1 INFESTATIONS

Within a few days, a single rat on board can eat through engine hoses, electrical wiring, and ruin food stores. At marinas, cruisers often put plastic bottles on their dock lines to fend off mice and rats. If the boat is cross-tied in a slip or med moored this practice can be useful. But tied alongside a dock with fenders or with a boarding plank the rodents will take the easy way aboard. At each marina, ask your neighbors if there is a rat problem and be prepared with a trap or two. At night, or when away from the boat during the day, keep the doors and unscreened hatches closed. If your boat is left unoccupied at a marina for an extended period, make sure that it is frequently visited, checked and aired. Have rattraps located where they can be checked by the dockhands.

The tropics have lots of termites, cockroaches, bees, spiders and other critters you don't need aboard. After buying supplies that come with cardboard containers, remove the cardboard on the dock and check the goods for bugs. It's probably smart to hose down the bulk purchased canned drinks on the dock before storing them aboard.

Stock and prepare your boat with pesticide bombs and borax type roach compounds such as *Combat*® or *Hot Shot*® Roach Powder before the cruise. Terro™ is a product that has been found to be effective against sweet eating ants. With the right protection you never need have roach or ant infestations.

Honey bees just love to nest in self furling masts, engine cooling vents and other inviting spots. Recently an unoccupied boat in the Rio Dulce of Guatemala had a massive bee infestation in the cabin. The bees had entered through an unscreened ventilator.

Dirt daubers like to build nests in small openings. It's a good idea to check your fuel and water tank vents occasionally. On rare occasions boats have become infested with termites. Mostly they are boats that have been left unattended for long periods.

In a few areas, it rains 200 or more inches per year. Tropical rains are usually brief, but occur several times a day and can be very intense. That means your boat is opened and closed more frequently than you have ever experienced before. There are a couple of problems associated with this. The first has nothing to do with infestation, but can be just as maddening. All kinds of important stuff and woodwork will get wet if you fail to wake up and close up the boat when the rain begins.

The other problem with high humidity and a closed up boat is mildew. Mostly it is a cleaning nuisance, but for some people, respiratory problems accompany high levels of mildew. Here's a tip. Clorox® and water solutions help, but a solution of 1 part vinegar, 1 part hydrogen peroxide and 1 part water works much better. The correct proportions are important and the solution doesn't work at all if you leave out the water.

Occasionally, a snake will find its way aboard a cruiser's boat. You're on your own on this one. On the other hand, welcome the geckos. They will help keep the population of spiders and other insects under control and are great for humorous surprises. If you're lucky, generations of geckos will remain with you throughout the cruise, perhaps for years. Their small droppings aren't so welcome, but as with all of cruising, compromises are part of the deal.

Chapter 26
Fishing, Catching Lobsters and Preparing the Catch

26.1 FISHING

Sometimes trawlers listed for sale have a parenthetical statement saying that a fish has never been brought onboard. That may appeal to waterway cruisers, but for those who want to do extended cruising, fishing is a perk for which a trawler can be well suited. Boats having open aft decks such as the yachtfish and classic trawler designs have good layouts for fishing, but with a little imagination, other types can also be fished.

When at sea, it pays to troll a lure. For the best results, the trolling speed should be 7 to 8 knots. Above 7 knots feathered subsurface lures work well. At lower speeds, surface popping lures and natural baits are a better bet. Be aware, however, that going from point to point does not necessarily mean crossing fertile fishing grounds. So, it is not unusual to troll hundreds of miles without a single catch.

Natural trolled baits are usually better than artificial lures, but they are a lot of trouble. In productive waters, it is possible to satisfy the need for fresh fish using only artificials. Here are a few artificial lure suggestions:

For dorado (dolphin-fish or mahi-mahi)
    yellow/green feather lures,
    white or yellow bucktails,
    pink and white feather lures (southern Caribbean)

Tuna, black fin, yellow fin
    white or yellow bucktails,
    blue/white feather lures,
    pink and white feather lures (southern Caribbean)

Wahoo
    red/black feather lures, heavy wire leader suggested

King Mackerel
    Drone spoons and other large spoons

Spanish, sierra or cero mackerel
    Clark spoons and other small spoons

Fish with a lightly set drag, but set the hook as soon as possible.

Because of the risk of ciguatera poisoning, barracuda (especially large barracuda) should not be eaten in many areas. With so many other types of good eating fish, we avoid catching them as much as possible. Barracuda will hit almost any lure, but they can generally be avoided by trolling in water over 120 feet deep.

For those new to ocean fishing, a fish identification reference book with color pictures will be helpful in determining which are good food fish and which are not. Bonito, skipjack tuna and some of the jacks are not usually eaten and bringing one aboard can create a big mess without benefit to either of you. However, a badly injured fish in this category can make good pet food.

Cruisers seldom go out just to fish, thus gear such as down riggers and planers, which require slower trolling, aren't very practical. Birds, however, (floppy noisemakers) may at times be trolled advantageously ahead of lures.

When at anchor, the dinghy can be used for slow trolling over reefs and rocks. This can be productive and enjoyable using a variety of small lures. (In some areas, eating reef fish such as large grouper and large snapper may carry a risk of ciguatera poisoning. Check with the locals.)

From the anchored trawler, night fishing for snapper can be productive. It's good to have a supply of squid, conch or other tough cut bait in the freezer for night fishing. Circle hooks work well. Adjusted the reel drag fairly light, set the clicker on and put the rod in a rod holder. A hooked fish will usually wake you.

26.2 PREPARING THE FISH

Pulling a big fish onboard and then cleaning it is a messy proposition no matter what. But here are a few suggestions that may help.

A large fish thrashing about on deck can flop or cause other stuff to flop over the side. We have found that a small rug or cover, put over the fish's head, greatly reduces the panicked flopping. Another trick that results in instant calming is to squirt a small amount of rum or other alcoholic beverage on the fish's gills. With aft mounted dinghy davits, a freshly caught fish can be put into the dinghy where at least part of the mess can be confined and more easily cleaned up.

But the biggest problem with catching large fish is in the cleaning. If it were possible to restrict the fish size to about 10 lbs, then a nice little cleaning board and drain might be rigged. But the fact is a big fish may be 4 or 5 feet long and the only place large enough to work is on the deck. Thus, it is a messy chore (especially on a rolling boat) and keeping the gore controlled is difficult.

A continuous running salt-water wash down hose is best, but a frequent rinse down from a bucket is a good alternative. A small tough rubber (concrete) bucket with a rope can be used to pull water aboard even while underway. Yet, under the best of conditions, it can take longer to clean up the boat than it did to catch and clean the fish. Still, when 20 lbs or so of fillets go into the freezer, the effort is well worth it.

It is surprising to find that many cruisers are unfamiliar with a good method of filleting fish. We have known skippers who avoid fishing because of the difficulty of cleaning fish (without filleting). Fish

Sometimes the fishing is really great. Here, off the coast of Venezuela, Joan holds up a nice Dorado while grandson Johann gives an assist.

as small as ½ pound are candidates for filleting. With a little practice, a 1 to 3 lb fish can be filleted in about 30 seconds.

A little side note. A cruiser with a fishbone caught in his or her throat may require emergency medical help. But, from out on the reef, getting help can be difficult. Boneless fillets are the best way to avoid that risk.

Try the following instructions and pictures for simple, quick fish cleaning. Don't be too concerned if the outcome of the first fish is a little ragged. After a few more tries it will get easier. Done properly, there is very little wasted flesh. On most fish species, be sure to remove the strip of pink to dark red meat that runs longitudinally down the center of the fillets. Leaving even a small amount will cause it all to have a strong taste.

Large fish can be filleted in fourths by making the first cut the length of the fish down the lateral line.

As described in the chapter on Provisioning, fish fillets can be placed in zip lock bags, filled with fresh water, the air excluded and frozen for months. With the exception of tuna, the fillets will be just as good as fresh caught.

Tuna meat tends to have a slightly stronger taste after freezing, but fresh blackfin or yellowfin tuna is hard to beat. If more than a meal is caught, invite the neighbors for grilled tuna and wasabi.

Whatever the recipe, avoid overcooking the fish.

26.3 CATCHING LOBSTER

In the U.S., catching lobster while diving can be done legally using only gloved hands. However, in many areas of the Caribbean the rules for taking lobster aren't so stringent. Several methods work well. They are:

   a wire loop (draw string) on a stick or rod,
   a tickle stick (~3 ft. and 5/16" diameter shaft)
   a tickle stick as above, but with a large fish hook fastened to one end,
   a pole spear
   a spear gun.

Step 1. Begin the filleting process by raising the pectoral fin. Then, make a diagonal cut toward the head and backbone.

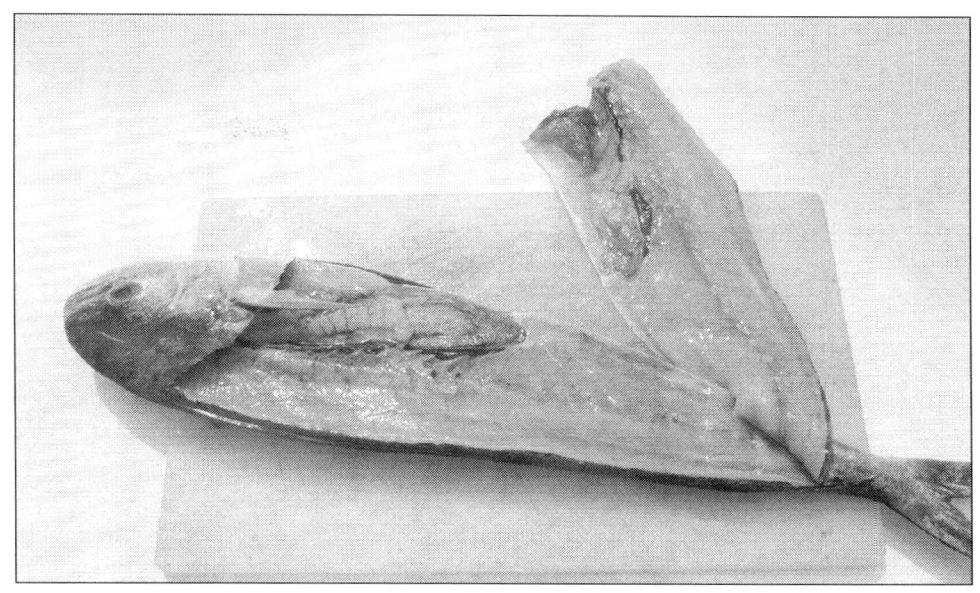

Step 2. After stopping the knife at the backbone, turn the knife and cut toward the tail. Cut as close to the backbone as possible.

We favor the method using a tickle stick with a large hook because the yield ca be higher. For example, inside a coral head there may be 3 or more lobsters in one hole. A pole spear stirs up panic after taking a shot and the other lobsters usually scatter. The wire loop tends to be cumbersome, snags on things and is difficult to get into position. But, using the tickle stick and hook method, all of the lobsters in a hole can often be taken. Here's how. After locating a lobster, the

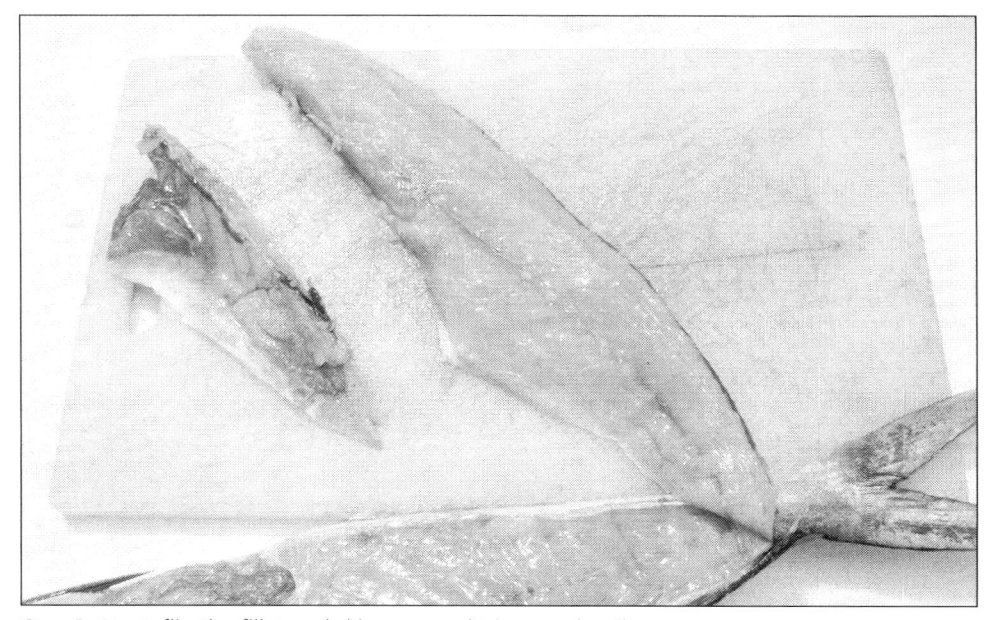

Step 3. Next, flip the fillet and skin over and trim out the ribcage.

FISHING, CATCHING LOBSTERS AND PREPARING THE CATCH

Step 4. With the skin side against the cutting board, place the knife near the tail and flat against the skin. Then, gently pushing the knife, cut the fillet from the skin.

hook must be moved slowly into position. The lobster will mostly regard the tickle stick as another lobster moving about. With care, lobsters can be herded into the ideal position for snagging. Then, with the hook located just behind the carapace and under the tail, a 2 or 3" firm jerk will snag the lobster. It can then be removed

Step 5. With a little practice, very little meat will be left on either the carcass or the skin.

from the hole without much disturbance. Then, go back for more.

In Mexico and Belize, lobsters can be found behind the barrier reefs and at the atolls in 5 to 15 feet of water. The best places to find them are Bahia de la Ascension, Bahi del Espirtu Santos, Turneffe Reef and Glover's Reef. Glover's Reef may now be a marine reserve, check the status before taking lobster. They can also be found behind the Belize barrier reef, but are spotty. It may take a little time to find lobsters, but they can be easily caught free diving.

At the Bay Islands of Honduras, a few lobsters may be caught at depths with scuba gear. In Panama, the locals free dive for lobster outside the barrier reefs in deeper water. Unfortunately, they take the shorts and egg bearing females as well.

26.4 PREPARING THE LOBSTER

In the old days, there was a thing about putting the whole live lobster in a pot of boiling water. There may still be a few diehards about, but most cruisers wring the tails and ice them down until dinnertime. The easiest method for wringing is to pass the blade of a sharp knife around the skin just inside of the carapace (pointed toward the front of the lobster). After cutting the skin, the tail can be wrung (about ¼ turn each way) and pulled free of the carapace.

Before discarding the carapace, break off approximately ⅔ of one of the antennas. Then, insert the large end of the antenna into the anus of the lobster tail about ¼". Twist the antenna a half turn and withdraw it from the anus. The vein or gut is thusly removed.

There are dozens of good recipes to experiment with. But lobster tails boiled and served with drawn butter are hard to beat. Try not to overcook these yummy critters.

26.5 RECIPES

Recipes belong in recipe books, not as filler in cruising guides. Oh, but we just have to put in two especially good ones.

Back in the early 70's, when we used to go out on dive boats in southern California, there was one boat that took all the dead lobster shorts (oops), extra fish and undersized abalone to make chowder. Then, after a long day of diving in cold water, the crew served up this wonderful restorative brew. The cook gave us the recipe and we have enjoyed it ever since.

Boil 'till cooked, 2 cups or more of bits of fish fillets, lobster, and shellfish (any combination) in fresh water. After they are cooked, drain off the water and add the following.

1 can	New England clam chowder
1 can	vegetable soup
1 pint (or more)	milk
1 large	chopped onion

Season to taste with Tarragon, thyme, oregano, salt and pepper.

Simmer a few minutes, until the onion is cooked, and it is ready to eat. You're going to love it.

The second recipe is for outstanding fish fingers. Roy and Dunia, m/v Ventura II, who have a beautiful fishing lodge (Roy's Zancudo Lodge) at Gofito, Costa Rica, passed this along to us.

Make fine breadcrumbs using a blender and day old bread.

Make a dip of well-mixed egg and milk.

Cut fish fillets into strips 3–4" long by about ¾" square.

Lightly salt the uncooked fish fingers.

Dip the fish in the egg/milk mixture.

Evenly coat the fish with the breading.

Deep-fry the fish fingers at 340° F until golden brown and a little crisp.

Along with hush puppies, tartar sauce and cole slaw, the fish fingers go so quickly it's hard to make them fast enough.

Happy foraging.

Chapter 27
Home Schooling

EVERYONE IS FAMILIAR WITH THE LARGE VARIATIONS in quality of education of the public school system. We are also unpleasantly aware of the social pressures and other problems of public schools. If a kid is overweight, homely, a geek, extra bright, not so bright, or just doesn't dress cool, then growing up is all the more difficult and the stigmatism can become a long term handicap. For a growing number of families the cruising life and home schooling hold the answers to those problems.

Many private organizations provide accredited home schooling curriculum, testing and oversight. These, as well as other information on home schooling, can be found on the Internet. The programs range from conventional course work to others having religious affiliations. Personal recommendations from cruisers may be helpful in choosing a school. Some states of the U.S. require greater oversight than others, but when done properly the child receives full credit for each year completed.

The formal curriculum is fast paced and quite broad, but the homework environment is relaxed and the student has many things to learn and experience outside of class.

Home schooling can be characterized as a broad-based programmed course of study that is individually paced. It requires three to five hours a day of dedicated effort by the parents. Parents often alternate on the various subjects to share the load.

Home schooling is also flexible. Study can be suspended for a few days or even a week or two when special travel events come up. For instance, a four-day trip to Angel Falls in Venezuela or a tour of Mayan ruins in Central America can be offset by a few six or seven day school weeks. The youngster gets a break from formal study and is enlightened to marvels of which most children are not aware.

Homework aboard

Learning to snorkel

Here is a little testimonial from this book's authors.

> We were privileged to home school our grandson through most of the third and fourth grades. During that time, *Francesca* cruised from South Carolina to Trinidad, Venezuela, Colombia and Panama. Homework and tests provided daily feedback to judge his progress. We then spent more time in areas where there was slower learning and less where he excelled. At the same time, he learned good study habits, touch-typing, a little Spanish, how to swim and snorkel, to appreciate reading for pleasure and visited many wonderful places. It was a great experience for grandchild and grandparents alike. We hope to do it again soon.
>
> Also, during our cruising years, we have come to know many families who have taken direct responsibility for their children's education. The evidence is anecdotal, but in all such cases, we have found the children to be well educated, better adjusted and more mature than most others who were schooled conventionally.

Home schooling and cruising may only be possible for a few years. If a young person later returns to public or private school, he or she will be worldlier, environmentally aware, educationally advanced, have good study habits and higher values. What more could a parent ask?

One of the many Spanish schools at Antigua, Guatemala. Each student is paired with an instructor. Cubicles are used most often, but the teacher and student may also take instructional walks, work at the park or beside a pool.

Here's a further note on educational opportunities while cruising. Most Latin countries have inexpensive schools in which to learn Spanish. The instruction is usually full immersion and fast paced with one student for each instructor. As an example, at Antigua, Guatemala there are numerous schools offering tuition, room and board for $100 to $200 USD per week. It may be possible to work this into a child's studies. Most people gain a conversational foundation in Spanish after about a month.

Chapter 28
Your Cruising Newsletter and Website

FAMILY, FRIENDS AND CRUISING GROUPS ARE ALWAYS ANXIOUS AND HAPPY to receive news of your cruising adventures. Consider writing up cruising experiences on a more or less regular basis. An email newsletter sent out every month or so has a calming effect on families. It also chronicles special enriching, adventurous, and perhaps even the difficult times for grandchildren to cherish.

Today, it is most usual for newsletters to be text only. Pictures require too much time to send via HF-SSB. Even when sending out newsletters through an Internet café, the number and quality of pictures have to be limited. Later, however, the newsletters can be incorporated into a website where they can be loaded with pictures. In that regard, digital cameras are a boon.

Newsletters should be kept to less than two full pages, preferably a page and a half. Rambling on in great detail about doing this or that may only cause the newsletter not to be fully read. Use just enough detail to make them interesting.

Emails sent to and through the SailMail system will be truncated to about 6000 characters. If newsletters are sent through either the SailMail or Winlink systems, the transmission and reception times can be long, especially if the recipient list is also long. It may be advantageous to send the newsletter to one person in North America and have them forward it to a longer distribution list.

Cruisers are a special group. Out of hundreds of millions of people in North America, only a tiny few get to experience extended cruising. Share the fun and give generations of family members things to dream about.

Chapter 29
Cruising the ICW (Intracoastal Waterway)

THE WATERWAY IS AN INVALUABLE TREASURE that aids us in running the U.S. East Coast and Gulf Coast in nearly all weather conditions. Most cruisers have to spend days and days cruising the ICW before jumping off to blue horizons. The reason for including this chapter is that experience has shown that most cruisers haven't figured out how best to run the waterway. Here are a few things that can help reduce frustration, workload and decrease the time and fuel required.

29.1 NAVIGATING THE WATERWAY

The Waterway day markers are positioned to provide navigable water for the largest craft that commonly ply these waters. That, of course, includes tugs and barges; some of which require a lot of room to negotiate turns. The first and most easily corrected problem for cruisers is the tendency to run the waterway by going from marker to marker. This crossover technique assures that a vessel is always in the channel and its usefulness at night with a spotlight is undisputed. But, during clear daylight hours either that technique or cruising the center, the right hand side or going wide in the turns, adds miles and miles to an overall trip. To avoid this, it is best to keep your charts at the helm station, always know your position, and *try to run the straightest course possible* without cutting day markers or interfering with other traffic. It is usually possible to crowd the day markers at the turns, but unless you are careful to watch for indications of shoaling, it may be prudent not to be too aggressive about it.

For vessels with a draft of 5 feet or less it is not usually necessary to navigate using the visual ranges. However, in areas where the charts indicate very shallow water just outside of narrow channels, it may be advisable.

29.2 BRIDGES

Thankfully, there is a continuing trend to replace swing and bascule bridges with high fixed bridges. Yet, there are many of the older bridges left that may require opening for passage. Most of these bridges open on request, but some open only at scheduled times ranging from 15 minutes up to an hour apart. A *Bridge List* that has the schedules and mile marker positions for the bridges from South Carolina to Key West may be found on our website at: www.cruisingfrancesca.org. The Bridge Lists are viewable as well as downloadable as Excel spreadsheet (.xls).

As bridges are passed that require opening, it's a good idea to enter GPS waypoints such that on the return trip your boat's speed can be adjusted to coincide with the scheduled bridge openings. This practice can save fuel, time and frustration.

We often hear captains calling bridges on VHF radio several miles before the bridge. This causes a lot of needless radio clutter and serves no purpose. Only rarely will a bridge operator delay or hold an opening (and they sure don't care to hear that a boat is approaching, but is 5 miles away). Depending upon the vessel's speed, it is usual to call the bridge for an opening when within ½ to ¾ of a mile.

Bridges with scheduled openings are not required to open unless someone requests it. Most times the bridge operators will make a helpful suggestion to the oncoming traffic, but on a few occasions we have been among several boats waiting; each thinking that the other had called for an opening. Then, at the time of the scheduled opening, nothing happened and it was too late. Those situations usually result in a feisty exchange of words between captains and bridge operators that ends up something like, "you operate your boat and I'll operate the bridge."

Approaching South Florida, unless there is a good reason not to do so, it is best to avoid the Fort Lauderdale area, especially on weekends. As one can see on the *Bridge List*, that stretch of the Waterway has 21 bridges, most have scheduled openings and most will be required to open even for smaller trawlers to pass. On weekends there is considerable congestion and many of the small go-fast boat operators have little experience. Some of the bridges have very low clearances that require even the small fishing boats to wait for an opening and it isn't unusual to be crowded with little room to maneuver. Regardless of your boat's speed capability it will take a full day to transit these 40 miles and while there are many crowded marinas, there are almost no places to anchor.

In good weather, most cruisers who wish to avoid the Ft. Lauderdale area, leave and re-enter the Waterway at the Lake Worth Inlet and the Port Everglades Inlet. Going north, it may be best to go offshore a few miles and take advantage of the Gulf Stream current. When heading south it is often possible to ride the coastal counter current by staying very close inshore (inside ½ mile).

We compiled the *Bridge List*, but it has not been updated for several years and there have been a number of changes since then. Please email noted changes to us so that we may update the list on the website. (email: KG4LRA@yahoo.com)

29.3 THE ROCK PILE

The number of boats that come to grief in this notoriously bad stretch of the ICW in South Carolina is astonishing and shameful. It is similarly shameful that this region is not marked with cautionary signs. *Francesca's* home port is at the north end of the *Rock Pile* and, when there, we often ask transient captains if they know of its existence. About half are not aware of it.

The *Rock Pile* is roughly an 18 mile long stretch of the Waterway from mm 348, about 1 mile south of the Little River swing bridge, to mm 365, at the highway 501 high bridge. The dangerous parts of this section cannot be observed except at low tide and at high tide (approx. 6 ft) the whole region looks completely innocuous. Don't be fooled.

There is a small, almost unnoticeable note on the charts that suggests there might be a problem, but take it to heart, it is a problem. The *Rock Pile* helps keep the boat yards and prop shops in the area in business. Even the locals, who know better, get tangled up in this rocky trap.

In this region, sections of the ICW were blasted out of solid rock creating a 100-foot wide channel. Over the years, however, erosion of the soil banks on each side makes the channel look very much wider at all but low tide. This is made worse by the fact that the bad sections of the rocky channel are not marked.

All cruising vessels transiting the area should announce their position and intention to transit the *Rock Pile* on VHF channel 16 after which they should proceed staying as near the center of the channel as possible. Barges are few and far between these days, but if you do meet one in the *Rock Pile*, you have two options. Depending upon where you are in the *Rock Pile*, the easiest and safest solution may be to turn around and give way to the barge. Otherwise, the barge operators are very experienced at negotiating this stretch and a call on VHF channels 10 or 16 may result in a cooperative, but necessarily very close passage. Be cautious, be careful and pass other vessels as close as may be done safely. North Myrtle Beach is a great place to visit, but an unscheduled, extended stop with bent shafts/props/struts, hull damage and a broken budget won't be pleasant.

29.4 ANCHORAGES

There are many great places to anchor along the Waterway, but there are many more not so great places to anchor. Skipper Bob publishes excellent guides to Waterway anchorages and Waterway facilities. His website can be found at http://skipperbob.home.att.net/

At many anchorages the tidal currents can be very strong and a poorly set or undersized anchor can lead to a bad night's sleep. Remember too that the tide reversal can foul the anchor and even pull an anchor free. Look for anchorages that are very roughly equidistant between inlets and tributaries that do not come from extensive drainage areas. These are regions of lesser current where the water rises and falls more gently and it is easier to sleep. Also remember, that in some spots, the tides can be more than 8 feet during a spring tide.

So often we read or hear that a particular favored anchorage provides good protection from the wind, yet considering the other factors it is not very suitable. With good ground tackle, protection from the wind should not be an especially high priority item. In our opinion it is far better to have good swinging room, good holding (and room to drag) than to worry about protection from the wind. For that reason it is often reasonable to anchor on the windward side of sounds and other large, less well protected areas, rather than small waterway tributaries.

29.5 FUEL PROBLEMS AND FUEL STOPS

A vessel that has been dormant for months at a time has a relatively high risk of developing fuel contamination from water condensation, biological activity and/or rust accumulation. The large sounds of the Carolinas and Georgia can be good places to stir up the fuel tanks and let the fuel filters clean it up. With 15 to 25 knots of wind against the current, the sounds can set up a surprisingly punishing chop. If it becomes too punishing, and it can, one can always turn back. But, rather than waiting to discover the trouble at sea, it is far better to experience and sort out dirty fuel problems in these relatively innocuous settings. Take advantage of a little rough water to check out your fuel system as well as the rest of the boat equipment and material stowage.

The times are-a-changing and fuel prices. . . well you know. Here are a few tips that can save lots of dollars. Avoid the need to buy fuel (other than to top off), in south Florida where fuel often costs significantly more. In the Keys, the two fuel docks near the west entrance of Boot Key Harbor have usually had better fuel prices than almost anywhere else in South Florida. Also, there are fuel truck services that will bring fuel to your boat at marinas and at reasonable prices.

The lowest fuel price in Florida may be found at the Florida Petroleum dock at Fernandino Beach, Florida. But be aware; the fuel dock is built to accommodate tugboats and shrimpers. It is difficult to get fenders arranged and to avoid dock rash. Also, the tidal current is swift and it is best to arrange the schedule to take on fuel during or near slack tide.

In South Carolina fuel prices vary, but not so greatly. In North Carolina, the best fuel prices have been found near the New River Inlet and at Coinjock.

29.6 GROUNDING

Every time we make the ICW trip we see grounded vessels and hear them calling a towing service. (We've helped many too.) Everyone makes a mistake now and then and boats with greater speed make mistakes more frequently and with worse consequences. If you ground, *Stop and Think* before making the knee jerk reaction to call for help. This will most often save you money and perhaps even damage to your vessel. Here are two scenarios that will help in understanding the problem.

Case 1. A vessel inadvertently cuts a day marker grounding heavily. Without thinking, the captain immediately calls for a tow. He then nervously waits 30 minutes or more for the arrival of a towboat. When the towboat finally arrives the tide has risen several inches, but the bow is still hard aground. Attempts to tow the vessel free results in the gnashing of teeth, gears and flying mud. In the recovery process the vessel looses more bottom paint, may ding a prop (or worse) and has gel coat finish damage.

Here is what probably should be done in such a situation. First evaluate the status of the tide. Next, consider whether it is likely that damage has been done. From Georgia through North Carolina the tide runs anywhere from 5 to 8 feet. If the tide is rising, all that the captain may have to do is get a soft drink and wait until the vessel floats free. That is not always the case, however. One must determine if the rising tidal current may push the vessel further aground. If so, it may be best to launch a dinghy and set an anchor. As a last resort a tow may be needed, but only when the time is right.

Case 2. Same situation, but this time the tide is falling. A towboat may be useful, but only if it can be on site within a very few minutes. The next best thing may be to wait for the next rising tide. Unfortunately, that may be at night when kedging, towing or powering off may be difficult, dangerous and accompanied by a greater potential for damage. Sailboats with a deep keel can get in real trouble with a 6 foot falling tide and hulls without protective keels can suffer prop, strut and rudder damage on a hard bottom.

Each case is different and one must assess whether the tide will be helpful or just make the problem worse. A towboat operator can also be thoughtfully helpful or make the problem worse by using horsepower instead of gray matter.

When trying to back off from a grounding situation one should remember that the props are likely pumping copious quantities of muddy debris at the engine's intake(s). The results can be clogged screens, damaged raw water pump impellers and overheated, damaged engines. After clearing from a grounding incident, watch the engine temperature and check the intake screens as soon as possible.

Clearly the best way to navigate the waterway is without grounding. Keep track of your position, marker to marker, and know where you are at all times. It is easy to get distracted with a cell phone conversation, radio communication, sandwich or whatever. While one person can handle the job, two people working together provide a greater margin of safety.

29.7 YELLOW FLIES (DIACHLORUS FERRUGATUS).

In some locations, and particularly during the late spring, these biting critters can be terrible. Yellow Flies are found near salt marshes all along the coast, but there is a section of Georgia (60-80 miles long) where they can be so numerous that we call it *Yellow Fly City*. In that area we have experienced times when there were hundreds of them in the fly bridge enclosure. It required both of us to keep fly swatters in continuous motion. At such times, along with many bites, the decks were nearly black with dead flies. Not a fun experience. At the least, boaters should be prepared with several fly swatters aboard.

29.8 WATCH YOUR WAKE

Occasionally, during our first two years of ICW cruising experience, we found ourselves being yelled at for our wake. Of course we tried to be as thoughtful and careful as possible, but there was just no way to run the throttles up and down for every floating dock, john-boat, and eroding bank. We also found that although go-fast boats would pass us, their cruising day was often exhausting for the crew and thus foreshortened. The conclusion was that, at least for trawlers, running at 7 knots produced little wake, was quiet, relaxing, there were fewer navigational mistakes, fewer throttle excursions, we saved fuel, nobody yelled at us and because our cruising day was longer, we usually passed the same go fast boats – day after day.

In Florida, it is a curious fact that there are *Manatee Zones* and *Idle Speed Zones* and there are *Manatee Zones* and *Idle Speed Zones*. By that I mean in some areas, even a minor speed infraction will be rewarded by a visit from the marine patrol. In other areas, the wakes have beaten down the "No wake, Manatee Zone" signs or the signs are so weathered it is questionable if they were really meant to be there. What's a captain to do?

The best answer is to take all of the signs at their face value. The slower speed won't make a wit of difference at days end. And, it is better to err on the safe side, for both you and the manatees.

Chapter 30
Useful References

Considering the limits of space and budget, selecting from the field of cruising guides and other potentially useful books is something of a task. In most regions there are several guidebooks to choose from and each book has its own special flavor. There are, however, a couple of excellent cruising guides for which there are no alternatives. Without these, gunk holing the western Caribbean would be difficult and risky. They are:

The Northwest Caribbean Guide, by Stephen J. Pavlidis, Seaworthy Publications

The Panama Guide, by Nancy and Tom Zydler, Seaworthy Publications

Other books that have been especially helpful include:

A Gentlemen's Guide to Passages South, by Bruce Van Sant, Cruising Guide Publications

Keeping Food Fresh, by Janet Bailey, Harper and Row

Lonely Planet Guides, for each country where inland travel is planned.

Reed's Nautical Almanac, Caribbean, Thomas Reed Publications

Spanish for Cruisers (Boat repairs and maintenance phrase book), by Kathy Parsons, Aventuras Publishing Company

Sport Fish of Florida, by Vic Dunaway, Florida Sportsman

Index:

A

Anchor(s) 146
    bridles 147
    chain 145
    drag alarm 149
    light 148
    rode 145
    scope 145
    setting 147
    snubbers 147
    watch 149
    windlass 48
Anchorage legal issues 152
Anchorages 150, 202
    bottom type 150
    escape plan 150
Anchoring 145
Anti-siphon loop 49
Assisting other vessels 177–180
ATM machines 181

B

Bahamas 88
Bank exchanges 181
Batteries 39, 109, 114
BBC World News 53
Bites and stings 156
Boarding Inspections 83
Boat selection 6–14

C

Checklist, maintenance 122–128
Ciguatera fish poisoning 158
Collision avoidance 44
Communications 42–43, 50–56
    emergency 54
    licensing 50
    satellite 54
    SSB 52–53
    VHF 51
Computer 35, 43, 52, 56
Contamination, water and produce 159
Costs of cruising 92–94
Credit cards 181
Crew list 80–82
Crew readiness 91
Cruise planning 87–94
Cutlass bearings 109

D

Dinghies 15–23
    at anchor 16, 150
    davits 17–20
    repairs 117
    security 21
    towing 17
Ditch bag 115
Dock power cord 118
Documentation 30, 78

E

Electric fence 170
Electrical system 11–12
    problems 118
email, SSB 42, 52
Emergency communications 54
Energy 37–42
    storage 40–42
    use 41
Engine 8
    alignment 112
    alternator 38, 116
    belts 107
    coolant fresh water (FW) pump 108
    coolant heat exchanger 107
    coolant reservoir cap 107

exhaust elbow 108
fuel injectors 109
heat exchanger zincs 109, 114
hoses 107
injector pump oil changes 113
mounts 114
oil & filter changes 113
oil cooler 107
raw water pump 108
raw water pump impellers 108, 114
starting problems 116
valve adjustments 112

F

Fire aboard 176
Fire extinguishers 114
Fish filleting 188–192
Fishing 187–194
Flies, biting 157
Flying home 84
Foreign destinations 78–84
Foreign money 181–182
Foundering and sinking 174
Freezers 46
Fresh water system 47
Fuel 95–105
    comparisons table 99–100
    efficiency 95
    filters 113
    management 99
    measurement 95
    special fuel concerns 104
    system calibration 95
    tankage 103
    tanks 12

G

Generator 38
    heat exchanger zinc 109
    raw water pump impeller 114
GPS 43, 111
Gulf Stream 89, 102

H

Home schooling 195–198
Hooka 48
Hull blisters 12
Hull configurations 7
Hurricane season 88–90, 130

I

Injuries, illness 172
Installations, new equipment 119

Insurance, vessel 25
Intracoastal Waterway (ICW) 200–205
Inventory maintenance (provisions) 62
Inverters 40

L

Lightning 168
Lobster, catching 190
Lobster preparation 193

M

Maintenance 106–121
Maintenance checklist 122–128
Maintenance in foreign ports 119
Malaria 156–157
Man overboard 173
Marine growth 116
Medical 154–162
    emergencies 155
    health–care abroad 154
Medicines aboard 160–162
Medicines abroad 154
Mildew 63, 186
Money 181–182
Mosquitoes 156
Movies 47

N

Newsletter 199

O

Ocean currents 100–103, 131
Optimizing range 100
Outboard motor 18–19
    fuel contamination 19, 117
    fuel storage 19
Outfitting 35–49
Outfitting costs 35
Outfitting for reliability 36
Overnighters 139–141

P

Parasites 158–159
Pest infestations 185–186
Pets 183–184
    food 60
    health certificates 80, 183
    selection 183
    veterinary care 184
Power generation 38
Power systems 37
Propeller damage 115
Provisioning 57–73

in the Caribbean 61
in U.S. and Canada 60
lists 64–73

R

References 206
Rudder packing gland 113

S

Safety
    at anchor 152.
    at sea 172–176
    equipment 48
    equipment, maintenance 114
Sailmail 43
Satellite communications 43
Scuba 48
Security
    ashore 166
    at anchor 164
    at sea 163
    dingy 21
Shaft packing gland 110
Single sideband radio (SSB) 42, 52–56
Spanish schools 197–198
Spare parts 74–77
    inventory & spreadsheets 75–77
Speed calibration 97
Steering system 12
Stings 157
Storage space 57
Strobe lights, life jacket 115
Surveyor 14

T

Tachometers 112
Taxes 24

Teak decks 11
Television 47
TNC 43,52
Tools 49
Towing
    dinghy 17
    vessels 179
Transmission
    B.W. drop center 10
    oil changes 113
    oil cooler 107

V

Veterinary services 184
VHF radio 41, 50–52

W

Washing machine 46
Water tankage 45–46
Watermakers 45, 111, 117
Weather 129–138
    email 135
    FAX broadcasts 133
    forecasts 132
    subscription services 136–137
    summer conditions 130
    voice broadcasts 132,137
    winter conditions 129
WiFi 44
Winlink 43, 52–53

Z

Zincs
    heat exchangers 109, 114
    rudder 126
    shaft 126